T0331397

ECONOMIC REFORMS IN THE SOCIALIST WORLD

Economic Reforms in the Socialist World

Edited by

STANISLAW GOMULKA
Reader in Economics
London School of Economics

YONG-CHOOL HA
Assistant Professor, Department of International Relations
Seoul National University

CAE-ONE KIM
Professor, College of Social Sciences
Seoul National University

Routledge
Taylor & Francis Group

LONDON AND NEW YORK

First published 1989 by M.E. Sharpe

Published 2015 by Routledge
2 Park Square, Milton Park, Abingdon, Oxon OX14 4RN
711 Third Avenue, New York, NY 10017, USA

Routledge is an imprint of the Taylor & Francis Group, an informa business

Library of Congress Cataloging-in-Publication Data
Economic reforms in the socialist world / edited by Stanislaw Gomulka,
Yong-Chool Ha, Cae-One Kim.
p. cm.
Includes bibliographies.
ISBN 0–87332–577–X : $45.00
1. Communist countries—Economic policy. I. Gomulka, Stanislaw.
II. Ha, Yong-Chool. III. Kim, Cae-One.
HC704.E28 1989
338.9′009171′7—dc20   89–6113
                                                              CIP

ISBN 13: 9780873325776 (hbk)

Contents

Notes on the Contributors

Byung-Joon Ahn Professor of Political Science, Yonsei University, Seoul, Korea

Suck-Kyo Ahn Professor of Economics, Hanyang University, Seoul, Korea

Wladimir Andreff Professor of Economics, University of Grenoble, Grenoble, France

Jean Benard Professor of Economics, University of Paris I Panthéon-Sorbonne and CEPREMAP, Paris, France

Ivan Bićanić Assistant Professor of Economics, University of Zagreb, Zagreb, Yugoslavia

Stanislaw Gomulka Reader in Economics, London School of Economics and Political Science, London, England

Gregory Grossman Professor of Economics, University of California, Berkeley, USA

Yong-Chool Ha Assistant Professor of Political Science, Seoul National University, Seoul, Korea

Branko Horvat Professor of Economics, University of Zagreb, Zagreb, Yugoslavia

Myung-Kyu Kang Professor of Economics, Seoul National University, Seoul, Korea

Michael Kaser Reader in Economics, Professorial Fellow of St Antony's College, Oxford University, Oxford, England

Cae-One Kim Professor of Economics, Seoul National University, Seoul, Korea

vii

Józef Pajestka Professor of Economics, Director of the Institute of Economic Sciences, Polish Academy, Warsaw, Poland

László Szamuely Associate Professor of Economics, Institute of Economic Research and Information, Budapest, Hungary

Jerzy J. Wiatr Professor of Political Science, Warsaw University, Warsaw, Poland

Christine P. W. Wong Associate Professor of Economics, University of California, Santa Cruz, USA

Preface and Acknowledgements

Socialist countries now account for about a quarter of the world economy, about a third of the world population and about half the world military power. What happens in those countries is therefore *par excellence* of importance to all of us.

This book is an outcome of a Conference on Economic Systems and Reforms in a Changing World, held in Seoul in September 1987. The Conference was significant in several respects. Foremost was the fact that this was probably the first such meeting of scholars from both socialist and non-socialist countries held to discuss socialist economic reforms worldwide. Secondly, major changes are now taking place or being initiated or planned to take place in the two largest socialist countries, the USSR and China. Our Conference was designed to evaluate the origins, the contents and the obstacles to these changes. The Conference was also notable in that the case of North Korea, which for a variety of reasons is usually absent from Western discussions of socialist economic systems, was included on this occasion. It is also significant that the Institute of Social Sciences of Seoul National University, which has for a long time recognised the need for promoting better understanding of socialist economic systems in South Korea, was the host of the meeting.

We are deeply indebted to many individuals and institutions without whose support this book would not have been possible. Our special thanks go above all to the authors who contributed a great deal of effort in preparing their papers and were later gracious enough to respond in a co-operative manner to suggested editorial revisions. We wish to thank those participants of the Conference who contributed by presenting papers or serving as chairpersons or discussants, but whose contributions could not be included in this book. We also wish to thank Professors George W. Breslaver, Gregory Grossman, and Robert A. Scalapino at the University of California, Berkeley, for their valuable advice at the planning stage of the Conference. Professors Lee, Hong-Koo, Ahn, Chang-si and Lim Hyun-Jin of the Seoul National University showed their deep interest in the Conference and fully supported the whole enterprise.

It is a pleasure to acknowledge the financial and in-kind contribution of the following institutions: National Board of Unification, Ministry of Education of the Korean Government, Korea Cultural Society, Ssangyong Economic Research Institute, DaeWoo Research Institute and Korea Traders' Scholarship Foundation. The Pacific Science Congress was instrumental in expanding channels for outside contacts. Our thanks go to Dr Lee Hyo-Seong, who prepared the Conference from beginning to end. We also express our thanks to the following individuals who worked behind the scenes: Lee Keun, Suh Yi-Jong, Park Kyung-Suck, Park Soo-Un, Lee Song-Hyong, Chae Hee-Yul, Mun Woo-Sik, Kil Jeong-Woo and Lee Chi-Yon for their gracious help with organisation and funding.

The task of selecting and preparing the Conference proceedings for publication rested with Stanislaw Gomulka. He wishes to acknowledge the contribution of Scheherazade Daneshkhu of the London School of Economics, who provided valuable subeditorial assistance, and Prue Hutton, Sue Kirkbride and Pat Nutt, also of the London School of Economics, for their help with typing and correspondence.

Sarah Roberts-West at the Macmillan Press and Adrian Stenton of Stenton Associates Editorial Services were most helpful with their suggestions, their willingness to accept last-minute changes and for seeing the work through its various publication stages.

Stanislaw Gomulka
Yong-Chool Ha
Cae-One Kim

Introduction

Seven decades have passed since a Soviet-type socialist system appeared on the horizon of the earth. The underlying idea of its founders was to avoid the shortcomings of capitalism, such as unequal distribution, exploitation, and economic egoism, by abolishing private ownership. To this end socialist ownership was married with central planning and management. Initially, the expectations of the founders of the system appeared to be fulfilled as the Soviet economy demonstrated the ability to grow rapidly with massive mobilisation of human and material resources. This strategy of extensive growth was also pursued with considerable success by other East European socialist countries.

However, the highly centralised control of the economy soon revealed its limitations. It was found that there were, in such economies, inherent sources of inefficiencies, disequilibria, and stagnation tendencies. The excessive centralisation caused rigidities, which precluded flexible and timely economic adjustment and froze innovation and initiative. One of the most critical problems was how to motivate people to work hard and efficiently with little or no competition and in conditions of relatively high economic security. It has become increasingly difficult to rely heavily on moral incentives. In these circumstances the adoption of new concepts and devices such as enterprise profitability, managerial flexibility, and material bonuses had to be considered.

This is the economic background to the reform waves in socialist countries since the late 1950s. The past experience of reforms in these countries suggests the presence of uneasy tension between the economy and the political system, which often led the countries into crises or fostered forces which interfered with the smooth implementation of reforms. Examples are those of China in the mid-1960s and Czechoslovakia in the late 1960s.

The existence of several waves of reform movements has made it increasingly difficult to find a socialist country which has been faithful to the original model. An extreme reaction to Soviet Stalinist model is Yugoslavia, which chose a self-governing socialism where the market is regarded as an instrument for planning. The New Economic Mechanism in Hungary allowed (though to a limited degree)

1

private ownership, and accomplished a substantial decentralisation with the introduction of an active market mechanism in resource allocation. Czechoslovakia also attempted to adopt a form of socialist pluralism in the late 1960s, and its current leadership has recently reopened reform discussions.

The Chinese reform efforts since the late 1970s have now entered a stable period and have attained some degree of irreversibility. Now the focus is shifting from rural areas to urban areas, and from agriculture to manufacturing and service industries. A very flexible position on private ownership and user rights of lands and other means of production is also being taken. In distribution, the so-called communist principle of 'each according to his need' has been replaced by the socialist principle of 'each according to his work', which implies that the necessity or unavoidability of a considerable degree of income and wealth inequality is now being admitted.

In the Soviet Union, Gorbachev has called for a comprehensive *perestroika* (restructuring), which is supposed to be substantially more than a mere adjustment or refinement of the central planning and decision-making structure within an essentially unchanged systemic environment, as was often the case in the past. The Soviet leadership has already experimented with various incentive schemes, but current reform measures seem to include a significant degree of decentralisation, in terms of enterprise autonomy as well as more opening of the economy to Western capital and commodities. All these efforts reflect the determined will of the Soviet Union to return to its rapid economic growth path.

In the Third World, the performance of socialist-orientated developing countries has not generally been outstanding. Excessively hasty, heavy-industry-centred industrialisation drives have had, as their consequence, large accumulated foreign debts and trade deficits. In some cases, the simple-minded pursuit of 'self-reliance' has blocked the way to benefits from external economic transactions.

In sum, the ethically attractive ideals of socialism have been, in the course of their realisation, going through the process of adaptation to different historical, political, and economic environments. This development is consistent with the view that there is no unique predetermined model of socialism. Whatever the model may be, the first important problem to be solved is how to promote human creativeness and technological innovation in order to enhance productivity and efficiency. Specifically, this problem is related to such issues as competition and incentives. It is now widely accepted that one of the strongest merits of a market mechanism is its positive effect on efficiency and productivity through the stimulation of competition. This explains why most economic reforms in socialist countries have tended to assign more active roles to market competition and material benefits. Another hot issue in economic reform is related to the foreign sector. An open-door policy aims at increasing efficiency through the international division of labour. However, given the background of the long tradition of highly centralised planning, the introduction of a market mechanism is no easy matter. Price reforms, for example, sometimes distort relative prices further and invariably produce high inflation.

All the above observations boil down to the question of how to strike a balance between plan and market, and the formulation of a workable combination of equality and efficiency under the dominant socialist ownership.

The primary concern of the essays in this book is to address this question in the light of the variety of reform efforts in socialist countries. The socialist countries covered include all those in which the reform effort has been substantial. These essays are arranged in groups covering major socialist countries and areas, with the last part providing a general overview.

Part I deals with China. Byong-Joon Ahn is concerned with the interplay of politics and economics in the process of China's economic modernisation. He traces differences and conflicts between political conservatives and reformers in agricultural, industrial and trade policies. In the political arena, Ahn observes an ongoing conflict between political liberalisation, leading possibly to political pluralism, and maintaining the Party's hegemony. China's political economy is characterised as a constant interaction between forces of equality and those of efficiency. The dilemma facing China is how to justify the increasing role of the market, and consequently a wide differentiation in income and economic status, with egalitarian ideology. The author maintains that strong measures by the top leadership will push forward reforms in China while avoiding any clear-cut theoretical formulation of the policy by using the flexible phrase 'socialism with Chinese characteristics'.

Suck-Kyo Ahn analyses different aspects of China's economic reforms since 1978. His focus is on ownership structure, models of resource allocation, incentive and motivation. Of particular interest is his documentation of Chinese efforts to differentiate stages of development in socialism. Rather than viewing socialism as a transitional stage to communism, two different stages in socialism are posited, advanced and backward, to be distinguished by the types of ownership.

In contrast to these two authors, Christine Wong is interested in micro-aspects of economic reform in China. She focuses on the role of local governments. Her findings show us how decentralisation efforts, including market reform, have been 'leaked out' by local governments before they reach economic agents, retaining and expanding control over enterprises through a variety of informal mechanisms, as well as through their control over geographically immobile factor resources.

In Part II, Soviet economic reforms are discussed. Stanislaw Gomulka provides us with a detailed analysis of the contents of Gorbachev's intended economic reforms. He sees the main thrust of Gorbachev's reform to be close to Hungary's New Economic Mechanism. Discussing the potential effectiveness of the reform, Gomulka notes the presence of an inherent contradiction between measures designed to promote economic efficiency and those intended to retain the large economic power of central institutions. One distinct feature of Gorbachev's *perestroika* is the fact that it is carried out in conjunction with political reform. The author views *Glasnost* as Gorbachev's effort to build political support from outside the establishment, among young people and intellectuals, partly in order to change the personnel of the establishment. Yet Gorbachev cannot, and probably does not wish to, risk any major loss of power by the Party. Gomulka suggests that what Gorbachev intends to do is to explore the feasibility of building a socialist equivalent of the South Korean model, whereby a market-based economy moves quite rationally under an authoritarian political system. An interesting question is whether and for how long such a combination may last.

The chapter by Gregory Grossman discusses the implications of the second (underground or parallel) economy for Gorbachev's reforms and – vice versa – the possible impact of reform measures on the second economy. His conclusion is that the second economy is so well entrenched that reform measures so far taken are unlikely to eliminate 'crypto-private' economic activity. Those involved in illegal activity will continue to benefit from underground business. Neither is Gorbachev's plan to restructure the first economy going to do any serious damage to the second, for confusion in the early phase of the reform will help the second economy to survive. In the longer term, the incomplete break from the past economic structure will enable the second economy to survive after some adaptation. Thus, the overall impact of the reform on the second economy is likely to be negligible.

Yong-Chool Ha, through a case study of the attitudes of the District and Provincial party secretaries to the 1973 Production Association reform, demonstrates that middle-level party officials are guided not so much by an abstract conception of party interests but by such factors as local interests, the degree of power consolidation by the top leader, and patron–client ties.

Michael Kaser succinctly presents some parallels in the measures taken by the Chinese and the Soviets for agriculture, private economic activity, foreign trade and financing. His comparative analysis helps an understanding of both the similarities and the differences.

There are four chapters in Part III: by Jerzy Wiatr, Ivan Bićanić, László Szamuely and Józef Pajestka. They deal with the key ideological, sociological and political issues related to economic reforms which are relevant to all socialist countries. However, their extensive empirical references are to East European countries.

Jerzy Wiatr's comparative analysis of the three cases of economic reforms in Eastern Europe arrives at the following four conditions for a successful economic reform: control by the political leadership over the course of economic reform; obtaining Soviet approval or sufficient independence; the extent to which both dogmatic-conservative resistance and radicalisation of the reform movement are overcome; and reconstituting political structure after the reform. His findings suggest that a strong political leadership is required to implement reforms fully. The same leadership, however, also has to make political adjustments, consequently diluting economic reforms. This inherent dilemma helps to explain the limits to reform in socialist countries.

Ivan Bićanić characterises Yugoslavia as an 'administratively overloaded economy'. Major economic decisions are taken by unaccountable administrators. These decisions are *ad hoc* and reactive in nature. Bićanić provides clues as to how the mechanism of administered economy is sustained. He argues that the quality of administrators is unusually low and that deep political reforms are necessary to solve the country's present social crisis.

László Szamuely argues that reforms cannot succeed if they are limited only to the economic sphere. Successful reforms must be preceded by a re-evaluation of the strongly entrenched faith in the correctness of the early mode of development, which is by now well outdated. At the social level, a deep-rooted egalitarianism which has undermined motivation for hard and efficient work must be corrected.

In the concluding chapter in this part, Józef Pajestka argues that the basic institutions required for micro-rationality of enterprises are real money, the market mechanism and the independent firm. He then identifies and discusses several major 'determinants' of change which are at work in Poland with a view to establishing such institutions.

In Part IV, cases of socialist countries outside Eastern Europe are discussed. Vladimir Andreff looks at the experience of twenty-one socialist-orientated developing countries to assess the economic performance of the Soviet model. His conclusion is that the adoption of a socialist model of industrialisation by a developing country inhibits economic performance, but also prevents economic crisis by delaying necessary adjustment efforts. The implication is very serious for the political influence of Eastern Europe and the USSR in the Third World. One may also add that the Leninist model may have helped elites of Third World countries to acquire and sustain political power. Once power is gained, however, they face a situation where institutions and ideology are not conducive to solving economic problems.

Hyung-Kyu Kang specifically focuses on North Korea. He observes that despite the officially expressed need to improve the functioning of the economic system, North Korean efforts to this end have, by comparison with those in Eastern Europe, been relatively modest. However, various within-system juggling efforts have become more visible in recent years. They include the adoption of Joint-Venture Law and an independent accounting system. Kang's conclusion is that in the final analysis, the North Korean economy has not yet moved far from the highly centralised system it always was. North Korea is therefore an example of a country where the existing political leadership sets a clear boundary to any meaningful reform.

In Part V, Jean Benard's concern is with the question of whether decentralised organisation of production can be consistent with centralised optimal pricing. He advocates the use of decentralised (market) pricing and approaches this problem by analysing the role of prices and various ways of price-setting in closed hierarchy and open hierarchy.

In the second chapter in this part, the last chapter in the book, Branko Horvat argues the case for making the distinction between etatism and a self-managed system under socialism as it really exists. Individual freedom, political and economic democracy, elimination of hierarchy and decentralisation of political and economic power are identified as essential components of socialism. Etatism is characterised by the political monopoly of one party, rigid political and social hierarchy, lack of pluralism, replacement of markets by bureaucratic controls, and lack of individual initiative. According to Horvat, most reforms in Eastern Europe and the Soviet Union are attempts to correct defects of etatism. He contends that a complete reversal from etatism to socialism is difficult, for it requires substantial loss of power by bureaucrats. Etatist reforms, he contends, will proceed from obtaining economic security to securing political liberties. However, it will not be easy to accomplish political liberalisation, due to the resistance of ruling elites. Thus, what is likely to happen is that etatist reforms will lead to economic decentralisation and industrial democracy, while substantial political reforms are postponed indefinitely (that is, for as long as possible).

Despite the great variety of issues and countries discussed, there are several propositions that are explicitly and implicitly shared in these chapters. One is that socialism manifests itself in various forms, and therefore reforms take place in different contexts. Of particular importance for reforms are the differing patterns of interaction between (domestic and international) politics and economics in socialist countries. This variation can explain much of the differences in speed, degree and shape of reforms, despite structural similarities.

Secondly, almost all the authors agree that major obstacles to reform are political and socio-psychological as well as economic. That is, a mere organisational change will not suffice; there is also a need for change in values, mode of thinking and behaviour.

Thirdly, any fundamental economic reform would require a redefinition of socialism in order to justify reform in ideological terms. The need for such a redefinition is due to the fact that the socialist etatist system left a long-lasting legacy of incompatibility between planning and market. But the introduction of market elements on a large scale naturally raises the task of differentiating socialism from capitalism and of justifying the compatibility of socialism with the social implications of the market.

This last point raises an interesting question: to what extent would the differences between capitalism and socialism still remain if and when economic reforms are implemented to their logical conclusion? This question is related to the existence of an 'optimal' economic system *à la* Tinbergen and the debate on possible worldwide convergence to such a system.

Cae-One Kim

Part I
The People's Republic of China

1 Political Economy of Reforms in China

Byung-Joon Ahn

1 POLITICAL ECONOMY OF SOCIALISM AND MODERNISATION

In general, the term political economy refers to the interaction between authority and markets,[1] or to the 'mutual interaction of state and market'.[2] This perspective can be usefully applied to Chinese reforms as well. But since China is a communist country, its political economy involves the specific interaction between the imperatives for sustaining socialism and the requirements of accomplishing modernisation, the two main goals of the state and the Party since the assumption of power in 1948.

The central proposition of this chapter is that China's reforms have resulted from that interaction; therefore a political economy perspective is best able to account for their contents and problems. One distinguishing feature of communist politics in general is the requirement that the Party has to 'build socialism' in order to realise a classless society in the future. At the same time the Party has to carry out economic modernisation in order to make up for underdevelopment in the past. More specifically, this means that the Communist Party has to carry out simultaneously both class struggle – or the socialist revolution – and economic development. In practice, however, emphasising socialism over modernisation (understood here as economic development) results in sacrificing modernisation and, vice versa, emphasising modernisation results in sacrificing socialism.[3]

Since Mao's death in 1976 the Chinese Communist Party has chosen to put more emphasis on the task of accomplishing 'four modernisations' than on carrying out the class struggle. In so doing, however, the Party has encountered a number of fundamental problems in justifying its choice as well as in pursuing its new task. Tensions have inevitably arisen between the Party's ideological commitment to socialism and its practical commitment to development.[4]

11

A most fundamental problem underlying these tensions has been one of legitimacy.

Traditionally, all socialist systems derive their legitimacy from Marxism–Leninism – or, as in China, from 'Marxism–Leninism–Mao Zedong Thought'. But once the first-generation leadership passes away and a post-mobilisation phase sets in, the basis for the Communist Party's legitimacy begins to shift from carrying out class struggle according to the dictates of Marxist ideology to achieving modernisation according to the requirements of problem-solving. When the inspirational and the innovative roles of Marxism–Leninism can no longer be expected to predominate, the Party tends to resort increasingly to three sources of legitimacy: (1) raising the material and cultural standards of the people; (2) arousing nationalistic sentiments; and (3) instituting some measure of 'democratisation', or at least a degree of liberalisation based on a system of legal procedures to ensure a reasonably secure and predictable life for every citizen.

There are many constraints on the Party in its search for legitimacy. No Leninist party, of course, allows unbridled democratisation to run its course. What it can do instead, without running the risk of inviting a head-on challenge to its one-party rule, is to pursue policies (1) to (3).[5] In China, the Deng leadership has attempted to do just this. It has taken the four modernisations to mean the quadrupling of the level of production in (i) agriculture, (ii) industry, (iii) science and technology, and (iv) national defence by the end of this century. This is now the Party's primary task; the endeavour has, however, eroded its ideological commitment to socialism.

For the purpose of modernisation, the party embarked immediately after 1978 on policy adjustments in various areas and later introduced a series of structural reforms in economic management, even drawing upon market principles from the West. Such attempts to seek economic efficiency have inevitably undermined central planning and management, thereby prompting its advocates to counterattack with the ideologically inspired call for maintaining economic equality. Moreover, as soon as some negative consequences of the open-door policy and other reforms appeared, the leadership aroused nationalistic sentiments by calling for the 'liberation of Taiwan' and by demanding the return of sovereignty in Hong Kong from the British in the name of an independent foreign policy. Such appeals to nationalism might have had adverse effects on China's access to Western capital and technology.

The Chinese leaders have also tried to allow some degree of pluralism in political life, but when the democratisation movement challenged the very legitimacy of party hegemony, they began to narrow the scope for liberalisation through laws and regulations. On the other hand, Deng and his followers have made serious efforts to cultivate the better-educated and professionally competent cadres, seeing among them future leaders.

Fourthly, the Chinese leadership has tried to legitimate its reforms by arguing that they represent 'socialism with Chinese characteristics'. But it has been facing an acute dilemma in trying to justify its political rule without resorting to the tenets of (non-Chinese) Marxism–Leninism, especially when capitalist phenomena such as economic inequality, unemployment, inflation and cynicism are re-emerging as a result of the reforms.

2   ECONOMIC REFORMS: PLANNING VERSUS MARKET

By and large, the economic reforms which have been undertaken reduce the role of central planning and increase that of market forces. The quest for efficiency has prompted the Beijing leadership – among other measures – to enhance material incentives and the role of the price mechanism. As this tends to undermine not merely economic equality but also the entrenched position of certain cadres, there have been some critics who defend central planning and collective (national) management on the grounds that these are the correct socialist institutions.

Purely in terms of economic rationality, such practices as the household responsibility system in agriculture, enterprise autonomy and self-financing in industry, and the price mechanism in the economy can be justified in terms of 'the socialist commodity economy'. Yet in terms of political feasibility, these practices have to be moderated to preserve some measure of ideological consistency and leadership cohesion. Thus, a combination of economic concerns and political forces have, in many ways, determined the state of China's post-Mao reforms.[6] But more than anything else, it has been the political will and the commitment of the leadership under Deng and his associates that have kept the reforms alive to this day.

Adoption of the modernisations programme in fact represented a return to the attempt which Zhou Enlai made at the National People's Congress in 1975.[7] The programme was also a reaffirmation of the party line reported by Liu Shaoi at the Eighth Party Congress in 1956. It is significant that the Party under Deng has decided to secure its legitimacy by accomplishing modernisations rather than by agitating for class struggle as Mao used to do. This shift, however, was by no means smooth. It was made only after power struggles between Hua Guofeng's followers and Deng Xiaoping's followers in 1976–8 cleared the way for Deng to assume leadership at the Third Plenum in December 1978. At that Plenum, Deng's associates did away with Hua's attempts at another 'leap forward' and decided instead to implement a policy of 'readjustment, restructuring and consolidation' for three years, beginning in 1979.

In order to raise agricultural productivity, the Party resumed experiments with the 'household responsibility' [*paokan*] system at various localities. Among these, the ones in Sichuan province under Zhao Ziyang's supervision were outstanding. By making contracts between the state and individual households, this system gave the households a free hand in disposing of whatever was left after selling to the state the quota specified in the contracts. Hence it established a direct link between work and reward. Now that the peasants were given incentives to work hard, they did work hard by improving management and technology. In 1978–82 the central government not only enforced this system throughout the entire country, but further encouraged the peasants to work by raising prices for quota procurements for the major crops – grain, cotton, and edible oils – by, respectively, 26, 20 and 24 per cent, while the respective prices for above-quota quantities were raised by 45, 56 and 43 per cent.[8]

In subsequent years, the authorities have allowed even more decentralisation of farming by extending the range of the contract system, diversifying agricultural production and promoting autonomous rural industries. In effect, these measures came to bury the Maoist model of people's commune. Taking economic decisions away from the commune deprived local political cadres of their power to intervene in the new system. Instead, households themselves have been given the power to take economic decisions.[9] As a result of these innovations, peasant income has doubled in less than a decade. In 1984 the commune system was suspended, thus accelerating the decollectivisation of landholdings and the specialisation and marketisation of farm products. Growth in employment and production was also generated by rural industries. By 1985 these industries employed 70 million people, or 19 per cent of the rural labour force, supplying 19 per cent of China's total industrial output.[10]

This agricultural reform has put a stop to the slogan of 'eating from one big pot', so characteristic of the Dazhai model, but it has created new problems. The most obvious is the re-emergence of inequality in income and wealth among households and regions. We shall return to this issue later.

The decision to expand reform to the urban and industrial economy was taken at the Third Plenum in October 1984. It was a far-reaching decision in that it aimed at decentralising more decision-making power, and even developing a market mechanism. But this reform is in many ways more complex than rural reform, for it involves deploying a new system of prices, which are to reflect relative scarcity. While continuing mandatory planning in critical sectors, such as energy, transportation and defence, the new policy called for shifting the decision-making power from the central bureaucracy to professional managers in local enterprises.[11]

Initially, the experiment involved autonomous management in some 4000 enterprises. Since 1978 these units have been paying about 55 per cent of profits as taxes to the state, but have been allowed to keep the remainder for investment or bonuses. The result was that enterprises in this category in light industry achieved an output growth rate of 56 per cent by 1982.[12] The 1984 decision was designed to expand the experiment to more enterprises throughout the country. To do so, it required a market-based price mechanism coupled with a system enabling managers to enjoy autonomy not only in production decisions, but also in personnel hiring and firing.

Since an abrupt switch to autonomous management and market pricing may cause unemployment and inflation, decentralisation and marketisation have been implemented gradually, and mostly in selected enterprises producing consumer or light industrial goods. As a result, China has become a mixed economy. For example, the government has reduced the number of major commodities which are distributed exclusively within the state commercial network from 256 to 20. Moreover, 65 per cent of agricultural products, 55 per cent of industrial consumer products and 40 per cent of industrial raw materials are no longer subject to fixed state prices.[13]

But establishing prices according to 'the law of value' has been exceedingly difficult, mainly because at such prices supply has not been able to meet demand. Further aggravating the situation has been bureaucratic resistance to change and corruption at all levels. Most serious of all, however, it has been difficult to cut the Party's prerogatives without damaging the support of the ruling coalition for reforms.

Indeed, there have been endemic conflicts in the industrial reform efforts. Struggles have occurred between different sectors, regions and bureaucracies. The response to these problems could have been either further decentralisation or recentralisation. The choice would have to be determined by political considerations.[14] This is the case because, as in the Soviet Union, central planning has in China become a vehicle for furthering political authoritarianism and the repression of individual rights.[15] Moreover, the choice touched upon the very foundation of the socialist economic system.

At the special party congress in September 1985, a senior Politburo member, Chen Yun, found it necessary to remind his audience that China is a socialist country. One of his remarks deserves full quotation: 'In pursuit of their own selfish gain, some party members put money above all else, regardless of the state's and people's interests, to the extent of violating the law and discipline.'[16] Apparently because of such arguments, legislation on the bankruptcy of enterprises and their autonomous management, independent of party control, has been delayed and it is not yet clear when and whether it will be passed.

As to the extent to which this 'planned socialist commodity economy' can be further marketised, there are continuing debates among economists and top leaders.[17] Since the fall of Hu Yaobang, Deng and Zhao have made every effort to limit the campaign against 'bourgeois liberalism' to within the Party, in order not to affect economic reforms adversely. To make reforms work more effectively, the current practice of 'guidance planning' concerning resource allocations must yield to the dictates of the market mechanism, or the laws of supply and demand. The more the leadership accepts this, however, the greater the difficulties it faces in legitimating its policy in terms of Marxism. One way or another, therefore, politics and ideology will determine the response to this dilemma.

3 TRADE AND FOREIGN POLICY: OPENING VERSUS NATIONALISM

China's trade and foreign policy has been closely tied with the needs of domestic reforms. In the pursuit of capital, trade and technology, China has adopted an 'open-door' policy towards the outside world. In its attempts to cope with the 'spiritual pollution' resulting from this policy, and to guard China's national interests, Beijing has been advocating an independent foreign policy with the emphasis on nationalism. At the cost of oversimplification we can therefore say that the requirements of economic reforms necessitate an open-door trade policy, but this, coupled with China's political and security interests, necessitates an even more nationalistic foreign policy.

The open-door policy has been best reflected in China's investment, trade and technology relations with Western capitalist countries, such as the United States, Japan and Europe, and in the establishment of 'special economic zones' and 'economic development zones'. In addition, the nationalist policy has been well illustrated by Beijing's approach to the Taiwan question, and to negotiations with London over the future of Hong Kong.

Making a significant departure from the Maoist policy of self-reliance, the reform leadership in China has consistently used an open-door policy to increase foreign investment, trade and technology transfer ever since the four modernisation programmes were launched. That China has incurred a debt of $20.6 billion by the end of 1986 attests to this fact.[18] Most of its trade has been with Western countries. China's top five trading partners in 1986 were, for exports, Hong Kong and Macau, Japan, the US, Britain and Singapore, accounting for 32, 15, 8, 5 and 4 per cent respectively. China's imports in that year came mainly from Japan, Hong Kong and Macau, the US, West Germany and the Soviet Union, accounting for 29, 13, 11, 8, and 3 per cent respectively.[19] China is also a member of the IMF and the World Bank, and participates in the GATT negotiations. As a consequence of these changes, the Chinese economy and the Western world economy have become more interdependent.

Since 1983, Beijing has embarked upon an ambitious export drive. For this purpose it has also resumed purchases of foreign technologies and investment goods, causing an increasing deficit in its balance of trade. To meet the shortfall in its balance of payments, it invited foreign investments and borrowed from international and commercial lending institutions.

The introduction of 'special economic zones' in 1979 marked another radical attempt to attract foreign capital. After Deng toured these zones in Shenzhen, Shantou, Xiamen and Zhuhai in 1984, he called upon the entire nation to 'learn from Shenzhen' and authorised the opening of fourteen additional coastal zones. There is no doubt that the primary purpose of this policy was to encourage foreign investments through direct or joint ventures in these zones.

Although the amount of investment that has been made in these zones has been less than expected and therefore puts the success of the policy in doubt, the leadership has not relented in its continuation.[20] This, in the eyes of Western observers, is indicative of the extent of the commitments that Deng and his associates have made to the open-door policy.

In contrast to this, it is important to note that Beijing began to distance itself from Washington in 1981, by initiating a search for a more independent foreign policy while seriously trying to improve its relations with Moscow. This was in part a response to the changes in the international environment. Such a recast of foreign policy was to a large extent motivated also by the domestic need to arouse nationalist sentiments. The assertion of an independent posture *vis-à-vis* both Moscow and Washington, and the revival of the policy of 'two systems and one nation' for Taiwan and Hong Kong, accorded well with China's appeals to nationalism.

China's recent approaches to Taiwan and Hong Kong in particular have served the twofold purpose of asserting independence and sovereignty while being assured of stable and steady access to Western capital and technology. The joint communiqué between Beijing and Washington on arms sales to Taiwan in August 1981 granted prestige to China, because it made the US pledge a gradual suspension of arms sales to Taiwan.[21]

The successful completion of negotiations on the return of sovereignty over Hong Kong in 1983, just when the campaign against 'spiritual pollution' got under way, gave Deng and his supporters enormous legitimacy in domestic politics. Yet the final deal, specifying that British rule would end in 1997 but that the Chinese would allow Hong Kong to continue its capitalist system for another fifty years, reflected nationalism as well as pragmatism.

When Beijing applies the formula of 'one nation and two systems' to Taiwan, however, it runs into steep resistance. Even on this issue Beijing has been flexible enough to expand indirect trade with Taipei and to allow the return of a hijacked Taiwanese plane through direct negotiations in 1986. While maintaining the rhetoric of 'liberation of Taiwan', Deng seems to give priority to the implementation of domestic reforms.

Finally, in order to pursue its economic modernisation China needs a 'prolonged peaceful international environment'; to this end Beijing has defended peace and stability, as well as the North–South dialogue on the Korean peninsula.[22]

It is clear that the moderately open-door policy and the moderately nationalist policy have complemented each other in meeting China's domestic and foreign needs. Whenever its vital national interests are at stake, however, Beijing's political and security considerations are likely to take precedence over the economy. On the other hand, as long as China continues to maintain its open-door policy to tap foreign inputs, the domestic economy will also be subjected to the vagaries of the international political economy.

4 POLITICAL REFORMS: HEGEMONY VERSUS PLURALISM

The progress of economic reforms invariably generates pressures for political changes, in part because the success of reforms depends on and breeds new types of leadership and management. As long as China adheres to Marxism–Leninism, however, the Party has to guard the Leninist tradition of hegemony. But the imperatives of rapid innovation and market-based reforms call for a large degree of pluralism in economic decision-making.

Since Mao's death the Chinese Communist Party has maintained hegemony, but in so doing it has gradually developed some corporatist relations with both the state and society, by allowing each a measure of autonomy and pluralism. The Party's attempts to substitute power-sharing with the state and society for class struggle in the cause of 'seeking truth from facts' have been regarded as political reforms, but when these attempts came to challenge the legitimacy of party hegemony, they were suppressed as being expressions of 'bourgeois liberalism'.

It should be recalled that the so-called 'democracy movement' enjoyed Deng's blessings in 1978–9, when he was building up a kind of public support for initiating the modernisation programme. Only when some radical students in this movement set out to attack the very notion of party leadership did Deng lay down the 'four cardinal principles' to which all people should adhere: (1) the socialist road of development; (2) the dictatorship of the proletariat; (3) the Party's leadership; and (4) Marxism–Leninism–Mao Zedong Thought.[23] These caveats had a dampening effect on the big debates and the character posters that were proliferating at that time.

Nevertheless, the policy of rehabilitating the old cadres and reorganising the bureaucracy has continued. In fact, the comeback to

original positions of the fallen leaders made it easier for the Deng
leadership to carry out reforms, without the kind of resistance which
is characteristic of the Soviet *apparatchiki*.[24] The Party's co-optation
of intellectuals and scientists into the new tasks of modernisation has
also helped to create a useful constituency for reforms. Deng himself
had already championed the intellectuals as an important productive
force in 1978.[25]

By carrying out reorganisation programmes in the bureaucracy,
Deng has sought to institutionalise collective leadership and succession processes.[26] This effort has involved the reshuffle of organisations and personnel. As a result, new organisations and faces have
assumed important functions and duties from the top down. Emerging from these endeavours has been a new division of roles between
the Party and the state. For example, Article Five of the new Chinese
Constitution stated that: 'all state organs, the armed forces, all
political parties and public organisations and all enterprises and
undertakings must abide by the constitution and the laws.'[27] A literal
interpretation of this provision must be that even the Communist
Party should abide by the Constitution and the laws.

The National People's Congress and its Standing Committee have
been active in performing legislative functions and in strengthening
legalism since the adoption of the Constitution in 1982. The Standing
Committee, under Peng Zhen's leadership, has often found itself in
conflict with the Party Secretariat under Hu Yaobang. Although Hu
committed ideological and political errors, the way he was forced to
step down in January 1987 provided telling evidence about a new
balance of power between the Party and the state.[28]

In all probability, with Hu's supporters consisting mostly of intellectuals, radical reformers must have clamoured to gain further
autonomy and pluralism in the name of political democratisation.
They may well have justified their demands on the grounds that such
democratisation was necessary to implement economic reforms successfully. For example, Professor Fang Lizhi contended that human
rights and liberty are not unique to the West, but are a common
historical legacy shared at birth by all human beings, including the
Chinese.[29] Emboldened by this doctrine, student demonstrations
spread to over twenty universities throughout the country in early
January 1987, calling for the granting of human rights and a multiparty system. Had these demonstrations been allowed to go on, they
would have irreparably eroded the Party's hegemony. This possibility
shocked many leaders, who had been trained in Leninist thought to

regard such a hegemony as essential for carrying out the socialist revolution. Unless the Party suppressed these demonstrations, Deng feared that a crisis resembling the one following the birth of the Solidarity labour movement in Poland would erupt in China.[30] He had to force Hu to give up the position of General Secretary and authorised another campaign to fight 'bourgeois liberalism'. These abrupt actions indicated that a coalition of leaders was formed strong enough to moderate the reform policy, if not to oppose it outright.

While trying to reassert the primacy of party control in this manner, it was also necessary for Deng to continue cultivating a new generation of younger and competent leaders, prepared to support and implement the reform policies. In the course of making preparations for the 13th Party Congress, therefore, Deng has been manoeuvring to make some senior leaders gracefully retire from the Politburo, in order to clear the way for a corps of younger leaders to assume positions of power. At the same time, Zhao Ziyang and his technocrats have continued with their plan to make enterprises autonomous of party and central control. They have come to criticise those who characterise the reform and open-door policy as signs of capitalism for holding ossified views. For them, 'reform was the only way to develop socialism'.[31]

Apparently, Zhao and his supporters are committed to continue their political reforms which contain certain aspects of pluralism, but only so long as they are necessary for economic reforms and do not challenge party hegemony. Should these reforms proceed again to the point where they begin to jeopardise the Party's leading position, the Party is expected to defend its hegemony by all means at its disposal, including massive coercion.

5   THE FORMULA OF 'SOCIALISM WITH CHINESE CHARACTERISTICS'

The analysis thus far of China's political economy indicates that there has been constant interaction between the forces of equality and those of efficiency. As long as China is committed to building socialism, the official ideology must emphasise equality, but the more pressing goal of accomplishing four modernisations compels the Party to emphasise efficiency even more than equality. In fact, in order to justify capitalist practices of the reform, the Chinese Communist Party has been paying only lip service to Marxism. At the same time, however, the Party has been persistently adhering to Leninism in defending its leading role in society. This has led to the fundamental dilemma that it is facing now: how to sustain its Leninist political role without advocating the Marxist utopia of achieving a classless society.

This dilemma is discernible in every area of reform policy. With respect to economic reforms, the advocates of central management continue to do battle with those of competitive markets. When inequalities deepen between individuals, households, social strata and regions, the battles become more intense, even violent. In trade and foreign policy, too, the advocates of opening compete with those of nationalism. Finally, with respect to political reforms, there have been struggles between those who cling to the doctrine of party hegemony and those who seek to allow some degree of pluralism. These struggles are by no means over.

On balance, China's political economy reveals more emphasis being placed on efficiency than ever before. The thrust of economic reforms has certainly been towards enlivening markets and autonomous price mechanisms rather than sustaining central management. The leadership has pledged itself to continue with the open-door policy despite some of its negative consequences. The Party has even gradually accepted that it must share power with the state and societal groups, thereby giving rise to what may be called an authoritarian pluralism.

The Chinese have been carefully building consensus on the basis of preserving the economic policies and reforms initiated at the Third Plenum in 1978, although considerable disagreements remain over the exact nature of these policies and reforms. The household responsibility scheme in farming is credited with increasing considerably the output of the agricultural sector. Similar attempts at decentralising the decision-making industry have been less successful so far, as they are seen to be creating new macroeconomic problems such as inflation, unemployment, deficits and inequality. How to strike a proper balance between central management and enterprise initiative remains a perennial problem.[32]

The Chinese call their reforms manifestations of 'socialism with Chinese characteristics'. They maintain that by adapting the universal ideology of Marxism–Leninism to China's contemporary realities, they are actually creating the kind of socialism which is particularly well suited to the needs of present-day China. Yet they have not defined in clear terms what is socialist and what is Chinese in this formulation. All we can say is that they are muddling through with neither clear-cut ideas nor a neatly defined formula as to where they draw the line between socialism and capitalism in the reforms. The precise meaning of 'socialism with Chinese characteristics' is thus left to be determined by further interactions between politics and economics in the future.

Notes

 1. Charles E. Lindblom, *Politics and Markets, The World's Political-Economic Systems* (New York: Basic Books, 1977) pp. 17–64.
 2. Robert Gilpin, *The Political Economy of International Relations* (Princeton, NJ: Princeton University Press, 1987) p. 8.
 3. Byung-Joon Ahn, *Chinese Politics and the Cultural Revolution: Dynamics of Policy Processing* (Seattle and London: University of Washington Press, 1976) p. 3.
 4. Richard Lowenthal, 'Development vs. Utopia in the Communist Party', in Chalmers, Johnson (ed.), *Change in Communist Systems* (Stanford, CA: Stanford University Press, 1970) pp. 33–116.
 5. Robert A. Scalapino, 'Legitimacy and Institutionalization in Asian Socialist Societies', in Scalapino, Seizaburo Sato and Jusuf Wanandi (eds), *Asian Political Institutionalization* (Berkeley, CA: Institute of East Asian Studies, University of California, Berkeley, 1986) p. 70.
 6. Elizabeth J. Perry and Christine Wong, 'The Political Economy of Reform in Post-Mao China: Causes, Content, and Consequences', in Perry and Wong (eds), *The Political Economy of Reform in Post-Mao China* (Cambridge, MA: Harvard University Press, 1985) p. 27.
 7. Byung-Joon Ahn, *Chinese Politics and the Cultural Revolution*, p. 251.
 8. Perry and Wong, 'The Political Economy of Reform', p. 10.
 9. Kathleen Hartford, 'Socialist Agriculture is Dead; Long Live Socialist Agriculture: Organizational Transformations in Rural China', in Perry and Wong (eds), *The Political Economy of Reform*, pp. 31–62.
10. *Far Eastern Economic Review*, 4 June 1987, p. 78.
11. *Renmin Ribao*, 20 October 1984.
12. Robert Michael Field, 'Changes in Chinese Industry since 1978', *China Quarterly*, no. 100 (December 1984) pp. 746–50.
13. *Far Eastern Economic Review*, 16 July 1987, p. 70.
14. Susan L. Shirk, 'The Politics of Industrial Reform', in Perry and Wong (eds), *The Political Economy of Reform*, pp. 195–222.
15. Mark Harrison, *Soviet Planning in Peace and War, 1938–1945* (Cambridge: Cambridge University Press, 1985) p. 261.
16. *International Herald Tribune*, 24 September 1985, p. 1.
17. *Far Eastern Economic Review*, 16 July 1987, pp. 69–71.
18. *International Herald Tribune*, 30 March 1987, p. 9.
19. *Far Eastern Economic Review*, 19 March 1987, p. 86.
20. Victor C. Falkenheim, 'China's Special Economic Zones', in *China's*

Economy Looks Toward the Year 2000, vol. 2: Economic Openness in Modernizing China (Washington, DC: Government Printing Office, 1986) pp. 348–70.

21. Byung-Joon Ahn, 'South Korea and Taiwan: Local Deterrence', in James W. Morley (ed.), *Security Interdependence in the Asia Pacific Region* (Lexington, MA: Lexington Books, 1986) p. 106.
22. Byung-Joon Ahn, 'The Korean Peninsula and East Asian Security', in Robert A. Scalapino, Seizaburo Sato and Jusuf Wanandi (eds), *Internal and External Security Issues in Asia* (Berkeley, CA: Institute of East Asian Studies, University of California, Berkeley, 1986) pp. 114–37.
23. *Deng Xiaoping wenxuan (The Selected Writings of Deng Xiaoping)*, 1975–1982 (Beijing: Renmin chupanshe, 1983) pp. 144–5.
24. Byung-Joon Ahn, 'Changing Leadership in China', in *Political Leadership in a Changing Society, Proceedings of the Second APPSA Conference, October 16–18, 1986, Seoul, Korea* (Seoul: The Asia-Pacific Political Science Association, 1986) pp. 29–40.
25. Byung-Joon Ahn, 'Chinese Communist Party Policy toward Intellectuals since 1949: A Critical Analysis', in Yu-ming Shaw (ed.), *Power and Policy in the PRC* (Boulder, CO: Westview, 1985) p. 312.
26. Harry Harding, 'Political Stability and Succession', in *China's Economy Looks Toward the Year 2000, vol. 1: The Four Modernizations* (Washington, DC: Government Printing Office, 1986) pp. 49–71.
27. *Beijing Review*, no. 50 (December 1982) pp. 11–17.
28. *International Herald Tribune*, 14 January 1987, p. 1.
29. Fang Lizhi, 'In China, as Elsewhere, People Are Born with Rights', ibid., 21 January 1987, p. 8.
30. *International Herald Tribune*, 27 February 1987, p. 2.
31. *Renmin Ribao*, 10 June 1987.
32. Robert F. Denberger, 'Economic Policy and Performance', in *China's Economy Looks Towards the Year 2000, vol. 1*, pp. 15–48.

2 Theoretical and Practical Aspects of the Economic Reform in China

Suck-Kyo Ahn

Ten years have passed since China launched a major economic reform at the Third Party Congress in 1978. Judging by economic results, it seems that China has chosen the 'right' model for its socialist construction. The much improved living standards of the Chinese people, especially since the beginning of the 1980s, seem to provide ample evidence in support of the new policy.

However, economics is only one aspect of the reform programme. The other side is more subtle and problematic since it concerns the ideological justification and the theoretical construction of the Chinese socialist model.

The problem arises from the fact that the transformation to socialism has not occurred according to the iron law of historical development as expounded by Marx. It took place at a time when all the socialist countries, but particularly China, were poorly developed.[1]

In 1984, China officially declared that it would adopt a 'planned socialist commodity economy' to be based both on the law of value and on public ownership. This necessarily gave rise to the ideological problem of harmonising the two diametrically different categories: central plan and commodity economy, each in competition with the essence of the other. Thus, ideological and theoretical disputes between the purists, or fundamentalists, and the pragmatists seem to be built into the present socialist model of China.

Bearing this in mind, we shall try in this chapter to trace out characteristics of economic reform in China, focusing on theoretical arguments of Chinese economists and some practical problems caused by the reform. This chapter deals with the aspects of the ownership structure of the means of production, the mechanism of resource allocation and the relation between income distribution and motivation of economic agents.

25

1 SOCIAL OWNERSHIP OF THE MEANS OF PRODUCTION

Social ownership is one of the most fundamental constituent elements of the socialist economic order. In China, state ownership became more dominant in the period from the founding of the republic in 1948 to 1956.[2]

In 1949 the state sector accounted for 34.7 per cent of total industrial output, the joint state–private sector for 2 per cent and the private sector for 63.3 per cent. Of the total retail sales in 1950, state commerce accounted for 14.9 per cent and private commerce for 85.1 per cent.[3] During the 1950s, the socialist transformation of the means of production took place step by step: the joint state–private sector had been encouraged at the cost of the private sector. The joint state–private enterprises were assured by the state of their sources of raw materials, the marketing of their products and reasonable profit. Profits were distributed by the shares. In the next phase, the capitalists of all enterprises drew a fixed annual interest of 5 per cent of their shares in disregard of profit.[4]

In the agricultural sector in 1949, only 0.1 per cent of all peasant households had joined agricultural producers' co-operatives, and only 3 per cent of all handicraftsmen had formed handicraft co-operatives.[5] The agricultural collectivisation went through three stages. The first was one of mutual aid teams. In the second phase peasants, while retaining private ownership of their land, pooled together for its common use and management. Income was distributed according to the amount of work as well as land, draught animals and farm implements. In the last phase these elementary co-operatives were integrated into advanced agricultural co-operatives of a fully socialist nature. In this way, public ownership of the means of agricultural production prevailed. The products of labour were distributed according to work, after deductions were made for the depreciation costs of the means of production, state taxes and a small amount of reserve fund and public welfare fund.

While only 2 per cent of the peasant households were in co-operatives in 1954, the figure rose to 14.2 per cent in 1955 and to 96 per cent by the end of 1956, with 88 per cent in advanced co-operatives.[6] In 1958 the agricultural co-operatives were reorganised in people's communes, where egalitarianism prevailed as the principle of distribution.

Such a speedy change of the ownership of the means of production was based on Mao's view that 'In a socialist society the basic contradictions are still those between the relations of production and the productive forces and between the superstructure and the economic base.'[7] However, the present regime seems to take the view that the radical changes of social relations of production undertaken by Mao were not at all conducive to economic development. In this regard, Mao's policy, especially during the ten years of Cultural Revolution, had become the target for intensive criticism.[8] According to Deng Xiaoping, the basic contradiction in China in the 1980s is no longer between the relations of production and the productive forces, but between the production capacity of the country and the people's demand.[9]

As to the prevailing two types of public ownership, collective and state, the following two aspects are often noted as important. One concerns the treatment of the ownership question in the Marxian version of communism, the other the impact of ownership on the motivation of economic agents to work well.

In his 'Critique Gotha Programme' Marx envisaged two phases of communism, lower and higher, both characterised by social ownership of the means of production. Only with such ownership would the 'exploitation of man by man' be eliminated. However, real socialism has been characterised by the coexistence of two different types of public ownership. To justify this divergence of ownership structure from the Marxian version of communism, some authors suggest that socialism should not be regarded as an autonomous phase of development.[10] According to one such author:

Current history poses a new question to us: Shouldn't socialism also be divided into several phases? . . . Recognition of this point is highly important because it helps to prevent a premature recognition of certain principles applicable only to the first phase of communism as defined by Marx.[11]

According to this view, advanced socialism (or the first phase of communism) is distinguished by unitary ownership by all the people, while backward socialism is characterised by the coexistence of the two types of public ownership. This is not to question that ownership by all the people and collective ownership are both socialist in nature. The difference lies in the degrees of maturity, the first representing a higher form and requiring a higher level of socialist consciousness for the economy to function well.

The second basic problem arising from the socialist ownership of the means of production relates to the proper motivation of economic agents, without which the development of the productive forces would be seriously hampered. There are basically two ways to solve the incentive problem. One is the return to private ownership, the other is decentralisation of economic decision-making. China is very cautious as regards the former, fearing that it might endanger the cause of socialism itself. This fear notwithstanding, there are signs of change. In the agricultural sector households are permitted to exercise certain disposable autonomy over private plots, and recently the bond market has been introduced on an experimental basis.

The most discernible feature of the economic reform in China is the fact that the lower and middle echelons of the economic hierarchy are endowed with increasing decision-making autonomy. Automatic remittance of all profits to the state has been replaced by profit tax, and enterprises have the power to dispose of the retained profits as they please. With this new practice, the right of disposal [*Vertfügungsrecht*] becomes increasingly distinct from the property right [*Eigentumsrecht*], an important new development which Marx apparently did not foresee.

2 MECHANISM OF RESOURCE ALLOCATION

The managerial system in China's economy, borrowed from the Soviet Union during the 1950s, laid primary emphasis on centralised management and leadership by the state. The decisions of individual enterprises with respect to production and investment were to follow the imperative guidelines set by the central plan. The policy of fixed prices dominated.[12] For example, the price of grain remained almost constant during the twelve years 1966 to 1978. Prices of agricultural products remained generally low, while prices of manufactured products were set relatively high.[13] Partly as a result of this policy, capital accumulation in the manufacturing sector was much greater than in the agricultural sector, and during the 1960s and 1970s the ratio between the living standards of workers and peasants stood at about 2 to 1. Furthermore, the prices of services provided in the urban sector had also been set low. The housing rent collected in 273 cities until 1980 covered only about a quarter of management and maintenance costs. Total state subsidies between 1971 and 1980 were consequently high, amounting to 22 per cent of the state's total revenue for that period.[14] As a result of such 'paternalistic' attitudes to enterprise by the state and the rigid management system, China's economy also suffered from low efficiency.

These are some of the problems which have necessitated price changes since 1979. At the Third Party Congress in October 1984, China officially declared that price reform was to be viewed as a decisive factor for the overall success of economic reform. As mentioned previously, China's economic system is now defined as a 'planned commodity economy' – some stressing the 'plan', while others emphasise the 'commodity economy'.

In a symposium held in China in 1985, the Hungarian economist János Kornai distinguished two categories of the regulatory mechanism of any modern economy: (I) administrative regulation and (II) market regulation. According to him, each of these mechanisms has two concrete forms: (IA) direct administrative regulation and (IB) indirect administrative regulation; (IIA) uncontrolled market regulation and (IIB) macro-controlled market regulation. It has generally been accepted that the IIB set-up is probably the most suitable for adoption in all socialist countries, including China.[15]

This means that state orders for outputs and allocations of inputs will assume a decreasing role, while the market mechanism plays an ever-increasing role, especially at the microeconomic level. In the future economic activities will, presumably, be increasingly co-ordinated with such economic parameters such as prices, tax rates and interest rates.

Aided by the new theories, China introduced various measures to ensure the working of the market mechanism. These are as follows:

(i)   The price reform is based on the 'block-double-track' system. This consists of a planned fixed price for the production quota of a commodity, and floating or free market prices for the above-quota production.[16] Since 1984, both fixed and market prices have also been adopted selectively with regard to the means of production.

(ii) As for manpower allocation, the State Council promulgated a series of regulations on reforming China's labour system in 1986, which aimed at eliminating the defects of the 'iron rice bowl' practice. Since 1949 – and especially since 1956 – labour has been assigned centrally, the state guaranteeing lifetime employment. With the implementation of the new regulations, state enterprises have, since 1980, been introducing a contract system.

This endows state enterprise managers with the power to deploy the workforce, while the workers enjoy certain freedoms in the selection of jobs. At the same time, the enterprises are permitted to dismiss employees who violate the contract.

(iii) To ensure the efficiency of management through competitive pressure on the market, new laws concerning the bankruptcy of enterprises have been enacted. They appear to follow the principle that 'those who have lost out in competition should be eliminated, no matter whether they are state-owned or collectively owned'.[17]

Now we turn to some of the key problems of the new reform.

(a) The first problem to be settled is how to delineate in clear-cut terms the scope of decentralisation of the decision-making power regarding prices. Here it is difficult, if not impossible, to harmonise the requirements of theory and practical operability, so as to avoid setting the scope in a more or less arbitrary manner. In the case of commodity exchanges between the state sector and the collective enterprises, it is in practice also difficult to establish exchange ratios which would reflect the 'socially necessary labour'. This has to do with the fact that fixed prices still dominate in the state sector, whereas collective enterprises can exercise certain autonomy in their price policy.

(b) Due to the two-track system of pricing, increases in allocative efficiency resulting from the more flexible prices are limited. The collective enterprises which exercise flexibility in their pricing policy are estimated to account for only 30 per cent of total industrial output. At the present stage, however, such a dual system is considered a necessary 'transitory measure', which 'will serve as a bridge spanning the old structure and the new one, smooth out the transition from direct administrative control to indirect market control'.[18]

(c) Any price decentralisation brings with it the danger that inflationary pressure will intensify. According to one estimate, if prices of basic products alone were to rise at an average rate of 10 per cent a year, the cost of machinery and light industrial products would rise 4 to 5 per cent a year.[19] It is therefore to be expected that concern for the general price level will be an important restraint on the price reform.

It seems to be the general perception of policy-makers and economists that two conditions, among others, must be satisfied to reduce the inflationary pressure of the price reform: the formation of a buyers' market and abolition of monopoly in the state sector. However, neither of these conditions can be easily satisfied, at least not in the short term.

(d) As for the reform of the employment system, the contract system, giving enterprises the right to dismiss employees can create or aggravate the problem of unemployment.[20] According to official statistics, the rate of unemployment is estimated to be 1.9 per cent. However, there is a 150 million surplus labour force in the countryside, and 30 per cent of the staff and workers in the enterprises of the urban sector constitute practically disguised unemployment. Furthermore, it is estimated that the labour force will increase at a rate of 2 per cent annually until the end of the century.[21]

These are some of the problems which might accompany the reform process in China. To sum up: China is likely to proceed with the reform of the allocative system. The speed of the reform, however, will be influenced by the capacity of society to absorb its various negative side-effects.

3 INCENTIVE SYSTEM AND MOTIVATION

As far as the roles of various kinds of work incentives and motivation structure are concerned, it has been suggested that under the capitalist mode of production, man's nature is quiescent. In other words, individual material incentives and disincentives are needed to set in motion man's rational self-interest. In communism, however, moral incentives and 'mass enthusiasm' are expected to propel an individual to exert him- or herself unstintingly for the good of the community.[22] Here again, Marx provided the relevant ideology. According to him, transformation of capitalism into socialism is accompanied not only by the change in the ownership of the means of production, but also by the conversion of individual labour into social labour. With this, factor labour ceases to be a 'commodity'. He noted that communism is 'the real appropriation of the human essence by and for man; . . . the complete return of man to himself as a social being'.[23]

Mao Zedong, who believed in creating a new species of (communist) human being, had worked hard at human engineering. Emphasis was laid, in the mass media and formal education, on political and ideological indoctrination, and the principle of egalitarianism influenced income distribution. During the ten years of the Cultural Revolution, the use of material stimulus was subjected to the particularly intensive criticism of being a remnant of bourgeois individualism.

Since 1978, however, the principle of egalitarianism and the system of moral incentives have been reflected upon critically, the argument being that they violate the 'objective law' of the present stage of Chinese economic development. In this respect Chinese economists assent to the argument of Engels, who implied the possibility of partial possession of labour power by the individual as an 'intermediate link' between capitalism and communism. According to this new theory, 'The division between labour performed by the labourer for himself and that performed for society is an expression of the dual nature of socialist labour in the field of distribution.'[24] In this way, the principle of distribution 'to each according to his work', or 'the exchange of an equal amount of labour for an equal amount of products', gains its ideological basis. Such a principle of income distribution is regarded as an objective necessity, since 'egalitarianism . . . would dampen people's enthusiasm and hinder the development of productive forces, making it difficult to implement the gradual transition to the practice of "to each according to his needs"'.[25] Table 2.1 shows how the incentive systems in China have changed since 1949.

However, income distribution based on the principle of performance would inevitably lead to an increase in income inequality. This might be especially true for the agricultural collectives, due to high variations in the quality of land. On the other hand, if the state taxes away a large part of the incomes of the high-yielding collectives and uses the revenue to subsidise the low-yielding collectives, this would probably discourage the productive activity of both types.

Assuming a certain trade-off between effort and imposed equity, China's policy-makers will have to continue tackling the theoretical and practical task of establishing a socially optimal compromise between the two policy objectives.

4 PROSPECTS

Statistical evidence shows that the economic reform in China succeeded, in the years since 1978, in substantially raising the living

Table 2.1 *Work Incentives in China since 1949*

Period	Material	Moral	Individual		Collective
1949–52	X		X		
1953–7	X		X		
1958–60		X			X
1961–5	X		X		
1966–70		X			X
1970–6[a]		X		X	
1976–7[b]		X		X	
1978–80	X		X		

[a] moral and collective dominate
[b] material and individual dominate

SOURCE Jans S. Prybyla, *The Chinese Economy: Problems and Policies* (University of South Carolina Press, 1981) p. 148.

standard of the Chinese people. During the 1979–84 period average consumption increased 7.3 per cent per annum, compared to only 2.2 per cent during 1953–78. From 1979 to 1983, total output of industry and agriculture increased 7 to 9 per cent per annum. In 1984 the growth rate jumped to 14.2 per cent. Encouraged by these results, China moved to an overall economic reform in the urban sector after 1984.

However, there is still a long way to go. Most of the Chinese economy is technologically backward; consequently, labour productivity is very low. For example, labour productivity in the engineering field is only 9 per cent of that in Japan. The corresponding ratios are estimated to be 4 per cent in the steel industry and 6 per cent in the electronics industry.[26] China's economy will be burdened with the task of increasing labour productivity, while at the same time absorbing actual and disguised unemployment.

As the economic reform proceeds further, the tension between the systematic requirements of socialist orthodox ideology and the requirements of functional efficiency of resource allocation is likely to continue. For the moment, it seems, the Chinese leaders share Lenin's view that 'We do not regard Marx's theory as something completed and inviolable'.[27]

Notes

1. 'Marx and Engels assumed that the proletarian socialist revolution would first be successful in the most developed capitalist countries. . . . Had this been the case, the transition from capitalism to socialism would have been much easier. But history takes a tortuous course. Up to now, no proletarian has triumphed in any of these countries' (Xue Muqiao, *China's Socialist Economy* [Beijing: Foreign Language Press, 1981] p. 1).
2. In 1956, the socialist state industry accounted for 67.5 per cent of gross industrial output (Xue Muqiao, *China's Socialist Economy*, p. 31).
3. Ibid., p. 18.
4. Such a fixed interest was abolished in 1967.
5. Xue Muqiao, *China's Socialist Economy*, p. 23.
6. Ibid., p. 35.
7. Mao Zedong, 'On the Correct Handling of Contradictions Among the People', *Selected Works* (Beijing: Foreign Language Press, 1977) pp. 393–4.
8. 'The Gang of Four argued that at no time can productive forces grow without a change in the relation of production, and advocated an unconditional, continual change in the social relations of production. This was an anti-Marxist view' (Xue Moqiao, *China's Socialist Economy*, p. X).
9. Ahn Suck-Kyo, 'Political Economy of the Economic Reform in China' (in Korean), *Sino-Soviet Affairs*, vol. VI, no. 1, Spring 1982, p. 47.
10. Xue Moqiao, *China's Socialist Economy*, p. 15.
11. Ibid., pp. 45–8, 63.
12. Xu Dixin, 'Transformation of China's Economy', in Xu Dixin *et al.*, *China's Search for Economic Growth* (Beijing: New World Press, 1982) p. 16.
13. Reflecting such a pricing system, profits of enterprises show wide differences between industries. Profits of selected industries in the raw material sector in 1979 were as follows: coal 2.1 per cent, iron ore 1.6 per cent, cement 4.4 per cent, timber 4.8 per cent, chemical materials 3.2 per cent; while profits in the processing industries were substantially higher – for example, 44.9 per cent in rubber processing, 38.4 per cent in dyes and paints, 61.1 per cent in the watch industry, 33.1 per cent in chemical products and pharmaceuticals (Liu Guoguang, 'Price Reform Essential to Growth', *Beijing Review*, no. 33, 18 August 1986, p. 14).
14. Ibid.
15. Liu Guoguang *et al.*, 'Economic Restructuring and Macroeconomic Management', *Social Sciences in China*, Beijing 1, 1986, pp. 10–11.
16. Specifically, the pricing system is as follows: (1) Unified state prices cover the products 'most important to the state plan' and the people's livelihood – that is, the small number of products under state mandatory plans. (2) Floating prices cover products which are 'relatively important to the national economy', and for which the state may set certain limits. (3) Free prices – including negotiated prices fixed through the consultation between producers and dealers, and market trade prices – cover most of agricultural and sideline products, household commodities and

labour services (Han Zhiguo, 'Symposium on Restructuring China's Economy: A Summary', *Social Sciences in China*, Beijing 3, 1985, p. 17).

17. According to a survey conducted in Shanghai and Chunggyung, 68 per cent of the people were for the introduction of such a law, 4 per cent against it and the remaining 28 per cent judged it to be worthy of consideration (Jian Chuan, 'Competition Touches Off Chain Reaction', *Beijing Review*, no. 35, 1 September 1986, p. 17).

18. Liu Guoguang *et al.*, 'Economic Restructuring' p. 17.

19. Liu Guoguang, 'Price Reform' p. 17.

20. To solve social problems arising from the contract system, two kinds of insurance system have been introduced: labour insurance for the unemployed and insurance for the retired. Insurance funds for the unemployed will be collected at a rate of 1 per cent of their wage bill. While waiting for new jobs, laid-off workers will receive 50–75 per cent of their previous wages. Those who have spent five years in their job will receive unemployment pay for two years, and those who have spent less than five years, for up to one year. The retirement insurance scheme will apply to new workers from the time they are recruited. Funds for pensions will be largely collected from enterprises at a rate of 15 per cent of their total wage bill, while contract workers have to pay into the fund 3 per cent of their wages (interview with Minister of Labour and Personnel, He Guang, 'Articles', *Beijing Review*, no. 37, 15 September 1986, p. 16).

21. *Far Eastern Economic Review*, 16 October 1986.

22. Jans S. Prybyla, *The Chinese Economy – Problems and Policies* (University of South Carolina Press, 1981) p. 175.

23. Cited in ibid., p. 146.

24. Xue Muqiao, *China's Socialist Economy*, p. 71.

25. Ibid., p. 76.

26. *Far Eastern Economic Review*, 16 October 1986.

27. Lenin, 'Our Programme', *Collected Works* (Moscow: Foreign Language Publishing House, 1960) vol. 4, pp. 211–12, cited in Xue Muqiao, *China's Socialist Economy*, p. v.

3 Between Plan and Market: The Role of the Local Sector in Post-Mao Reforms in China[1]

Christine P. W. Wong

INTRODUCTION

The Chinese economy has long been characterised by multilevel planning, with local governments controlling nearly half of total industrial output and allocating substantial resources.[2] Because of the continuing important role played by local governments, market reforms in the 1980s have not brought a straightforward transfer of decision-making authority from central government to enterprises. Instead, there has been a good deal of 'leakage' in the reform process, with local governments retaining and even expanding control over enterprises through a variety of informal mechanisms, as well as through their control over geographically immobile factor resources. This chapter looks at the local sector and how market reforms have affected it. The term 'local' will mean administrative levels below the central government: province, municipality, prefecture, county, township and village.[3]

Defining reform as a redistribution of decision-making, with '+' indicating gains and '−' indicating losses, we can, in a three-level economy, enumerate the following five different reform types:[4]

	1	2	3	4	5
Central units	−	−	−	−	−
Intermediate units (local governments)		−	+	+	+
Primary units (enterprises)	+	+	+		−

These types are arranged in an order of declining 'thoroughness' of

36

the reforms, which is defined according to the reforms' stated objective of transferring decision-making power to enterprises. In the best case (type 1), decision-making power is transferred from both central and local governments to the enterprises. In the worst case (type 5), 'positive intermediation' occurs, where the units of local government gain at the expense of both central government and the enterprises. In between the best and worst cases are scenarios where 'leakage' occurs, with local governments usurping some or all of the decision-making power passed down by central government (types 3 and 4). The success of market reforms in China obviously depends on the type that is obtained in the decentralisation process, as well as on the behaviour of local governments.

Previous decentralisation of the Chinese economy (especially during 1958 and 1970) were of type 4 ('administrative decentralisation'). While post-Mao reforms have broken decisively from that tradition by transferring much greater decision-making power to enterprises, there has also been a good deal of 'leakage' to the intermediate units. In fact, it will be argued that decentralisation through 1983 was closer to type 5 than to type 1. In the more recent period market pressures have eroded local control in some respects, but much remains to be done to ensure that reforms continue to make progress towards the objective of increasing enterprise autonomy.

This chapter looks at the local sector and its role in the reform process. Two sets of interrelated questions are explored. The first set concerns the nature of decentralisation and the size of the local sector in the reform period. The second concerns the behaviour of the local sector: how is it managed? What is the relationship between local governments and enterprises? And what are the implications of local control of resource allocation?

DISTINGUISHING FEATURES OF THE CHINESE ECONOMY AND PLANNING

During the 1960s and 1970s, the local sector was a 'catch-all' category that absorbed the spillovers from the state (central) sector, when the market sector was virtually nonexistent. Through successive rounds of decentralisation and rapid local industrialisation, it grew to rival the state sector in size. By the mid-1970s it had developed substantial growth momentum based on resources generated within the sector itself. To understand the key role played by the local sector, it is

Table 3.1   *Size Distribution of Industrial Enterprises in Selected Countries*
(per cent)

Size of enterprise	China 1982	United Kingdom 1979	United States 1977	South Korea 1981	Japan 1972	India 1976–7	Yugo-slavia 1981	Hungary 1981
Employees								
5–33	59.2	65.2	56.4	70.6	80.2	51.7	6.6	2.2
33–75	19.5	15.7	20.3	14.4	10.7	35.3	15.8	4.8
75–189	12.2	10.8	12.4	9.2	6.1	7.8	32.1	18.7
189–243	8.5	1.4	3.8	1.5	0.8	0.8	12.0	9.2
More than 243	0.6	6.9	7.1	4.3	2.2	4.4	33.5	65.1

NOTE   Data are percentages of the number of enterprises with five or more employees in the country.

SOURCE   World Bank, *China: Longterm Development Issues and Options*, 1985, Table 1.1.

necessary to look at the structure of Chinese planning.

A number of features distinguish the Chinese economy from other socialist planned economies. The first is the extremely large number of industrial enterprises. The *Chinese Statistical Yearbook* counts a total of 437 200 enterprises at the end of 1984: with 84 100 in the state sector (SSB, 1985, p. 305). Even though this number excludes most enterprises in the rural sector, it is extremely large compared to socialist economies in Eastern Europe.[5] Moreover, the number has increased by over 25 per cent in the reform period, with the addition of nearly 90 000 enterprises since 1978, almost entirely in the collective sector.

The second feature is the preponderance of small-scale enterprises. By World Bank estimates, only 0.6 per cent of Chinese enterprises have more than 243 workers, compared to 65.1 per cent in Hungary and 33.5 per cent in Yugoslavia (see Table 3.1). It is difficult to convert Chinese enterprise size categories for cross-country comparisons since they are based on annual output, productive capacity, or fixed assets. However, even if the World Bank numbers underestimate the portion of large-scale Chinese enterprises by as much as five- to tenfold,[6] it remains true that the size structure of Chinese industry is very unusual for a socialist planned economy, though not for a developing country. In addition, while the trend in other socialist countries has been towards merging enterprises into ever larger units, in China the share of output from small plants has grown steadily from 45 per cent of gross value of industrial output in 1970 to about 55 per cent today.

Given the large number and small scale of industrial enterprises, the Chinese planning system has by necessity evolved differently from those in Eastern Europe. Through the mid-1960s and 1970s, when rapid industrialisation at the local level was adding large numbers of small enterprises, the impossibility of incorporating them into the planning structure led to the creation of a multitiered, regionally based system where much of the responsibility for planning and co-ordination devolved to local governments. In this system, enterprises were divided by their importance and by ownership. Large-scale, key enterprises remained in the central plan, while non-key enterprises were left to planning and co-ordination at provincial, prefectural and county levels.[7]

The approximate distribution of enterprises by administrative level is presented in Table 3.2. At the top are some 2500 enterprises controlled by the central government and its ministries, which produce 30–40 per cent of total industrial output. In addition to key enterprises in the defence industry, this group comprises the largest producers in important industries. In 1980, for example, it included 84 coal-mining administrations (with 553 mines), 20-odd iron and steel enterprises, 53 large and medium cement plants, 50-odd producers of sulphuric acid, 5 producers of soda ash, and 10-plus key forestry regions (*Xiandai Zhongguo Shidian*, pp. 312–13).

In the second tier are enterprises run by provinces and cities. These include 30–40 000 mostly small and medium enterprises in the state-owned sector, as well as over 100 000 collective enterprises. Collective enterprises in this group range from very small (with a few employees) to very large (with over 1000 employees). Even though the bulk of these collective enterprises belong to vertically orientated light industrial systems, they are also subject to a high degree of local control.[8]

In the third tier are enterprises in the prefectural and county systems. These include perhaps 40–50 000 state-owned enterprises and some 20–25 000 collective enterprises. These enterprises are mostly small-scale and operate largely free of state plan control. At the bottom are rural collective enterprises run by townships and villages (formerly communes and brigades). In 1983 the State Statistic Bureau included 186 100 township enterprises in its industrial statistics (1985, p. 313). In addition, there were several hundred thousand enterprises at village level and below.[9] The shares of

Table 3.2   *Estimated Distribution of Industrial Enterprises by Ownership and Administrative Level**
(1983)

	STATE		COLLECTIVE	
1)	2 500 large enterprises controlled by central government (30–35%)			URBAN (75%)
2a)	30–40 000 small–medium enterprises controlled by provinces and city governments (25–30%)	2b)	100 000+ 'large' and 'small' urban collectives (10–12%)	
3a)	40–50 000 County and prefectural enterprises (13–15%)	3b)	20–25 000 'large' and 'small' collectives (3–5%)	RURAL (25%)
		4)	186 000 Enterprises owned by townships and villages (7%)	
	(78%)		(22%)	

* Figures in parentheses denote shares of gross value of industrial output.

SOURCES   Breakdown of collective sector output by urban and rural: SSB (1985), pp. 306, 315.
Estimated breakdown of urban–rural GVIO: Liu Suinian, 'The Issue of Concentration and Dispersal in China's Economic Development', in Liu Guiguang (ed.), *Zhongguo Jingji Fazhan Zhanlue Wenti Yanjiu* (Research on the Issues of China's Strategy for Economic Development) (Beijing, 1984) p. 502.

industrial output by enterprise categories are derived from reported breakdowns of output by sector and urban–rural division.

In this hierarchical ordering of enterprises there is a rough correspondence between enterprise size and degree of incorporation into the central plan. In general, the share of enterprise output included in the central plan declines as we move down the hierarchy. In 1977–8, for example, when the central plan included some 50–55 per cent of gross value of industrial output, it accounted for close to 100 per cent of output in centrally administered enterprises, but less than 20 per cent in rural collective enterprises.[10] Interpolating from these two extremes, we estimate that the central plan accounted for perhaps one-half to two-thirds of the production in provincial and city enterprises, and one-fourth to one-third that in county and prefectural enterprises during the late 1970s.[11] By 1984, with the share of gross industrial output included in the central plan declining to 30–40 per cent, there had been a corresponding decline in planned shares of output in all categories, though not necessarily proportionally. With most enterprises and so much of the industrial output outside direct control by the central government, the success of market reform in the post-Mao period depends critically on whether local governments introduce appropriate changes, *pari passu*, at the lower levels.

THE LOCAL SECTOR IN THE POST-MAO PERIOD

In the post-Mao period, there is some uncertainty about the size and behaviour of the local sector. On the positive side, the rapid response of local production to market stimuli has greatly improved the supply of many consumer goods as well as producers' goods such as coal and building materials.[12] The more rapid growth of the non-state sectors during the reform period is generally attributed to the greater dynamism of local economies. On the other hand, a good deal of anecdotal evidence indicates that in at least some spheres, local growth has come at the expense of the state sector and to the detriment of overall economic efficiency. Because of competition from local producers, for example, state procurement plans for a variety of agricultural products – including tobacco, wool, raw silk, animal skins, and high grades of cotton – are substantially underfulfilled. As a result, production in large-scale, modern processing plants is being displaced by less efficient production in local small plants (Wu Junglian, 1986; CASS, 1985). More importantly, the rapid growth in local investment in the 1980s has been squeezing out state investment projects, even in the bottleneck sectors of transportation and energy production.[13]

While there is little question of the continuing significance of the local sector, its true size is difficult to ascertain. In 1984, Chinese planners estimated that about 30–40 per cent of total industrial output was included in the central plan. Another 20 per cent was said to be produced 'primarily according to market principles'.[14] This latter figure was also the estimated portion of industrial output traded at market prices.[15] The 40–50 per cent of industrial output that falls outside both the central plan and the market constituted the upper limit for the size of the local sector, though its actual size was probably somewhat smaller.[16]

A major source of difficulty in estimating the size of the local sector is the paucity of information on the relationship between local governments and their enterprises. During the pre-reform era, when enterprises had virtually no autonomous decision-making authority, whatever was outside the central government sphere of control could safely be treated as within the local sphere.[17] This applied, for example, to the disposal of funds nominally retained by enterprises, such as those for depreciation and technical renovation. Throughout the Cultural Revolution, these funds were frequently pooled by local governments for use in local investment projects. With the reform strengthening enterprise autonomy, however, the use of these funds may have slipped out from under local government control. Since over 70 per cent of all extra-budgetary funds are retained by enterprises, the nature of local government–enterprise relations is an important determinant of local sector behaviour. Unfortunately, this relationship appears to be a rapidly changing area for which data are difficult to obtain. Moreover, there is undoubtedly a great deal of regional variation in the nature of these ralationships. In the absence of definitive information, the charges that local governments are continuing to wield primary control over local resources, use 'commandist workstyles' in managing local economies, and so on, have to be viewed against reform efforts to reduce their influence.[18]

THE NATURE AND EVOLUTION OF LOCAL PLANNING: THE CULTURAL REVOLUTION LEGACY[19]

As it evolved in the 1960s and the 1970s, local planning occupied an intermediate position between central planning and market allocation. Initially, local planning grew out of the need to augment state plans, when decentralisation transferred to local governments the responsibility for co-ordinating production. Although the planned components of production were usually supplied with planned allocations of major inputs, enterprises were expected to find supplementary supplies from local sources. In the absence of markets for goods, local planning developed to co-ordinate supplies of materials allocated under state plans with local resources.

The market-like character of the local sector grew out of the need to obtain resources outside plan channels, as local industries grew beyond local supply capabilities. It was local industrialisation that spurred the growth of interregional barter trade during the 1970s, where market-like prices developed. In turn, the availability of an extra-plan channel where surpluses could be exchanged for needed resources provided incentives to orientate local production along 'economic' lines. By its very nature and evolution local planning extended into the market fringe, both for supplies and for outlets for local production. In that local planning formed the bridge between planning and the market it was a precursor of 'guidance' planning, a concept that is much in vogue today.

At the same time, the market-like characteristics of local economies should not be exaggerated. During the Cultural Revolution, many restrictions limited the scope of extra-plan, interregional trade and prevented local economies from fully exploiting their comparative advantages. Instead, local planning was conducted along bureaucratic lines, and transactions within the local economy were usually guided by command principles. By all accounts, in the pre-reform period China operated as a command economy, albeit one that was fragmented into many vertical and horizontal pieces.

Plan-making was a separate and discrete process at each level. This lack of co-ordination can be illustrated with an example from Shashi, a medium-sized city in Hubei province. In 1977 the city was supplied with 13 408 tons of steel from state allocations. Of this, only 3100 tons came through block transfers for general allocation to the 267 city-owned enterprises. The other 10 000 tons were directly allocated by central and provincial departments and designated for three centrally owned, ten provincial-owned and fourteen city-owned enterprises under *sheng zhigong* (provincial direct supply).[20] These latter materials were routed through the prefectural materials bureau, completely bypassing the city's material supply system. In this way, central and provincial plans passed through Shashi without interacting with the city plan (Shashi Materials Bureau, 1984, p. 166) and enterprises located side by side were separated into discrete planning systems and supply channels, with virtually no interaction.

From the perspective of central planners, local activities were considered 'extra-plan' and lumped together with market activities.

Local production was not incorporated into national plans except for the portions under compulsory procurement by state agencies. From the local perspective, local plans encompassed central plans and added on to them the quantities needed to ensure sufficient supplies for fulfilling central plans as well as meeting local needs. Because of this multilevel planning, production in industrial enterprises was often divided into three sections: one under central plans, one under local plans, and a third, unplanned portion.

While local planning facilitated the mobilisation of local resources and provided some flexibility to an otherwise quite rigid and ineffectual system, it also led to a compartmentalisation of resources that greatly exacerbated the tendency of bureaucratic systems towards autarkic development. In terms of the local sector's role in the reform process, the most harmful legacy of local planning is the behavioural pattern local governments developed during the Cultural Revolution. Having gained control over large amounts of resources, local governments are in many places actively resisting reform efforts to turn over resource allocation to market forces and to transfer decision-making authority to enterprises.

MECHANISMS OF LOCAL CONTROL IN THE REFORM PERIOD

In the pre-reform period, local governments could directly control production, supply and sales in local enterprises through the allocation of material supplies. The pooling of enterprise profits and depreciation allowances also enabled them to allocate investment funds. In the reform period, while compulsory and guidance plans are still formulated by local governments, these direct control mechanisms have declined in importance, since the development of goods markets have allowed enterprises to be less dependent on administrative allocations. A 1984 survey of 429 enterprises found, for example, that although local levels accounted for nearly half of the compulsory plans assigned to them, compulsory planning accounted for an average of only 24 per cent of total production in these enterprises (CESRI, 1986, p. 53). Instead, with the decline in the use of direct mechanisms, there has been a shift to informal mechanisms of control, which have been left largely untouched by market reforms.

The most important informal mechanism available to local governments is their control over factor resources. The allocation of workers and appointment of managers gives local officials substantial leverage for influencing enterprise behaviour. In the absence of national capital markets, there is widespread consensus that local governments continue to exercise significant control over the allocation of investment finance. In spite of the near-universal introduction of enterprise profit-retention schemes, a good deal of evidence indicates that local enterprises, especially at lower administrative levels, enjoy less financial autonomy than enterprises at higher administrative levels. The 1984 survey mentioned above found a profit-retention rate of only 21.6 per cent among small-scale enterprises, compared with an average of 57 per cent for large and medium-sized enterprises in the sample. Given that these small enterprises had an average of only 100 000 yuan for production development funds from retained profits, they were left highly dependent on external finance (CERSI, 1986, p. 171).

Apart from the growing funds collected from enterprise profits and taxes which fiscal decentralisation has transferred to local coffers (see below), local officials continue to exert substantial influence over bank lending, since the regional structure of the banking system places bank officials at the mercy of local officials for a variety of supporting facilities, including housing for the bank staff (Zhou Xiaochuan and Zhu Li, 1987). In addition, other studies found that profit-retention contracts are often violated, with local officials arbitrarily requisitioning enterprise funds for investment in local infrastructural facilities, development of new products, or to support local welfare expenditures (Zhao Yujiang, 1986; Ding Jiatiao, 1985). In a report reminiscent of complaints during the Cultural Revolution, one writer told of officials in Sichuan province issuing quotas for local development projects in imitation of 'advanced experiences' elsewhere. In order to fulfil these quotas, local units were forced 'blindly' to start projects that were inappropriate to local conditions, and banks were coerced into granting loans in support of these investments (Zhu Xiaowen, 1985).

With local governments continuing to exercise control through these informal mechanisms, market reforms in the post-Mao period have left enterprises with a 'dual dependence'.[21] Not only are enterprises forced to be more responsive to market pressures, they also remain highly dependent on the administrative bureaucracy to provide vital support. With the economy moving away from the use of physical allocations to emphasising financial indicators, enterprise dependence on the bureaucracy has similarly shifted from plan bargaining to the financial sphere, in bargaining over profit quotas, subsidies, investment funds, and so on.

THE IMPACT OF REFORMS: THE FIRST PHASE (1979–83)

Through their formal and informal control over the three principal sources of extra-budgetary funds (enterprise funds, bank loans, and local government revenues), local governments greatly expanded their allocative powers when reforms spurred the growth of extra-budgetary funds from 36.1 billion yuan to 89.1 billion yuan from 1978 to 1983 (JJNJ, 1983, pp. III–90; 1984, pp. IV–43). In this section it is argued that decentralisation during the first phase of reform resulted in an outcome that was somewhere between type 4 and type 5, not only with local governments gaining substantial resources but also with some 'positive intermediation', since enterprises became even more dependent on local officials.

Under the profit-based bonus schemes in use during 1979–84, profit-retention rates were set at low levels of the bureaucracy and were subject to negotiation between enterprises and their supervisory agencies.[22] Under this system, the welfare of workers and managers became very much dependent on the goodwill of local officials, who held the authority to set profit-retention rates for the enterprises. Beyond setting these rates, local officials had a good deal of control over the *level* of after-tax profits through their price- and tax-setting authority. For any given level of output and X-efficiency, the level of after-tax profits is directly related to the level of prices and taxes.

The ability of local governments to set prices is a legacy of Cultural Revolution policies. In order to allow small-scale, local enterprises to cover costs, local governments were allowed to set higher 'temporary' prices for local products. In the reform period this price-setting authority has been formalised under the principle of *gaojin gaochu, baoben jingying*, whereby enterprises can charge high (market) prices for their output if inputs were procured at high (market) prices. Since much of local production is based on market-allocated inputs, local outputs are not constrained to state prices.

For any local administrative unit, this price-setting authority is dependent upon: (1) the amount of resources available for allocation at below-market prices; (2) its ability to procure output at below-market prices, which is linked to the first; and (3) the gap between state and market prices. For both inputs and outputs, as long as a divergence exists between the market price and the state allocation price, local governments can set the average price level in one of two ways. They can set the mix of the two prices, by stipulating the portions to be sold at each price for outputs and by setting the portions allocated at each price for inputs. Or, more commonly, they can set *local* prices at some intermediate level.

Market liberalisation during the first phase of reform greatly increased the price-setting authority of local governments, since the growing gap between market and state prices provided them with a growing margin for changing prices. Obviously, this price-setting authority varies with the administrative level. At the provincial level, where the pool of materials that can be allocated is large relative to total demand, officials have substantial price-setting authority. At the township level, this authority may well be negligible. In 1982, allocations accounted for 70–80 per cent of total materials supplied at provincial level, 60–70 per cent prefectural and municipal level, and less than 50 per cent at county level (Li Kaixin, 1983, p. 1).

While the rates for both income and industrial-commercial taxes were standardised nationwide, local governments in fact had substantial power to change them. When an enterprise ran into financial difficulties it could turn to tax authorities for help, by asking for temporary tax reductions or exemptions. In spite of numerous attempts to recentralise this tax-relief-granting authority, it rested at levels as low as the county. Efforts to make tax offices independent of local governments appeared to have been quite unsuccessful, with tax officials frequently taking the view that it was their duty to aid development of the local economy.[23] Interestingly, the 'harder' prices faced by enterprises at lower levels (where officials have less price-setting authority) were often partially offset by 'softer' taxes, with closer working relationships between the tax bureau and the economic planning agencies at these lower levels.

Throughout this period of reform all the changes transferred more resources to local control, without any countervailing pressures to force local governments to behave in more economically efficient ways. Indeed, with fiscal reforms transferring the bulk of local enterprise profits and taxes to local revenue incomes, local governments had improved incentives to expand the local economic base. Not surprisingly, these changes brought an explosive growth in investment in revenue-generating activities, accompanied by an outburst of local protectionism. Protectionist tactics ranged from excluding outside products from local markets to threatening local enterprises with cutoffs of funds and bank loans, supplies of fuel, and so on, should they dare to buy the products of competitors (Li Yue, 1982, p. 12).

Even though fiscal reforms that made local governments more revenue-orientated should have reduced their willingness to subsidise loss-making enterprises, several factors militate against the beneficial impact this was intended to have in forcing enterprises to adjust to market pressure. One is the fact that local governments try to maximise net revenues, which consist of profits and taxes paid by the firm. They would be willing to allow the survival of money-losing firms as long as sufficient tax revenues were generated to offset the losses. Since taxes were wholly unrelated to enterprise efficiency, this thwarted the reform's intent. In addition, local governments were often under heavy pressure to preserve or create local jobs and to respond to social and political concerns, and cost-cutting seemed less pressing in an era of growing revenues. Through the first phase of reform, some local governments took extraordinary measures to protect high-cost enterprises from bankruptcy, in clear violation of the attempt to shut down inefficient enterprises.[24]

THE SECOND PHASE OF REFORMS IN THE PERIOD SINCE 1984

In recognition of the problematic role played by local governments, the second phase of reform introduced two measures to reduce local government control and break down administrative barriers to resource flows. The first was the measure to promote the 'economic role' of cities. The other was the reform to 'substitute taxes for profits'. Neither has succeeded to date in fundamentally altering the administrative set-up.

The movement to promote the economic role of cities was intended to utilise their natural co-ordinating functions to break down the rigidities and irrationalities of the hierarchical system. Under this measure, some central and provincial enterprises have been transferred to city management. In some provinces the administrative level of prefecture has been abolished, and counties have been reassigned to supervision by cities. Some improvements have been reported under this measure, most notably in eliminating some of the circuitous shipment of goods caused by routing shipments along administrative lines (State Materials Bureau, 1984, *passim*). In other areas, transferring enterprises to city management has improved the horizontal co-ordination of enterprises formerly belonging to different planning systems. However, progress towards reducing regionalism and 'departmentalism' has not been universal, since cities are themselves 'local' units and the change has sometimes merely substituted one administrative unit for another, with little alteration in work style.

A more concerted assault on local control came in the tax-for-profit reform that was introduced in 1983–4. The main thrust of this reform shifted state-owned enterprises at all administrative levels from the system of remitting profits to paying a series of taxes.[25] The objective was to formalise the financial interaction between enterprises and their supervisory agencies and end the era of profit negotiation under previous enterprise incentive schemes. Apart from 'hardening' enterprise budget constraints, this measure would have the effect of stripping local governments of an important source of control.

The reform would also reduce the financial incentives for local expansion. By pooling all enterprise income tax revenues and apportioning them among the different levels of government regardless of enterprise ownership, it would separate local government revenues from the ownership and profitability of enterprises.

Finally, the reform was to reduce the scope of local government intervention in enterprise operations by mandating that many small-scale enterprises be contracted out to private or collective management. Accompanying the tax-for-profit reform was the announcement that over a three-year period, beginning in 1985, all small-scale, state-owned enterprises with fixed assets of less than 1.5 million yuan and annual profits of 200 000 yuan or less would be contracted out to individuals or groups (Zhao Ziyang, 1984). If fully implemented, this measure would turn over to private or collective management as much as half of the 81 000 state-owned enterprises classified as 'small-scale'.[26]

Not surprisingly, due to its potentially significant impact in redistributing income and resources across administrative units, the tax-for-profit programme ran into much opposition. By the end of 1987 it was quietly scrapped in favour of a return to profit-contracting.

CONCLUSION

The existence of local governments with substantial allocative power has been detrimental to economic efficiency for three reasons. First, the fragmentation of control under local governments continues to impede resource flows. The slowness of the development of capital markets may be partly attributable to local opposition. Despite a promising start, investment trust companies have not developed into serious competitors to state-owned banks as financial intermediaries, perhaps because of their inability to cross over administrative barriers in their investment activities.[27] Reports of interregional investments seem to be confined to 'interregional co-operation' projects undertaken by local governments to secure raw material and energy supplies.

Secondly, when local governments are making the bulk of investment decisions, resource allocation is not following 'market regulation', since they aim to maximise net revenues rather than profits. Even with market reforms incrementally improving the information carried by prices, tax signals continue to be problematic guides for investment. In addition, local governments make investment choices based on administrative rather than purely economic considerations. In many areas the pressure to create jobs remains strong. And as the earlier example from Sichuan demonstrated, local officials are often susceptible to 'emulation drives' and model-building practices that run counter to economic rationality.

Thirdly, local governments reduce competition by shielding enterprises from market pressure and by intervening in interregional trade. In addition, they slow down the market adjustments by helping to perpetuate sellers' markets in a variety of producer and investment goods through their vigorous investment activities. These investment projects may in the long run make prices downwardly sticky: the development of buyers' markets may spur new attempts at regional protectionism rather than price-cutting, as local governments try to protect their newly created productive assets. They may even reach oligopolistic compromises that divide markets geographically to avoid competition. For all these reasons, it is necessary to curb local control in order to achieve reform objectives.

To date, attempts at curbing local control through administrative restructuring have been largely ineffective. It is probably in the realm of price-setting authority that market forces have had the greatest impact in eroding local control – by reducing the amount of resources that local governments can allocate administratively, at below-market prices, and by reducing the gap between plan and market prices for many goods. Since local governments derive substantial leverage through their ability to set prices, these changes have reduced their manoeuvrability. However, market forces alone cannot close the price gaps; this can be done only through a combination of raising state prices to realistic levels (where average costs are covered) and eliminating sellers' markets. Numerous adjustments in state prices since 1982–3 have helped to close the gap for many products, especially consumer goods, where buyers' markets had developed.

Furthermore, market forces cannot always be expected to turn sellers' markets into buyers' markets, even with improved resource mobility. Too many factors persist in the economy to fuel excessive investment, including soft budget constraints at the enterprise and local government levels. In the reform period, sellers' markets have persisted for many producer and investment goods, where price gaps remain large. For rolled steel, for example, the market price continues to be two to three times the state price.

Price reform is therefore necessary to realign prices to cover average production costs and to eliminate the gaps between state and market prices. A price reform that reunifies the price structure will substantially limit the barganing power of local governments over their enterprises and go a long way towards 'hardening' the enterprise budget constraint.

Given the importance of taxes in conferring bargaining power on local governments, tax reform is also necessary. The 'softness' of the present system must be eliminated by introducing standardised taxes. The authority to grant tax relief must also be recentralised to higher levels to reduce the incidence of abuse. Under the present revenue-sharing system, local officials can often afford to be generous in granting tax reductions or exemptions because the loss of revenue is shared with higher levels. This system is particularly subject to abuse at lower levels, where local officials see this as an opportunity to 'rob' the state treasury by reducing total tax payments. To wrest control of tax rates effectively from local officials, then, a new system must be set up to separate local taxes from state taxes, with separate collection agencies.

Even though these changes are necessary to reduce local influence, they will not be sufficient. The greatest mechanisms of control available to local governments are those over factor resources, whose geographical immobility confers tremendous power on local officials.

Until market reforms extend into the development of factor markets, local governments will continue to wield substantial control in the Chinese economy.

Notes

1. An earlier version of this chapter was published in *Journal of Comparative Economics*, vol. 11, 1987, pp. 385–98 (copyright © 1987 Academic Press, Inc.). It is reprinted here with permission.
2. The multilevel planning system is discussed in a number of recent studies. See Wong (1985, 1986a), Granick (1986) and Tidrick and Chen (1987).
3. This enumeration draws from Neuberger (1985), pp. 18–26.
4. This is a problematic category because of the great diversity among the units, in terms of size and relationship to central government. The common bond that allows us to group them together for the purposes of this chapter is their competition for resources *vis-à-vis* central government.
5. The number is over 1 000 000 if rural enterprises at all levels are counted. Chinese industrial statistics include only township enterprises, excluding those at the villages and production teams as well as the considerable number of private and co-operative enterprises set up in recent years.
6. In 1984 there were 6400 large and medium enterprises by Chinese definitions (= 1.46 per cent total). The average employment in these enterprises far exceeds 243 workers.
7. For a history of the evolution of this multitiered system, see Wong (1985).
8. For a detailed description of the collective sector, see Wong (1986a), pp. 582–4.
9. For 1983, the *Agricultural Yearbook* listed 744 000 rural collective enterprises engaging in industrial production. 43.5 billion yuan of output from village and team enterprises was counted as agricultural output (1984, pp. 71, 79).
10. Estimates for the central plan's share of gross value of industrial output and for tier one enterprises are from Wong (1986a), pp. 586–8; rural collective share is from RMRB, 21 August 1980.
11. These estimates are supported by anecdotal accounts. The portion of industrial output under state plans was 70 per cent for Wuxi Municipality, 30 per cent for Wuxi County (Zuo Mu, 1980, p. 32), and one-third for Guangdong's Nanhai County (Chinese Association of Material Economics, 1984, vol. 2, pp. 343–4).
12. For example, during the 1978–84 period local mines accounted for nearly 80 per cent of the increase in coal production (MTNJ, 1982, pp. 9, 16; 1983, p. 61; 1985, p. 50).
13. This has been argued by Naughton (1985), Wong (1985) and others.

14. Briefing given to the American Economists Study Team, December 1984, reported by Naughton (1986), p. 625.
15. Estimate made by Zhang Zhuoyuan in a seminar at the University of California, Berkeley, October 1984.
16. If the local sector approached this limit, however, the 20 per cent market portion came entirely out of the central plan's share, since the local sector included 45–50 per cent of industrial output on the eve of reform in the late 1970s.
17. This also ignores resources under control of state organisations, such as highway departments and the water conservancy bureau. For our purpose of looking at resources available for 'empire-building', these organisations probably behave similarly to local governments.
18. For examples of these charges, see Ding Jiatiao (1985), Zhao Yujiang (1986) and Zhu Xiaowen (1985).
19. Information for this section draws from Wong (1985).
20. 'Direct supply' or *zhigong* enterprises are keypoint enterprises that receive higher-level support. For a detailed discussion of the complex ownership and control structure in Chinese industry, see Wong (1986a).
21. This is a term used by Kornai (1986) to describe the condition of firms in the reformed Hungarian economy.
22. For discussions of the problems of these profit-sharing schemes, see Naughton (1985) and Wong (1986b).
23. Fieldwork information, June 1982. Also, numerous articles in CZ and CMJJ corroborate the pervasiveness of these attitudes.
24. For example, in one rural county in Guangdong, money-losing fertiliser plants were helped to set up breweries and cement workshops to improve their overall profitability (fieldwork information, June 1982). These and other examples are reported in greater detail in Wong (1986a).
25. This discussion draws heavily from Wong (1986b). Details of the tax-for-profit system are also provided in Naughton (1986).
26. This is estimated on the basis of the 1983 profile of these enterprises: they had annual output of 3.1 million yuan and fixed assets of 2 million yuan, and remitted taxes and profits of 430 000 yuan (SSB, 1984, and BR, 1985; 9, p. 10).
27. For a brief account of the development of investment trust companies, see Naughton (1986), pp. 615–18.

List of Abbreviations

BR   *Beijing Review*
CASS   Chinese Academy of Social Sciences
CESRI Chinese Economic System Reform Institute
CMJJ   *Caimao Jingji* (Finance and Trade Economics)
CZ   *Caizheng* (Finance)
JJGL   *Jingji Guanli* (Economic Management)
JJNJ   *Zhongguo Jingji Nianjian* (Economics Yearbook of China)
JJYJ   *Jingji Yanjiu* (Economic Research)

MTNJ *Meitan Nianjian* (Coal Yearbook)
RMRB *Renmin Ribao* (People's Daily)
SSB   State Statistical Bureau

References

Agricultural Yearbook of China, 1984 (Zhongguo Nongye Nianjian) (Beijing: Agricultural Press).

Chinese Academy of Social Science, Institute of Industrial Economics (1985) 'An Investigation: Reform of the System of Monopoly Sales of Tobacco and Liquor', JJYJ: 11.

Chinese Association of Material Economics (1984) *Wuzi Jingji yu Guanli Wenji* (Compendium of Essays on Material Economics and Management), vol. 2 (Beijing: Materials Press).

Chinese Economic System Reform Institute Comprehensive Investigation Group (ed.) (1986) *Gaige: Women Mianlin de Tiaozhan yu Suanzhe* (Reform: The Challenges and Choices We Face) (Beijing: Chinese Economics Press).

Ding Jiatiao (1985) 'The Separation of Government and Enterprise Factors is the Key to the Reform of the Urban and Rural Collective Economies', JJGL: 5.

Economic Yearbook of China, 1983, 1984 (Zhongguo Jingji Nianjian) (Beijing: Economic Management Press).

Granick, David (1986) 'Prices and the Behavior of Chinese State Industrial Enterprises: Focus on the Multi-Price System' (unpublished).

Kornai, Janos (1986) 'The Hungarian Reform Process: Visions, Hopes and Reality', *Journal of Economic Literature* XXIV (December), pp. 1687–1733.

Li Kaixin (1983) *Wuzi Guanli* (Materials Management): 4.

Li Yue (1982) '[We Must] Build a Mass Production Structure by Unifying Vertical and Horizontal Systems', *Kexue Jingji*, 1982: 4, pp. 19–23; reprinted in *Gongye Jingji*: 23.

Liu Suinian (1984) 'The Issue of Concentration and Dispersal in China's Economic Development', in Liu Guiguang (ed.), *Zhongguo Jingji Fazhan Zhanlue Wenti Yanjiu* (Research on the Issues of China's Strategy for Economic Development) (Beijing: People's Press).

Naughton, Barry (1985) 'False Starts and Second Wind: Financial Reforms in the Chinese Industrial System', in Elizabeth J. Perry and Christine Wong (eds), *The Political Economy of Reform in Post-Mao China* (Cambridge, MA: Harvard University Press).

Naughton, Barry (1986) 'Finance and Planning Reforms in Industry', US Congress, Joint Economic Committee, *China's Economy Looks Toward the Year 2000, vol. 1: The Four Modernizations* (Washington DC: Government Printing Office).

Naughton, Barry, 'The Decline of Central Control over Investment in Post-Mao China'.

Neuberger, Egon (1985) 'Classifying Economic Systems', in Morris Bornstein, *Comparative Economic Systems* (Homewood, IL: Richard D. Irwin, Inc.).

Shashi Materials Bureau (1984) 'Use Cities as the Basis for Reforming the System of Material Circulation', State Materials Bureau, *Kaichuang Wuzigongzuo Xinjumian Jingyanxuanbian* (The Collected Experience in Opening up New Situations in Materials Work) (Beijing: Materials Press) pp. 166–182.

State Statistical Bureau, *Zhongguo Tongji Nianjian* (Chinese Statistical Yearbook) 1984, 1985.

Tidrick, Gene, and Chen Jiyuan (eds) (1987) *China's Industrial Reform* (Oxford University Press).

Wong, Christine P. W. (1985) 'Material Allocations and Decentralization: Impact of the Local Sector on Industrial Reform', in Elizabeth J. Perry and Christine Wong (eds), *The Political Economy of Reform in Post-Mao China* (Cambridge, MA: Harvard University Press).

Wong, Christine, P. W. (1986a) 'Ownership and Control in Chinese Industry: the Maoist Legacy and Prospects for the 1980s', in US Congress, Joint Economic Committee, *China's Economy Looks Toward the Year 2000, vol. 1: The Four Modernizations* (Washington, DC: Government Printing Office).

Wong, Christine P. W. (1986b) 'The Economics of Shortage and Problems of Reform in Chinese Industry', *Journal of Comparative Economics* December.

The World Bank (1985) *China: Longterm Development Issues and Options.*

Wu Jinglian (1986) 'Economic Instability and the Dual System', CMJJ 6:1–8.

Xiandai Zhongguo Jingji Shidian (Contemporary Handbook of Chinese Economic Affairs) (1981) (ed.) Ma Hong (Beijing: Chinese Academy of Social Science Press).

Zhao Yujiang (1986) 'The Present Problem of Controlling Extrabudgetary Funds', Chinese Economic System Reform Institute Comprehensive Investigation Group (eds), *Gaige: Women Mianlin de Tiaozhan yu Suanzhe* (Reform: The Challenge and Choices We Face) (Beijing: Chinese Economics Press).

Zhao Ziyang (1984) 'Report on the Work of the Government at the Second Session of the 5th National People's Congress', *Renmin Ribao* (People's Daily), 2 June.

Zhou Xiaochuan and Zhu Li (1987) 'China's Banking System: Current Status and Perspective on Reform', *Journal of Comp. Econ.*, 11, pp. 399–409.

Zhu Xiaowen (1985) 'Two Problems to Which We Must Attach Importance in Developing Rural Enterprises', *Sichuan Ribao*, 5 June.

Zuo Mu (1980) 'On the Role of Local Planning and the Relations between Plans and Markets', *Jingji Yanjiu*: 7; translated in JPRS *Economic Affairs*, 86, pp. 28–35.

Part II
The USSR

4 Gorbachev's Economic Reforms in the Context of the Soviet Political System

Stanislaw Gomulka

Since spring 1985 a warm wind of change has begun to envelop the Soviet Union, raising the prospect that the country's immensely large and highly centralised institutional structure, particularly its economic sector, may soon begin to shrink and decentralise. This institutional structure has changed remarkably little since the early 1930s. It was established, it may be recalled, by a small group of single-minded communist revolutionaries to serve the implementation of their drastically new social order. The new institutions, initially at least, operated in a political and cultural environment very much hostile to that order and, in part because of that hostility, in a manner exceptionally authoritarian for nearly all and extremely unpleasant – indeed, tragic – for a large number of the Soviet people. That manner changed much for the better after Stalin's death in 1953, when official ideology also became less rigid and more tolerant of other ideas. However, Khrushchev's de-Stalinisation process was effectively stopped when Brezhnev came to power in 1964.

In the meantime the peasant-dominated country of 1928 had been transformed into a fairly modern one, becoming in the 1950s a large industrial power and, of course, a military superpower. The people, the post-war generations in particular, have become well educated, especially in the sciences and technical subjects, relatively well informed and generally fairly sophisticated. These social changes, as well as higher real incomes, have bred tastes for high-quality consumer goods, travel abroad and a meaningful participation in the country's social, economic and political life. But these new, higher-order needs are precisely those which the old institutions and policies were designed to limit or suppress. The pressure for changes in these institutions and policies was thus building up for some time.

However, what gave special urgency to these changes at this time was, I think, not this pressure from below, which seems still to be moderate and containable, but a sense of crisis at the top. This crisis was caused by a sharp fall in the rate of Soviet economic growth to, approximately, the magnitude of the US rate. This fall came in the mid-1970s, at a time when the levels of Soviet national product and consumption per person still remained much below US levels. Subsequent desperate attempts to increase the growth rate and revive the process of economic catching-up have so far failed, and this failure has raised the spectre of the standard of living in the socialist USSR remaining visibly and indefinitely below that in the capitalist West. If that was accepted as inevitable, the attractiveness of the Soviet social system, both at home and abroad, would be put at serious risk. The sense of crisis among the Soviet elite has been additionally compounded by an even sharper slowdown in economic growth in other socialist countries of Eastern Europe, by these countries' rather large dollar debts, and by massive demands for liberalisation and full citizenship rights in Poland. Furthermore, the US 'Star Wars' programme has brought home the point that a permanent technological gap may also involve a high security risk.

Given this background, significant new initiatives by any post-Brezhnev leadership should have been expected. The changes initiated by Gorbachev, however, appear to be faster, deeper and wider than most Soviet and outside observers anticipated.

The new General Secretary immediately startled his fellow-citizens by being unusually frank and outspoken about the problems he and they have inherited. To cure them, he insists, a deep and comprehensive *perestroika* (institutional 'restructuring' or 'reorganisation') is an urgent necessity for the USSR. Radical economic decentralisation is to be a vital part of that restructuring. Political democratisation, apart from being good in itself, is also to be a key instrument of – and a necessary condition for – successful implementation of that economic reform. A number of questions immediately arise. What is to be the content of these intended reforms? Are they feasible? Do they put into question the standard Western view of limited reformability of the Soviet system? What are the major obstacles to such reforms? Given the presence of these obstacles, what actual impact are the attempted reforms likely to have on the USSR and Eastern Europe? These are some of the major questions which are now being widely asked and discussed throughout the world, above all in the Soviet bloc. At this early stage of the reform, there may be many answers to these questions. An attempt to develop preliminary and tentative answers is the subject of this chapter.

1 ECONOMIC REFORMS: WHAT THEY ARE OR ARE LIKELY TO BE

Two laws under the proposed programme had already been adopted before the crucial June 1987 Central Committee meeting which dealt specifically with the programme. One concerns individual (private) enterprise (19 November 1986), the other foreign trade organisations and joint ventures (21 January 1987). An important draft document on state enterprise was published in February 1987 and has since been the subject of national debate in the mass media before the Supreme Soviet turned a version of it into law on 30 June 1987. In preparation is a new law attempting to redefine the role of the central economic institutions. Its thrust will be to limit the executive powers of the State Planning Commission [*Gosplan*] and the State Supply Organisation [*Gossnab*], the two main pillars of the present system, and to widen the role of the central bank and the Ministry of Finance. The provisions of these two laws, on state enterprise and the economic centre, are crucial for defining the content of the whole reform. They have been hotly debated within the inner circle of the government and its economic advisers in the course of 1986 and the first half of 1987. Their approval in principle by the June 1987 Central Committee meeting opened the way to substantial changes from 1 January 1988, with full implementation intended by 1 January 1991.

Although many specific arrangements are yet to be decided, a preliminary overview of the proposed reform may be made. First, the reform is to be substantially more than (as was often the case in the past) a mere reorganisation of central planning, incentives and decision-making within an essentially unchanged, highly centralised economic system. Secondly, the reforms will be introduced gradually over the years 1987 to 1990 rather than at one go, as in Hungary (January 1968) or Poland (January–February 1982). Their provisions are still set to ensure that many important products and investment projects will continue to remain under direct central control. However, a substantial part – perhaps the bulk – of that sector of the economy which is producing marketable goods and services would be decentralised and, at least to some extent, subjected to the discipline of the market. That market-responsive part of the economy would typically be free of any direct government intervention; it would instead be influenced indirectly, by means of centrally imposed or regulated incentive schemes, imposed prices or price-formation rules, exchange and interest rates, fiscal measures, and so on. Thus Soviet reformers now see a regulated market not only as capable of performing the usual job of inducing individual producers and consumers to make appropriate allocative choices, but also as a medium through which the centre would affect those choices in the 'socially desirable' direction.

In other words, effectively (still) central allocation of resources and the competitive market are regarded as reconcilable. This idea as such is not new. It has, in fact, been promoted by economic theorists of market socialism such as Taylor, Lange, Lerner, Brus and Kornai during the last half century but was recently described by Kornai (1987) as 'naive'. In the present (imperfectly) directly centralised system of the Soviet economy, markets do already play a significant role.

It is now admitted, however, that a market-directed socialist economy requires a far greater decentralisation of decision-making to enterprises than at present, as well as the abandonment of centrally imposed plans for enterprises. Under the proposed system the centre apparently still hopes to 'manage' – or, to use Brus's phrase, 'regulate' – the market to such an extent that the managerially and financially independent enterprises would be supplying, and the consumers would be demanding, the types and quantities of products which the centre either desires or, at least, does not object to. It may be disputed whether it is in the social interest to have a system in which central preferences continue to exert a dominant influence. Whether the market can, under such a system, perform well in its efficiency-enhancing and plan-implementing roles is another matter, although one of crucial practical importance. Be that as it may, the Soviet economy under the new system would bear a strong resemblance to the Hungarian economy under the New Economic Mechanism (NEM), although it would probably retain significantly more elements of the old system, at least initially, than the NEM has retained.

A reform of this type aims to improve allocative efficiency, induce innovation, increase exports to competitive dollar markets, and reduce shortages at home. However, the purely economic gains are to be restricted by the requirement that any systemic changes must not excessively compromise both the traditionally socialist principles of full employment and a low economic (income and wealth) inequality and the communist principles of retaining the pre-eminence of the economic and political preferences of the centre as well as the dominant and, if need be, privileged position of the state and collective ownership. The Soviet reformers are now prepared to admit that competitive markets in the capitalist West have in practice proved able to impose a more effective discipline on enterprises than can Soviet central planners directly. This practical experience is indeed the major reason for the reform in the USSR as well as throughout the socialist world. But the central planners wish to secure the efficiency benefits of that greater disciplinary effectiveness of the market, while at the same time still striving desperately to retain for themselves, rather than for individual consumers, the role of dominant economic actors.

The specific reform measures which are to be adopted in the USSR therefore fall into two categories. One category consists of measures designed to promote economic efficiency and industrial democracy. Most prices are to be market-influenced, enterprises are to be largely self-financed, bankruptcies are to be allowed, and most managers are to be appointed by the workers themselves. These measures are intended to promote improvements by making positive (material) incentives stronger and negative ones (threats) more credible. They are also intended, through the use of 'realistic' prices, to make economic performance more transparent. The second category consists of measures of direct and indirect influence designed to promote the centre's preferences. Many key inputs, such as foreign exchange and investment credit, will continue to be centrally allocated, most wages and prices will remain subject to central control or regulation, large product and enterprise-specific subsidies to loss-makers and large taxes of profit-makers will be used to avoid unemployment and to keep inter-enterprise economic inequality low, managerial appointments will need approval by party committees and ministries, the market structure will remain highly monopolistic. The empirical evidence from Hungary (Kornai, 1987) and Poland (Gomulka and Rostowski, 1984; Brus, 1988; Fallenbuchl, 1988) suggests that systemic features of the second category lead to such widespread bargaining between state enterprises and the centre and such low inter-enterprise competition that the efficiency-enhancing measures of the first category are fundamentally weakened, rendering the latter largely ineffective. A different outcome in the USSR seems unlikely.

In China and Hungary it is largely in the private sector and, to some extent, in the more competitive segments of the non-private sector that the reforms have been an unambiguous success. Soviet reformers, however, apparently do not intend to follow the Chinese in the late 1970s, and the Yugoslavs and the Poles in 1956, in permitting the dissolution of state co-operative farms and the return to private farming on a large scale. The reasons are probably mainly ideological, although the Soviet economists to whom I spoke (Moscow, spring 1987) stressed the difficulties in selling or renting to individual farmers large buildings and expensive machinery, of which there is much more in Soviet agriculture than there was in the Chinese communes or the Polish and Yugoslav co-operatives.

Less radical measures are being urgently considered. Some of these are already being implemented, including giving the farms the right to decide what they are to produce. Farm managers are to be allowed to split their co-operatives into separate accounting units to be run by self-selected teams, such as individual families, in order to establish a clear link between work and pay. These families are to be given larger plots for private use. The private plot sector will also be somewhat enlarged by allowing city-dwellers to acquire disused farm buildings and allotments in rural areas. These measures, while having some positive effects, would appear to be too limited to bring about the necessary improvements in what is possibly the least efficient sector of the Soviet economy.

A major headache of Soviet society is the services sector. It is hoped that the recently adopted law on 'individual labour activity' will bring an improvement in this particular area. The activities permitted under the new law include making of clothes, shoes, carpets, furniture; building and repair of dwellings, servicing of consumer durables, teaching school or university subjects and providing medical services. However, it is interesting that the hiring of labour by individuals remains strictly illegal. State employees may indulge (with some exceptions) in private activity only in their free time, and all fit people of working age must have a state job. The law forbids the making of duplicators or photocopiers, presumably to hinder the spread of samizdat publications. It also forbids the teaching of subjects not included in the official curriculum of any state educational establishment. The rate of tax, at 60 per cent of any private income in excess of the equivalent of £5000 per annum, seems to have been set to impose a fiscal constraint as well on the growth of the private sector. Clearly, in this particular and potentially very important segment of the reform, the USSR is so far much more hesitant than are China, Hungary, Poland and Yugoslavia.

2 WHY HAS THE USSR MOVED IN THIS DIRECTION?

The official case for a 'radical reform' of the Soviet economic and political system has been developed by Gorbachev and his close associates and advisers over a period of five years or so, but articulated openly only during the last two or three years. Perhaps the most intellectually interesting are Gorbachev's Reports to the Central Committee of the Soviet Communist Party on 27 January and 27 June 1987. These reports are in many ways as critical of the post-Stalin economic and political system as is most Western analysis.

Gorbachev's case rests primarily on the evidence of a substantial economic and technological slowdown of the Soviet and East European economies since about 1975, a phenomenon which I have already mentioned (Gomulka, 1986, 1988; *The USSR*, 1987). Although in 1928 the USSR entered the economic race with the capitalist West from an inferior starting point, the political legitimacy for the new communist elite was derived to a large extent by the success in achieving high growth rates in the years 1929–41 and 1947–75, raising hopes that the USSR could achieve the highest standard of living in the world. Such achievement would substantiate the crucial ideological claim of the inherent superiority of the Soviet social system by using the Soviet Union's own criterion.

The slowdown came at a time when the USSR reached, in *per capita* terms, only about 40 to 50 per cent of the US Gross National Product and about one-third of the US level of consumption (and about a half of UK consumption). These data may be disputed on a number of grounds. In particular, they do not reflect adequately the poor quality of Soviet products. The welfare of the Soviet citizen is, on the other hand, increased by high job security and also, perhaps, by a fairly high degree of equality, but it is reduced on account of highly limited choice and long queues at shops. Given the inferior starting point, the data may be regarded as evidence of very considerable economic success. The problem, however, is that since about 1975 the relative position of the USSR, in terms of these two key macroeconomic indicators, has been practically stable. It is true that since 1975 an economic slowdown has occurred also in Western European countries and in Japan. However, the rates of innovation in these countries continue to be sufficiently high to bring about eventually a total or nearly total elimination of the *per capita* consumption gap with the USA, a gap which in any case is already relatively small (Gomulka, 1988).

As a consequence of these post-1975 developments, Gorbachev and his colleagues are now haunted by the possibility of the developed market-based economies of the capitalist West retaining a considerable advantage in technological levels and a large one in the standard of living. Soviet leaders and economists have begun to notice with disgust that the aggregate dollar purchasing power of the USSR and Eastern Europe, given by their dollar exports, is about the same as that of Belgium and Luxembourg. They are especially concerned by the Soviet and East European dollar exports of manufactured goods, including military equipment, remaining embarrassingly insignificant despite a major effort to increase them. These exports are now lower than – to give an example – similar exports by South Korea alone. The political crisis in Poland in 1980–3 and the recent Western challenges in military technology have also given notice that the economic weaknesses of the Soviet-type system may have potentially grave implications for the internal political stability of the Communist Commonwealth and the realism of Soviet worldwide aims.

The main purposes of Gorbachev's reforms must be for the USSR to regain enough internal dynamism to resume economic catching-up to the developed West and for Soviet people to sustain (or regain) their confidence in the Soviet communist system. He seems to be taking the view that the unceasing waves of new Western inventions in the form of attractive consumer products, especially those which the Soviet economy cannot produce quickly or does not produce at all, are constantly putting to the test the patience of the Soviet consumer, undermining as a result the credibility of socialist efficiency claims and feeding the inferiority complex of the Soviet worker. In the modern world of mass communications and easy travel, these effects are not readily tolerable and in the long term may even be potentially dangerous for the Soviet political system. Reaching military parity with the USA was a supreme goal that has been achieved. But in the expected absence of a war involving the two superpowers, the significance of this achievement begins to fall and the interest of the Soviet population must therefore begin to shift more and more to comparative achievements in economic and cultural domains. The question is whether Gorbachev, like the reformers in Hungary, Poland and Yugoslavia before him, does not expect too much from too little – a matter to which we shall return.

3 MAJOR POLITICAL AND SOCIAL OBSTACLES TO REFORMS

In his plenary report of 27 January 1987, Gorbachev himself admitted that 'change for the better is taking place slowly, the cause of reorganisation is more difficult and the problems which have accumulated in society more deep-rooted than we first thought.' On another occasion he nevertheless dismissed the thought that there is internal political opposition to his proposed reforms in the leadership, the Party and the government apparatus, or in society at large. Opposition to reform exists, but the reasons for it, according to him, are mainly psychological rather than political or social. Gorbachev suggests that intellectually everyone is convinced of the merits of *perestroika* and is therefore in favour of it, but due to the force of old work habits, everyone, himself included, is also against it (see his address at the April 1987 Congress of Soviet *Komsomol*). There may be a grain of truth in this view, but it cannot be called a satisfactory analysis. It is understandable that Gorbachev wants to play down the political opposition against, and play up the support for, the proposed reforms. He is in any case often refreshingly frank about the great strength of the opposition coming from the group interests which are likely to be affected by the proposed changes.

The subject of obstacles to reform under Soviet-type socialism is both complex and fascinating but not particularly well researched, partly because it has until recently been strictly forbidden for Soviet and East European social scientists to investigate them in a systematic manner. However, the history of reform attempts is rather long, and in its course a significant body of helpful analysis and evidence has been produced.

The obstacles most widely stressed as major are political, ideological and social. A reform based on marketisation of the economy and decentralisation of decision-making does imply a considerable redistribution of political and economic power. The potential losers are the central and intermediate levels of economic administration: *Gosplan*, *Gossnab*, branch ministries and industrial associations. Some of their decision-making powers are destined to be diffused to enterprises; others to be taken over by financial central institutions, such as the Ministry of Finance and the central bank. The top decision-makers, the Politburo and the (much reduced) apparatus of the Central Committee, will of course continue to be in overall charge of the economy. They intend to reduce the power of subordinate ministries, substitute a rather ineffective bureaucratic discipline of enterprises with the market discipline which they hope will be more effective, and keep for themselves key allocative and policy decisions. In this way the top leadership may justifiably hope to improve control over the direction and performance of the major segments of the economy. This top leadership also stands to gain politically at home and abroad from the beneficial impact of economic reforms on allocative efficiency, on the choice and quality of goods and services, and on innovation. On the other hand, the centre may lose some power, or a sense of power, when it abandons making detailed resource-allocation decisions in favour of wider use of indirect (parametric) instruments and markets. However, this potential loss may be dismissed as of minor significance if the economy is not responding well anyway to the directives of the centre, which appears to be the current Soviet predicament.

There is yet another potential loss that has to be considered carefully. This is related to the effects any substantial economic decentralisation and marketisation may have on the internal stability and, indeed, the survival chances of the traditional, one-party political system. The top leaders have to ask themselves whether the reforms or their absence entail greater risks of such an ultimate category. The answer to that question is only in part influenced by the political standing of the Communist Party, which tends to be higher in countries where it came to power through internal revolution, as in the USSR, China or Yugoslavia. The issue is rather complex, since sometimes the communist leaders regard reforms as a means of winning political support, as apparently was the case in Hungary in 1968 and Poland in 1981–2, and sometimes a wide measure of support is seen as helpful or even necessary before political risks of reforms can be accepted. Soviet leaders must find comfort in the fact that the political position of their Communist Party is apparently overwhelmingly dominant in the country, and that the two-million *nomenklatura* group controlling all the key hierarchies of Party, economy and state is well disciplined and has in the past been on the whole prepared to trust and follow the leaders at nearly every turn (Voslensky, 1984). Still, in the present-day USSR much power is diffused throughout all levels of the large hierarchies; the attitude of individual members of the *nomenklatura* group to the policies of the centre may therefore be expected to have a major cumulative influence on the effectiveness of these policies. A strongly negative attitude to reforms would be a major obstacle to their successful implementation, probably sufficiently important to encourage dangerous splits within the Politburo and the Central Committee themselves.

Gorbachev and his allies, in order to succeed and survive, must therefore build effective defences around their 'revolution from above', and in particular be in a position to dilute or otherwise overcome the potential obstacle in the form of an 'opposition from within'. Their policies of more communicative government [*glasnost*] and some limited political democratisation may be interpreted as novel means to achieve that end. Their primary aim seems to be to win over for the reforms a wider stratum of supporters – especially amongst the party activists and the party rank and file, but also among the young and the talented outside the Party. These supporters may then be expected to become the messengers of the new gospel, pressing for appropriate changes at workplaces throughout the country, from enterprises and farms to universities and the mass media. The *nomenklatura* group, especially the party apparatus, the military and the KGB, would then as a consequence of such criticisms be put under pressure from both above and below, to be followed (if need be) by demotions and replacements. The political campaign of *glasnost* and democratisation, well directed and controlled, is possibly above all an instrument to help the top leaders to mobilise, discipline and renew their cadres and, through the cadres, society itself. The campaign may superficially seem inconsistent with the old doctrine of 'democratic centralism', but given its central direction it is in fact only a novel way of implementing this doctrine which, Gorbachev states, remains very much in force. Still, the liberalisation which the campaign entails, even if limited, is a real gain to the population for as long as it lasts.

An outside observer visiting the USSR is particularly impressed by changes in the mass media. The media are apparently instructed not to just say what the new reform ideas are but also to make an attempt to engage the population in discussing them fairly openly and to provide serious arguments for the reforms. Inviting such discussion is now seen as important in a society which is fairly well informed anyway on internal problems. Any political leader who aspires to win and hold a good measure of support from such a society must now be considerably more open and truthful than his predecessors ever needed to be. An inexpensive way to gain trust among the intelligentsia is to allow writers and historians to reveal some of the hidden truth about the Soviet Union's murky past. But to gain trust among other groups as well, Gorbachev probably also needs to be much more truthful about the present.

Winning wide political support for economic reforms may still prove an exceedingly difficult task. Reform, when it begins to be effective, is likely to bring benefits to the skilled, the enterprising and the industrious. Since the reform measures are to be phased in gradually they cannot be really effective in the short run, and possibly not in the medium term either. The medium-term expectations of potential supporters are therefore quite likely to be frustrated, as in Poland or Hungary. These supporters are an elite of a sort and hence probably a numerical minority. Suppose it is true, as alleged, that the majority of Soviet workers perform poorly in inefficient enterprises, making the wrong or poor-quality things. Many of these workers may fear the consequences of being left at the mercy of high uncertainty concerning incomes, prices and possibly jobs. A high rate of inflation was, indeed, a first major effect of reforms in other socialist countries. (In Poland it was also almost the only effect.) Some of the negative expectations are therefore likely to be confirmed.

Any economy, whether centrally planned or market-based, is too complex to be really well understood. Consumers, producers and planners operate and take decisions in an information environment in which a great deal of data needed for the decisions are false, missing, or uncertain. The decisions themselves are influenced by both economic considerations and cultural and institutional factors, and their separate influences are virtually impossible to identify. It is therefore not surprising that different economists tend to have very different predictions as to how a centrally planned economy such as the Soviet one may respond to a particular reform measure. This wide variation in predictions is causing political decision-makers to be cautious, to prefer testing ideas one by one or in small packages rather than imposing large changes in one go and risking the chaos of uncertain duration and cost, even if a desirable order of things would be highly likely to emerge from this in the long term.

The practitioners of this evolutionary approach, however, face the difficulty that modern economies have to be (more or less) consistent internally in order to function well. Command-type economy and competitive market mechanism are two such consistent systems. Testing small changes within each of them – changes characteristic of the other system – may therefore be a deficient way of seeking improvement. Each system tends in any case to reject such changes. French enterprises tend to ignore national (indicative) plans, whilst Soviet enterprises have tended to respond little to changes in prices and to ignore the self-financing principle. An evolutionary reform of a centrally planned economy, therefore, cannot be effective unless and until the package of market solutions begins to exceed what in Eastern Europe has come to be called a 'critical mass'. It is not clear precisely what reform measures the critical mass must contain, but the analysis of reforms in Hungary and Yugoslavia, and certainly in Poland, suggests that even these countries have a long way to go before reaching that point on their reform paths. In fact, it would appear that a truly reformed, competitive socialist economy would differ, if it existed, only very little from a capitalist market-based economy, except that under such socialism the hired labour employed by the private sector would be less than half of the total labour force, security of job tenure might be higher, and institutions of industrial democracy at the enterprise level would in some respects be more developed than they are under mature capitalism in the late twentieth century.

4 CAN THERE BE ECONOMIC REFORMS IN ISOLATION FROM OTHER REFORMS?

The official Soviet view seems to be that economic reforms cannot be really successful unless they are accompanied, or even preceded, by measures intended to enhance significantly both industrial and political democracy. This implied willingness to diffuse and share power would appear to run very much against the practice of communist-dominated governments. Gorbachev's emphasis on the existence of a link between economic improvements and social and political reforms is therefore one of the most intriguing and paradoxical aspects of his *perestroika*. I have already indicated what a possible interpretation of this important paradox may be.

Gorbachev, according to this interpretation, intends to implement much of his economic programme. In particular, markets are to be given some of the economic disciplinary powers of the intermediate levels of the administration. This arrangement, he apparently hopes, will in the long run give the centre more resources to play with and more time to concentrate on taking important decisions. The intended redistribution of economic power is away from intermediate levels, including ministries, Central Committee departments and *Gosplan*, towards both enterprises and the top leadership. Once enterprises are given more powers, some of it can be even diffused further down: to representatives of workers themselves. Significant power-sharing is, however, intended to be limited strictly to enterprises. Some wider political liberalisation, in particular a more open but still very much controlled mass media, may also be useful to the centre, as noted above, as a means of disciplining lower and intermediate levels of the party and state hierarchy more effectively and gaining wider support.

The new party leaders seem to be concerned by evidence that the post-Stalin policy of neither terror nor democracy has reduced the fears within the *nomenklatura* group and, consequently, started to turn it into a constellation of vested interests. Since massive terror is not an option, these vested interests can be more easily identified and more effectively confronted only through a dose of local democracy, generating pressure from below and providing the ammunition for the guns of the mass media to apply pressure from above. The aim is to make the *nomenklatura* as a whole a more disciplined and more effective instrument of the top central powers. This democratisation, however, is and must remain a measured affair. The *nomenklatura*, whether old or renewed, remains after all the primary constituency for the top leaders: their most important power base. It is in any case in the leaders' and their Party's common interest not to give rise to expectations and demands for democratic reforms which may be satisfied only in a competitive, multiparty political system. It may be safely assumed, I think, that both Gorbachev and his renewed *nomenklatura*, as well as most of the twenty million membership of the Soviet Communist Party, will do their best to keep political reforms limited and expectations in check, in order not to face the dilemma of either refusing these demands – risking a major political crisis – or accepting them and risking a truly major loss of power.

Gorbachev appears to be a shrewd leader who understands the dangers of doing too little as well as those of going too far. Although highly liberal and modern by Soviet standards, he certainly does not appear to be a Soviet Dubček. At the same time, his insistence on the link between economic efficiency and political democratisation is novel in the USSR, and – if he persists in talking about it and, more importantly, acts on it – potentially undermines the present Soviet political system. This is the prospect that is electrifying for the Western observer and, I presume, confusing for the Soviet citizen.

My interpretation of Gorbachev's reforms assumes that he is still very much a communist leader who, however, finds it necessary to shake and destabilise the old system somewhat in order to preserve it more effectively. This means above all the preservation of two features of the system: (i) the dominant political and ideological role of the Communist Party and its cadres and (ii) the continuing cultural integration of Soviet nations based on Russian language and culture. So far I find this assumption compatible with Gorbachev's unusually critical analysis of the past and, by Soviet standards, his fairly radical reform proposals for the future. To have a balanced view of Gorbachev and his *perestroika*, it must be noted that there is not even a hint that the above-mentioned two principal features of the Soviet political system will be allowed to be publicly questioned. This in itself must be a signal to the Soviet population, as well as to the outside world, that the fundamentals are to remain unchanged.

Suppose, then, that the Soviet political system remains much the same as it has been – more enlightened and less repressive but nevertheless dictatorial, continuing to impose a rigid ideology and deny most of the large non-communist majority in the USSR and Eastern Europe any substantive political rights. The perplexing question is whether it is feasible to have a communist-dominated country which combines such a Soviet-type political system and a truly market-based economy – that is, whether it is feasible to have a communist equivalent of, say, South Korea until recently or Spain under General Franco. Given the intense interest of communist elites in preserving their power while at the same time improving economic performance, it would seem that such a combination is not only feasible but should become the dominant social order to emerge in state socialist countries during their transition, over the next several decades, to more democratic forms. This view, although it may eventually prove wrong, is certainly not undermined much by the recent evidence from the USSR that some limited democratisation may be a necessary precondition for starting the process of marketisation. Somewhat more telling evidence against it is the experience of Yugoslavia, Hungary and Poland, which suggests that marketisation gives rise to anxieties and resistance among many social groups and, as a consequence, that the centre may not be able to go far enough along that route, even if it wanted to, unless the policy is legitimised by clear evidence of majority support.

That support may, however, be difficult to generate and identify in the absence of democratic institutions. In their absence the many individuals who wish to be protected against the risks of a market economy may be expected to form a (powerful) alliance with the members of the communist authorities who wish to preserve their power by continuing to offer such protection (see Part III of this book, on reforms in Eastern Europe). A paternalistic protection develops, taking the form of fiscal measures, price controls, management of the market structure, preferential allocation of credit, foreign exchange and key materials, and so forth. A high incidence of such protection has obvious direct inefficiency implications. It also encourages the proposed enterprise-based appointment committees to continue the practice of hiring managers with good ministerial or party connections rather than entrepreneurial talent, with further indirect inefficiency implications.

Paternalistic protection of enterprises is, nowadays, a worldwide phenomenon, but its extent seems to be related – among other factors – to the type of ownership of the enterprises involved in it, private ones receiving on the whole less protection than state-owned ones. The relationship itself is influenced by the prevailing climate of social ideas in general and the ideology of the ruling political party in particular. Socialist ideology and state ownership tend to breed strong expectations of and demands for paternalistic protection amongst workers, and strong motivations and justifications for exercising that protection amongst political decision-makers. As a consequence, a social contract of a particular type develops between the workers and the socialist state. The contract's long and entrenched presence in the USSR may be expected to restrict the freedom of Soviet reformers to move the Soviet economy in the direction of a socialist equivalent of the Spanish or South Korean model. The reform experiences in Eastern Europe so far provide ample evidence in support of that view (see the chapters in this book by Bićanić, Pajestka and Wiatr). What may be expected realistically is that Gorbachev's reform, with its limited ideological desocialisation, marketisation and some privatisation, will begin to push the Soviet economy towards that socialist equivalent, but in a very gentle and gradual manner.

5   WHAT IMPACT WILL THE ATTEMPTED REFORM HAVE?

Given the various risks and barriers to marketisation of the Soviet economy, its transition to 'self-financing socialism' is likely to be a long process, taking perhaps many decades. As in Yugoslavia, Hungary and Poland, so also in the USSR state enterprises may become a little more cost-conscious, but not nearly enough for this improvement to have any significant impact on the qualities or quantities of their products. A major improvement would require a radical restructuring of the economy in terms of the production processes used and the labour skills employed. Such restructuring would in turn require a deep, market-aided surgical operation involving a widespread closure of inefficient production lines and whole enterprises, massive retraining of management and a far-reaching redeployment of investment resources and the labour force. A radical operation of this Thatcher-type category is nowadays advocated by many economists in Eastern Europe, but it seems to have been ruled out already by the authoritative Soviet reformers who, for reasons I discussed above, tend to be cautious and evolutionary.

The Soviet programme of growth acceleration in the 1990s does envisage a radical restructuring of the economy and a major increase of the rate of innovation (*The USSR*, 1987). However, it is not at all clear how these aims are to be achieved. Any attempt to achieve them through market-aided 'surgical operation' would require the creation or development of proper, competitive markets, especially for intermediate inputs, investment goods, credit and foreign exchange. In this case all prices would have to be market-clearing, so that rationing for enterprises is eliminated and their independence is possible. The amounts of resources transferred from profit-makers to loss-makers should be much reduced, so that the former are in a position to grow fast. The multi-unit enterprises would have to be broken down into independent firms so that the number of such firms is increased manyfold in order to promote competition. Most of these measures are not, however, contemplated for the 1990s.

The changes which may realistically be expected to arrive in the course of the next several years will be above all the result of greater monetarisation of the economy, in the form of greater price flexibility and an enhanced role for financial planning at the expense of planning in physical or quantitative terms. There should also be a significant impact of some privatisation of the economy and decentralisation of decision-making, especially in the provision of services and in agriculture. About a third of all prices are expected to be allowed to move relatively freely to levels at which demand equals supply. Market shortages of many produced or imported consumer goods should thus be reduced or eliminated. The shortages of intermediate and investment goods, now an immense problem, may also become somewhat less acute. Any improvement in this area will be related to the extent to which two major principles are implemented: (i) that government demands for goods are formulated in value terms, and not in terms of specific quantities (so that financial planning dominates over physical planning), and (ii) that these money-denominated demands are not adjusted automatically in response to changes in prices (so that money is not passive, or budget flexibility limited). Both these principles are at the heart of the proposed reform, but go very much against present practice. Their adoption in Hungary and Poland has been and continues to be strongly resisted, for reasons which also prevail in the USSR.

Soviet reforms, however inadequate and poorly implemented, should nevertheless legitimise the criticisms of the traditional economic system, stimulate reform debates and promote reform-minded politicians to positions of power throughout Eastern Europe. At the moment there is still considerable ambiguity about the precise content of Soviet reforms and uncertainty about the political fate of Gorbachev himself. In Czechoslovakia the conservative leadership has nevertheless decided to reopen reform discussions. This was a highly uncomfortable decision to make, as it required a reinterpretation of the Dubček reforms of 1968, the suppression of which gave the leaders their present positions of power (see Chapter 8 in this book, by Jerzy Wiatr). The most liberal of the typically very cautious East European leaders, those of Hungary and of Poland, will probably feel less restrained. Although their reform programmes do fall far short of what is required, they are the most radical programmes of the 1980s in Eastern Europe except Yugoslavia. They have now a good chance of becoming a model to be followed throughout the Comecon area. This is already happening, to some extent, in Bulgaria. East Germany is the only country in Eastern Europe strongly resisting any thought of substantial economic decentralisation, marketisation and privatisation. But there is perhaps no need to reform an economy which is seen to be performing well, although the reasons for this success are probably German-specific rather than system-specific.

Possibly more difficult to handle for the communist leaders of Eastern Europe are Gorbachev's political rather than economic ideas. His repeated calls for political democratisation are unlikely to be misunderstood in much of the USSR, where they would be widely perceived as serving the instrumental purposes of the higher echelons. However, these calls are inflating expectations and may even be destabilising in Soviet republics with strong nationalistic traditions, such as Armenia or Estonia; in the countries of Eastern Europe with some traditions of political democracy, such as Czechoslovakia and Poland; or those exposed daily to the mass media of their democratic neighbours, such as East Germany and Hungary. The evidence of a growing popularity of Soviet mass media in Eastern Europe is apparently, and paradoxically, causing concern for local governments. These concerns may well be shared by Soviet leaders, for whom any evidence of Gorbachev-inspired political instability in Eastern Europe (or the USSR, for that matter) would be regarded as a serious warning that he is moving too fast and too far.

Acknowledgements

I wish to thank the British Academy for sponsoring my visit to the Soviet Union in March and April 1987. As a guest of the Soviet Academy, I benefited much from my seminar presentations and individual discussions at several of the Academy's economic institutes and at the Moscow State University. I am grateful for comments and suggestions by Wlodzimierz Brus, Michael Ellman, Philip Hanson, Jacek Rostowski and Mark Schaffer, as well as participants in the Comparative Economics Seminar at the London School of Economics.

A version of this chapter appeared in *The LSE Quarterly*, vol. 1, no. 4, Winter 1987. Permission to reprint much of that version was granted by Blackwell. The present version takes account of the comments by the discussants of the original paper at the Seoul Conference, September 1987.

References

'Basic Provisions for the Radical Restructuring of the Management of the Economy', *Pravda*, 27 June 1987.

Brus, W. (1988) 'The Political Economy of Reform', in P. Marer and W. Siwinski (eds), *Creditworthiness and Reform in Poland* (Indiana University Press).

Ellman, M. (1987) 'The Non-State Sector in the Soviet Economy' (mimeo).

Fallenbuchl, Z. (1988) 'Present State of the Economic Reform', in P. Marer and W. Siwinski (eds), op.cit.

Gomulka, S. (1986) 'Soviet Growth Slowdown: Duality, Maturity and Innovation', *American Economic Review*, May.

Gomulka, S. (1988) 'The Gerschenkron Phenomenon and Systemic Factors in the Post-1975 Growth Slowdown', *European Economic Review*, February/March.

Gomulka, S. and J. Rostowski (1984) 'The Reformed Polish Economic System 1982–1983', *Soviet Studies*, vol. 36, no. 3, July. Reprinted in S. Gomulka, *Growth, Innovation and Reform in Eastern Europe* (Wheatsheaf Books and University of Wisconsin Press, 1986).

Gomulka, S. and J. Rostowski (1988) 'An International Comparison of Material Intensity', *Journal of Comparative Economics*, vol 12, 475–501.

Gorbachev, M. (1987) 'Report to CPSU Central Committee', *Soviet Weekly Supplement*, 27 January.

Gorbachev, M. (1987) 'Report to CPSU Central Committee', *Pravda*, 26 June.

Hewett, A. (1987) 'The June 1987 Plenum and Economic Reform', *PlanEcon Report*, 23 July.

Kornai, J. (1986) 'The Hungarian Reform Process: Visions, Hopes, and Reality', *Journal of Economic Literature*, vol. 24, December.

Law of the State Enterprise (Association), 30 June 1987.

Law on Individual Labour Activity, *Pravda*, 21 November 1986.

Smith, S. W. (1987) 'Soviet Reform: The Pricing Problem', (mimeo) August.

The USSR: Acceleration of Socio-Economic Development (USSR Academy, Moscow, 1987).

Voslensky, M. (1984) *Nomenklatura: The Soviet Ruling Class* (London: Bodley Head).

5 The Second Economy: Boon or Bane for the Reform of the First Economy?[1]

Gregory Grossman

1 STRUCTURE OF INFORMAL RIGHTS AND RELATIONS ON THE EVE OF REFORM

Mr Gorbachev's rise to the general-secretaryship of the CPSU has led to a veritable flood of unprecedentedly candid information from the USSR. Coming from all levels and parts of the Soviet polity and society, this information tends to focus on the ills of the Soviet economy, and serves to underpin Gorbachev's twin remedial imperatives of 'acceleration' [*uskorenie*] and reform or 'restructuring' [*perestroika*].

Not least among the highly publicised ills – most of which, incidentally, have long been known to specialists – is a vast and varied set of self-serving activities that transgress the legal or ethical bounds of socialist life and work that come under such rubrics as 'non-labour income', 'economic crime', 'shadow economy' [*tenevaia ekonomika*], bribery, and the like. In the aggregate, these activities add up to a world of unofficial and often illicit private income and wealth, an underworld of production and trade, a set of black and grey markets – indeed, a whole 'second economy' which reaches into almost every corner of social existence.[2]

There is no need to be rigid about terminology. By second economy we mean the aggregate of economic activities (production, trade, and so on) which meet at least one of the following criteria: (a) they are pursued directly for private gain, whether legally or illegally; (b) they are pursued knowingly in contravention of the law in some significant respect(s), whether for private gain or socialist benefit. Accordingly, we refer to the rest of the economy – the official,

79

socialist, formal, legal portion of it – as the first economy. Their common boundary is admittedly fuzzy.

Personal income derived from such production activity, and from certain informal or illegal activities that are more by way of transfer than production (for example bribes, theft), is informal income. Personal wealth accumulated in consequence of informal income is informally acquired wealth.

In a given place and time the nature and extent of the second economy and of informal income are determined and defined largely by the laws, institutions, and practices of the first economy. As these change, either by gradual evolution or by drastic reform or 'restructuring', the second economy and informal income and wealth can be expected to change as well, and from then on to evolve in their own directions. Moreover, officially initiated changes (reforms) in the first economy may be occasioned by the presence of the second economy and informal income – for example, to legalise certain activities, and/or to capture a part of hidden income for fiscal purposes – as in Hungary and, more recently, in the USSR.

Like all ongoing institutions of production and income-generation, the second economy and its concomitants create powerful vested interests which in turn may exert substantial conservative influence on social policy and change, especially in periods of officially sponsored reform. While not the same as the vested interests deriving from the official (formal, legal) positions, rights, privileges, and property holdings of individuals and groups, the two are mutually related and reinforcing. For a given individual or group, informal/illegal benefits are often derived from official circumstances, such as a particular job, occupation, ascriptive characteristics and location, which provide opportunities for underground activity and informal income. Thus in the USSR (and other Soviet-type countries), in contrast to many underdeveloped countries with large informal sectors, the recipients of informal income are typically not economically marginalised social elements working in a distinct sector, but full-fledged participants in the formal economy which richly nurtures their informal/illegal activities and incomes.

While many people work, steal, and earn informally as 'loners' or in small, isolated groups, often this kind of activity and income depend heavily on the actor's participation in one or more horizontal, informal social networks. (To be sure – especially given the bureaucratic formal structure and economic shortages – the Soviet first economy also functions with considerable resort to connections, exchange of favours, and other aspects of informal networks. Moreover, the two sets of networks intermesh. It could hardly be otherwise.) The horizontal networks of the second economy not only cut across the bureaucratic and political hierarchies of the formal system, but interlock with that system by dint of numerous vertical patron–client relations. The patron, often some official, grants his permission, or at least his forbearance, and extends some measure of conditional protection. The client pays in cash or kind, and not infrequently buys his way into the particular niche. Indeed, second-economy operations of even modest size require multiple and periodic payoffs – to administrative superiors, party functionaries or secretaries, law-enforcement personnel, innumerable inspectors and auditors, and diverse actual or potential blackmailers.

The correlative structure of individual property rights is worth noting. In Soviet law, individuals have the right to own what is called personal (as against private) property – objects for personal or household use, residences, summer homes, passenger automobiles and other passenger vehicles, and simple tools needed to ply a permitted trade or profession. More significantly, one may own tools for small-scale agricultural or gardening activities, in so far as these are permitted, and (within narrow limits) some livestock, fowl, and structures in conjunction with same. Finally, the ownership of currency, a narrow range of financial assets, collector's valuables (for example philately, art) and some forms of intangible property (copyright, patents) is also allowed. This formal property right is often conditioned or limited in various ways, such as on the individual's or household's proper performance in the socialist sector, or on legal acquisition of the funds with which the objects are purchased.

But there is also another set of valuable rights which might be termed informal property rights. By informal property right we mean legally unsanctioned and even illegal, yet in reality effective, control over assets for private profit or other form of access to future streams of informal/illegal income and consequent wealth. Such an informal right may be an expected and *de facto* accepted by-product of a legitimate job (a very common situation). Indeed, as we have seen, the legitimate job may have been purchased, in which case the informal property right even has a (black) market value – probably discounted for the various attendant risks assumed by the jobholder. Moreover, the seller of the given job may have to purchase *his own* official job, of which the sale of subordinates' jobs (and collecting periodic tribute from them) may be a most valuable illegal attribute, and so on up the hierarchical ladder, generating informal property rights on every rung.

Informal property rights also attach to the control of what we call crypto-private firms – private businesses with socialist fronts and true underground private businesses, those without socialist fronts and therefore carefully hidden from view. Crypto-private businesses are common in the USSR. Informal property rights in them and in underground businesses are bought and sold as capital transactions, sometimes with outside private financing. What makes such informal property rights *property rights* is a powerful if brittle combination of (a) customary law of the Soviet underground, nurtured by a philosophy of live and let live, and even with its own adjudication arrangements; (b) the informal networks plus corrupt patronage by officialdom; and (c) widespread corruption all around.

Resting on combinations of this general type, as well as on the failings of the first economy and on wholesale misappropriation and abuse of socialist assets, the second economy and informal property rights flourished during the Brezhnev era. In their wake followed considerable redistribution of real income for many and large illicit fortunes for quite a few.

Another characteristic of the pre-Gorbachev years was the rapid inflation of the currency overhang, especially after 1979. We have addressed its mechanism and hinted at its dimensions elsewhere.[3] In his speech at the June 1987 Central Committee Plenum Gorbachev stated that currency in circulation had increased 3.1-fold during the three quinquennia 1971–85, or 7.8 per cent per year. This means that it increased at an annual rate three times that of real GNP or of real consumption (both as computed by the US CIA), and half again as fast as official retail sales at *current* prices. The public's savings deposits increased even faster over the fifteen years – 4.7-fold, or almost 11 per cent per year on average. These data, confirmed by a wealth of circumstantial evidence, leave little doubt that a serious currency overhang confronted the new administration as it took power, at least with reference to the first economy. (In the second economy, where prices are uncontrolled and, therefore, market-clearing, the surfeit of purchasing power brings about open inflation of prices and incomes.)

The monetary overhang may well be one of the main obstacles to a successful economic reform of the official economy under Gorbachev. On the one hand, it serves as a convincing political reason for caution in relaxing price control, thus ensuring that the reform of the first economy will remain little more than a halfway measure for some time. On the other, it tends to sustain the vigour of the underground economy and the persistence of considerable 'non-labour incomes', including corruption.

2   EFFECTS OF THE SECOND ECONOMY ON CHANCES FOR A MARKETISING REFORM

It is a commonplace with the population of the USSR and Eastern Europe, and increasingly so with their political leaders as well, that by its vigour and perdurance the second economy amply demonstrates the existence of major and profound institutional defects in the official economic system. Notably, when hard pressed on the economic front, one government after another has turned to small-scale private activity for assistance: from the New Economic Policy (NEP) in the Soviet Union of the twenties and the legalisation of the private peasant plot in the mid-thirties, to domestic measures following the events of 1953 in the GDR and those in 1956 in Poland and Hungary, and on to the encouragement of the 'family contract' by Gorbachev.

Naturally, the average person tends to associate the shortcomings of the existing order and the lessons of the second economy chiefly with conditions of his own everyday life and work, and with the equity – or inequity – of distribution of material benefits and opportunity around him. There is a growing consensus in the USSR and Eastern Europe that economic betterment *and* social justice lie in the direction of *some* kind of economic 'reform', broadly (if vaguely) understood as a general institutional and systemic movement in the directions of decentralisation and greater or lesser marketisation of the socialist sector, legalised privatisation or quasi-privatisation (for example small co-operatives), and tolerated informalisation of smaller-scale activities.

In sum, the very presence of the second economy has provided a major argument for the necessity of economic reform, yet it has also prepared the way for economic reform in some more specific senses.

(a) Perhaps most importantly, its many negative features notwithstanding, it has served as a living example of an alternative to the official centralised-planned-command system. It has underscored the efficacy of decisions orientated towards profit and market demand, as against hierarchical command and technocratic imperatives. In the actual multicoloured markets (Katsenelinboigen's phrase)[4] and in the bartering of supplies among firms, it has no doubt tended to affect the individual's conception of economic value, affirming market worth derived from demand and trade-off as against administratively set, cost-based price. (In our experience, emigrants from the USSR sometimes say 'real value' to mean black-market value.) It has tended to monetise both material reality and individual economic thinking. Of course, there is no attempt here to idealise the second economy, merely to bring out the ways in which it may help pave the way to a (more or less) marketising reform.

(b) The second economy also helps to dispel the not uncommon view that generations of Soviet rule have extirpated nearly all private initiative and enterprise. An observer of the second economy cannot but be impressed by the constant evidence of widespread enterprise, ingenuity, flexibility, and speed in pursuit of private gain, despite formidable obstacles and great personal risk. Illegality does not, of course, necessarily detract from enterprise or initiative; compare Adam Smith's famous words that the smuggler 'would have been, in every respect, an excellent citizen, had not the laws of his country made that a crime which nature never meant to be so'.[5] We may also note that many second-economy operations are conducted on quite a large scale, sheltered as they are by the aforementioned informal property rights. Examples of such large-scale operations can be found in nearly every branch of the economy, as crypto-private and underground businesses, semi-legal construction gangs [*shabashniki*], pseudo-socialist miners' co-operatives, crypto-private subsidiary establishments of kolkhozes. These often deserve to be characterised as entrepreneurial, and not only because they may involve large investment of private (albeit illicitly acquired) capital. Anyone who has looked into, say, the organisation of illegal manufacture of blue jeans in the Soviet Union will probably agree.

The difficult task facing Soviet reformers in trying to harness personal enterprise and initiative for legitimate social ends is three-fold: (i) broadening the currently still very narrow range of legally permitted private activity – that is, converting some of the informal property rights into formal ones; (ii) preventing officialdom from diverting the process towards its own corrupt ends; and (iii) harnessing these personal qualities for the socialist sector itself in the face of many obstacles and pitfalls.

(c) Another important attribute of a modern market economy is that of trust between transactors. In today's commercial and financial practice the word comes first; only later come the reams of legal paper. In Soviet underground practice, in larger-scale transactions along horizontal lines, the word comes both first and last, because nothing can be put on paper for obvious reasons. In our interviews with former participants in this world, we have often asked how large and highly complicated operations can rest on the spoken word alone. Invariably the answer has been 'trust', sometimes followed by 'after all, we are businessmen, not *apparatchiks*'. Violent enforcement seems to be rare. Rather, the ultimate sanction for breach of trust is ostracism from the informal network, from the underground world of business, probably followed by loss of the patron's protection as well and, hence, vulnerability to criminal prosecution for past breaches of the law. The point, however, is that learning to operate on trust – and building up one's own probity – is also a step in the direction of a market economy.

(d) Turning to a different theme, we take note of the seeming growth of acquisitive, consumerist, and materialist tendencies in the Soviet population during the Brezhnev era. Our authority for this statement is a mass of virtually uncontroverted impressionistic accounts both in the Soviet press and in oral and written *émigré* reports. This trend interacted with the growth of the second economy, the redistribution of income, and the accumulation of a good deal of new private wealth during the Brezhnev period, as already noted. Whatever can be said about this development from a moral or ideological standpoint, the promise it bears for the marketisation of command system is positive. A more acquisitive public makes for a market economy that is more governable by macro- as well as microeconomic instruments, and less in need of administrative (and coercive) means of control.

Such are some of the potential positive contributions of a long-entrenched second economy to a substantial reform of a Soviet-type economy. Weighing in heavily on the opposite side, however, is the aforementioned opposition to reform of the *status quo* owing to widespread vested interest in the second economy and its inevitable concomitant corruption of formal power, as well as in other forms of informal property rights.

Still on a negative (anti-reform) side, one should mention such basic problems as widespread disrespect for law and cynicism towards matters formal and official, which, if not generated by the second economy, have surely been ingrained and enhanced by it, and which will do little for the vitality of whatever economic *Rechtsstaat* the reform may bring forth.

More specifically, stealing from the state, one of the chief material foundations of the underground economy (and even of the legal private one), is a deeply ingrained economic institution as well as a personal pattern of behaviour. But where nearly all assets are state-owned, *laisser faire* is also *laisser voler*. This cannot be ignored in the design of any reform of the first economy, and its effects are likely to be more restrictive than conducive to a far-reaching reform.

Given the monetary overhang and its unequal personal size distribution, the second economy, legal as well as illegal, exerts a strong upward push on prices, as Soviet experience amply shows. What is less visible is that it also exerts an upward push on unit labour costs, in that the employer-state has to compete with the more lucrative parallel sector for the worker's time, effort, morale, loyalty, and sobriety. Here, too, the second economy works against the chances of reform by raising fears of open price-wage inflation and inviting administrative means for its suppression.

To some extent it may be possible to turn the second economy to the benefit of the first with the help of appropriate institutional arrangements, such as leasing the state's productive facilities to groups of workers. Hungary has gone farthest in introducing a variety of such devices. Rather cautiously, the Soviet Union is beginning to experiment along similar lines, primarily in agriculture and construction. Ideology apart, one problem with such attempts is the fuzziness of the line separating neo-socialism from crypto-capitalism-cum-corruption.

3   THE SECOND ECONOMY IN THE TRANSITIONAL [*PERESTROIKA*] PERIOD

The transitional period can be said to have begun with the issuance of the anti-alcohol decree of May 1985.[6] At the time of writing, it has been marked by the following major formal measures: the law against 'non-labour incomes' (May 1986),[7] the law on 'individual labour activity' (November 1986),[8] the resolution regarding (non-agricultural) co-operatives (January 1987),[9] 'the basic principles of a radical restructuring of managing the [national] economy' (adopted by the Central Committee Plenum in June 1987), the law on the state enterprise (confirmed by the Supreme Soviet in June 1987),[10] and a set of resolutions on finance, prices, planning, and so on, adopted in July 1987 (collected in *O korennoi perestroike upravleniia ekonomikoi*, 1987).

Perestroika's first major two measures – those against alcohol and non-labour incomes – were expressly prohibitionist and punitive rather than liberalising, and very harshly so. The signal that both sent out, a year apart, was that *perestroika* is not only about the broadening of economic freedom for entities socialist and private, but also about the coercive restriction and containment of the individual's freedom of choice as both consumer and producer, at least in some respects. The latter message was implicitly reinforced by publication of the law on individual labour activity, which went only a short distance towards greater permissiveness in this area.

(a) Gorbachev's anti-alcohol campaign is not the first in Soviet history since the abolition of alcohol prohibition in the early years of the Soviet era, but it is by far the most resolute and harsh and is handled primarily by the police and other administrative means. It addresses a most serious social and economic problem. One can hardly gainsay the campaign's underlying assumption that there will be no real sanitising of the material, medical, and moral aspects of Soviet society without a sharp reduction in alcoholism and drunkenness. At the time of writing, over two years since the campaign's inception, the longer-term results are still far from obvious. Lately, there has been much complaint from various Soviet sources, from Gorbachev down, that the campaign is flagging; calls for its reinvigoration are being raised.

It is not our task here to inquire into the campaign's manifold social aspects. Rather, we focus on the effects on the second economy, and through that on the implications for economic reform. The facts and numbers that follow are by courtesy of Professor V. G. Treml of Duke University, USA, the leading Western authority on the economics of alcohol in the USSR. According to Soviet data, *official* sale of alcoholic beverages, in terms of pure alcohol, fell by about one-half between 1984 and 1986. (All comparisons in this section refer to these two years.) This is no mean achievement, of course, aided though it was by steep increases in official prices (68 per cent for vodka) and by physical rationing of vodka in some localities. But all observers agree that *consumption* of alcohol declined much less owing to the sharp increase in home-made alcoholic beverages, especially home-distilled vodka or *samogon*. One leading Soviet authority insists that there was *no* overall decline in consumption, the whole drop in official alcohol sales being compensated for by the rise in *samogon* consumption.[11] Professor Treml does not go so far. He estimates a decrease in absolute alcohol consumption of about one-fourth, still very substantial. His calculations show that in 1986 the consumption of *samogon* exceeded that of official vodka for the first time ever.

One major consequence of the anti-alcohol campaign has been a considerable rise in informal income from *samogon*. (Note that official prices of the ingredients of *samogon*, of which the most important is sugar, have not risen, with minor exceptions.) There has also been a considerable rise in black-market sales of both official vodka and *samogon*, both at increased prices, of some ingredients of *samogon*, such as yeast, and also sale of places in the now long queues at liquor stores.[12]

Not the least of the effects, however, has been the implicit rise in the rouble value of remuneration in the second economy. Because such labour is commonly paid not in cash but with vodka, and because gifts of vodka are commonly used to induce labour to perform specific tasks in the first economy as well, the rise in both official and black-market prices of vodka in fact means a rise in the rouble wage of a unit of labour in such cases. This effect at the wage margin, as it were, may eventually, directly and indirectly, exert upward pressure on intra-marginal – and, therefore, average – rouble unit labour costs as well.

Finally, to the extent that the state does not recoup – from increased sales of other commodities (including sugar for *samogon*) or of services to the public – the fiscal revenue and industry profits lost on sales of alcohol, there would be a corresponding increase in the currency overhang, with consequences on the second economy and reform along the lines sketched out above. In the event, however, it appears that the increases in official prices of alcoholic beverages may have brought in enough additional net profit and fiscal revenue per litre roughly to compensate for the reduction in sales volume.

(b) The May 1986 law against non-labour income was, of course, aimed directly at the illegal part of the second economy – that is to say, at most of it. (Even the peasants' private plots did not escape its sting, as we shall soon see). Immediately, it raised difficult issues of conceptualisation and delimitation. Are the earnings of the truly hard-working *shabashnik* construction gangs to be qualified as 'non-labour' because of various inevitable illegalities in their methods (for example, supplies from the black market)? Or perhaps merely because such earnings are very high by Soviet standards, though often too high in terms of the speed and quality of their work? And what about the earnings of millions of state employees who are patently overpaid in relation to their performance? Is not part of their remuneration also non-labour income? Or the interest received from state bonds and the winnings from state lotteries? These and similar issues quickly came to be debated in the press. Needless to say, they have not been resolved.

Enforcement of the law began with much publicity and zeal. Clearly, the relevant local authorities had to show results (the incriminating information had been at hand all along), while at higher levels the opportunity was seized to eliminate politically less acceptable officials of high and medium calibre on charges of corruption (usually valid, no doubt). A by-product of this campaign was the demonstration of the extent to which illicit but productive activities had permeated the total economy. The press began writing about the disappearance of various useful and even essential services (for example medical services) because the risk of accepting the wonted inducements became prohibitively high. But the biggest outcry surrounded the sudden disappearance of a large part of farm produce from the so-called kolkhoz markets (relatively free peasants' markets) and the corresponding surge in prices. Not only did this occur at the height of the summer's bounty but, paradoxically, the bulk of the produce in these markets originates with the perfectly legal personal plots of collectivised peasants and state-farm workers.

Yet the underground was, in fact, heavily involved: 'up to' 80 per cent of all the produce had been moved to market by bribing the drivers of state-owned trucks (since the peasants are forbidden to own commercial vehicles),[13] and a high proportion of sales in larger cities was in fact by the illegal middleman.[14] Both kinds of 'criminal' perform useful services from the standpoints of the consumer and the producer alike, and although they are easily spotted, they used to bribe their way to market. Now, however, the heat was on the police, the useful services were cut off, and much of the produce disappeared from the market. In late July 1986, in Khabarovsk, Gorbachev commented on the shockingly high market prices, law enforcement was apparently somewhat relaxed, supplies resumed their flow, and a round was scored for the second economy. The episode is now known in the Soviet press as the 'excessive zeal of July [1986] [*iul'skii peregib*].

(c) The law on permitted individual labour activity (ILA) was apparently to be published simultaneously with that against non-labour income, bringing the carrot along with the stick, as it were, but it was delayed by six months because of high-level disagreements. What emerged in November 1986 is a very limited advance on earlier legislation, particularly that of 1976 relating to artisans and craftsmen. The 1976 law produced only meagre results owing to official hostility, high taxes, and other impediments.

The 1986 law lists some thirty permitted kinds of ILA in the area of goods and services production (not commerce). Of these only a few are newly opened for private activity: for example motor-vehicle repair and the use of personal cars as private taxis, in both cases legalising what already had been widespread and long-standing practice. The law provides that activities neither expressly permitted nor expressly forbidden may be legalised at republic level, but the actual licensing of ILA is left to local authorities; herein may lie a serious obstacle to the law's success, as explained below.

In addition to retaining a narrow range of permitted activities, the law limits the potential scope of ILA in several other dimensions. Any person who by virtue of age and health is expected to be employed in the socialist sector may engage in ILA only outside the working hours of their official job. (In the past, this kind of restriction has often been circumvented by the purchase of fictitious employment in some socialist enterprise.) Only family members may help (also outside official working hours, of course). Non-family personnel may not be employed at all. Either locally set annual licence fees [*patenty*] or revenue taxes according to a national scale must be paid;

both can be very high. It is promised that material inputs, tools, premises, equipment, transport, and so forth will be available, but will they?

The law on ILA came into effect on 1 May 1987. Before that, private business provided nearly all of the same goods and services to the public (and, not insignificantly, to the socialist sector, too), mainly through the underground economy. Thus the law may well result more in legalising pre-existing production activity, bringing it into the open, than in net additions to it. This in itself may be beneficial to most (if not all) those concerned, and might allow the treasury to capture tax revenue that now escapes it, apparently a major purpose of the law. However, the coexistence of private, even dwarf-sized, businesses with the Soviet state will hardly be an easy one.

Turning to the resolution on co-operatives of January 1987, we first note that the new regime clearly prefers co-operatives to individual labour activity as a means of mobilising local enterprise and initiative outside the state sector to provide locally needed goods and services. After all, in the USSR co-operatives are socialist while private business is not. But the impression given by Soviet sources that the co-operatives are a new departure, spawned by the new thinking and pragmatism, is not correct. Non-agricultural producer co-ops, already traditional in pre-revolutionary Russia, date back to the dawn of the Soviet era and were relegitimated in Stalin's day very much for the same reasons and purposes as they are being relegitimated by Gorbachev. Their membership peaked in 1955 at two million, after which dismantling set in, with final liquidation of all producer co-ops (with minor exceptions) in 1960. The announced reasons for the liquidation was that they became ready for promotion to a higher organisational form, that of state ownership; many were transformed into or absorbed by state-owned firms. The real reason – as related to us by participants or otherwise knowledgeable *émigrés* in the course of interviews – was that many of them were crypto-private (pseudo-co-operatives): hotbeds of misappropriation and misuse of socialist (co-op) property, sources of private enrichment, and causes of severe corruption of officialdom.[15] So Khrushchev closed them. Will they be much different under Gorbachev? One wonders.

The new laws regarding ILAs and co-ops are still quite recent; definitive judgements of their success are premature. The main theme of the Soviet media has been to praise model instances in operation, but to complain bitterly of the paucity of applications to local authorities and especially of the reluctance on the part of local authorities to license them. Their resistance is quite understandable. To them, traditionally and typically, private activity has been fair prey for 'squeeze', for sharing in the economic rent inherent in the business. And the bigger rent is to be found in illegal undertakings, which shun the tax collector, ignore price control, and liberally misappropriate socialist assets. Here, protection money is to be raked in; here, graft is to be squeezed out. In other words, what has been the local authorities' informal property right, sometimes actually acquired by purchase, Gorbachev is now devaluing with his anti-corruption campaign and measures to bring underground activity into the open. Little wonder that they drag their feet.

This 'antagonistic contradiction' (to use a phrase in context) between Gorbachev's *perestroika* and his treasury on the one hand, and the self-serving impulses of local authorities on the other, with the would-be entrepreneurs in the middle, may well find its resolution in a compromise: ILAs and co-ops may indeed be lawfully established in good numbers; the statistics will be gratifying to the partisans of liberalisation, but in many cases the new entities will be partly below and partly above ground. They will provide fronts for crypto-private undertakings, milch cows for corrupt local and industrial authorities, rich but uneasy gold mines for the entrepreneurs – all in the venerable tradition of the Soviet second economy.

4 REFORM OF THE FIRST ECONOMY AND THE SECOND ECONOMY

Thanks to the adoption in June 1987 of the aforementioned 'Basic Principles for a Radical Restructuring . . .' and 'Law on the State Enterprise', the passing in July of the resolutions on finance, prices, and so on, and to the many speeches and articles by Gorbachev and his advisers and followers, one can now make out the general direction in which he intends to proceed: towards introducing market forces, if not towards a full-fledged socialist market economy. Certainly, the formal adoption of the two fundamental documents by the Central Committee Plenum and by the Supreme Soviet, respectively, is a significant procedural victory for *perestroika*. But it is only one battle won, and an early one at that. How fast and steadfast, with what setbacks, interruption, and detours, and with what detail, the progress towards a reformed Soviet (first) economy will progress, is still unclear. There will be many battles and skirmishes yet, as there will inevitably be innumerable exogenous shocks. It will take many years for the reform process to be – not completed, for such a process never really is, but brought to a point of sufficient accomplishment and reasonable stability. What the institutional state of the economy at that point will be, if the economy ever gets there, is still shrouded in great uncertainty. Will it be a socialist market economy (and how viable would one be in any case)? Or only a halfway solution, because this is all Gorbachev (or his successor) wants, or because this is all he can get?

For a long time yet, however, the reform will be at best at a halfway stage, thanks to excessive purchasing power, continuing price control, difficulty to shift from materials allocation to 'wholesale trade', non-convertibility of the rouble, and many other factors. Thus there will still be basic disequilibrium and hence much room for underground activity and informal incomes.

In the meantime, confusion seems to reign in the economy because of the enormous turnover of executive and political personnel, the new legislation, and the staccato pace of organisational change. So far, *perestroika* amounts to a blanket injunction not to operate in old ways, but gives little concrete indication how to operate without them. This confusion plays into the hands of the enemies of reform. It also works to the advantage of the second economy, particularly the underground, accustomed as it is to move quickly to fill gaps in the official economy. Hampering the second economy in this regard are the continuing campaign against non-labour incomes and, perhaps more seriously, the impairment of the old lattice of horizontal networks and vertical patron–client ties by dint of the shake-ups of the past two years. However, time is on the side of the underground. Networks and ties are usually rebuilt with time; given economic need, corruption and clientelism bide their time.

But perhaps the greatest assurance that the underground will survive is the sheer fact that socialist (state) property will remain within easy grasp, constant temptation to profit in the old familiar ways. At any rate, a revolution in civic morality can hardly be round the corner.

Of course, survival of the underground economy does not guarantee the retention of any individual's or group's informal income. If *perestroika* does little to cut down illicit activity and income, it may still do much to redistribute them. Those who fear losses know what they stand to lose; those who may gain informal income do not yet know it with any certainty. So the overall effect of the second economy is still against reforms. Gorbachev's battleground, like the economy itself, is both above and below ground.

Notes

1. The research underlying this chapter has been generously supported by the Ford Foundation, the National Council for Soviet and East European Research (contract 620-5), Wharton Econometrics Forecasting Associates, and by several units of the University of California, Berkeley. This support is gratefully and cheerfully acknowledged.
2. Some ideas of the magnitude of informal (or 'private') incomes in the USSR can be grasped from the findings of questionnaire survey among over 1000 families of recent Soviet *émigrés* in the United States, conducted by Professor V. G. Treml of Duke University and the present author as part of the 'Berkeley-Duke Project on the Second Economy'. The data centre on 1977 and refer only to urban areas. They have not yet been re-weighted for greater representativeness of the sample in relation to the Soviet urban population. Grouped by region, they also reflect the great spatial variation in the importance of the second economy and informal incomes. The figures presented below refer only to families in which both husband and wife were present and at least one of them was officially employed at the time. The first figure is the mean amount of informal income *per capita* per year, in roubles; the second is the same as per cent of mean total (formal and informal) income *per capita* per year; and the third indicates the number of *persons* covered in the given sub-sample.

	r./yr	*%*	*N*
RSFSR and Baltic republics	541	29.6	1 051
Belorussia, Moldavia and Ukraine	874	40.2	558
Armenia (ethnic Armenians only)	2 065	64.1	560
'Europeans' residing in Transcaucasia and Central Asia	887	49.7	488

Since the late 1970s, for reasons partly mentioned in the text, the importance of informal income in relation to formal (official) income seems to have increased, at least until the start of Gorbachev's campaign against 'non-labour incomes' in 1985. For general accounts of the Soviet second economy see Grossman, 1977 and 1979.
3. Grossman, 1986. For a characterisation of the Brezhnev era in ways germane to this paper see Millar, 1985.
4. Katsenelinboigen, 1977.

5. Adam Smith, *An Inquiry into the Nature and Causes of the Wealth of Nations* (Modern Library edn, 1937) p. 853.
6. *Pravda*, 17 May 1985.
7. *Pravda*, 25 May 1986.
8. *Pravda*, 21 November 1986.
9. *Ekonomicheskaia gazeta*, no. 9, 1987, pp. 11 ff.; also no. 18, p. 23.
10. *Pravda*, 27 June and 1 July 1987, respectively.
11. G. G. Zaigraev in *Kommunist*, no. 11, 1987, p. 37.
12. Treml estimates *samogon* production in 1986 at 1.0 to 1.3 billion litres of pure (100 per cent) alcohol. At *samogon* black-market prices of 12–16 roubles per litre of standard alcohol content (40 per cent), and therefore 30–40 r./l. of pure alcohol, the gross 'street value' of output comes to 30–52 billion roubles. Compare this with total *official* retail sales of all goods of 332 billion roubles in 1986. The value added must be quite close to the gross value, for the cost of ingredients (chiefly sugar) is very low, though risk may be a substantial cost component (especially when the product is marketed and not just self-consumed). The sharp rise in the attractiveness of *samogon* production has stimulated an underground private industry of production of stills (distilling apparatus), some of it within state machine factories (*Sotsialisticheskaia industriia*, 16 August 1987, p. 4).
   On the significance of alcohol in general, and *samogon* in particular, in the USSR and its second economy see Treml, 1982 and 1985.
13. Figure from deputy procurator-general of the USSR, N. Bazhenov, quoted in *Pravda*, 14 July 1986, p. 3.
14. Figure and reference to be supplied.
15. As one of our experienced interviewees put it: 'It is frightening to think what had been going on in those co-operatives' [zhut' chto tam tvorilos']. In fact, similar 'frightening' things are still going on, decades after the liquidation of co-ops in 1960. See, for example, the recent account of the takeover of a considerable portion of gold mining by private business-men operating through pseudo-co-operatives of miners (miners' co-ops remained legal) and with the help of large bribes to high officials in the industry (*Sotsialisticheskaia industriia*, 13 May, 12 June, 20 June, and 28 June 1987).

References

Grossman, Gregory (1977) 'The "Second Economy" of the USSR', *Problems of Communism*, 26, September–October, pp. 25–40.
Grossman, Gregory (1979) 'Notes on the Illegal Private Economy and Corruption', pp. 834–55 in US Congress, Joint Economic Committee, *The Soviet Economy in a Time of Change* (Washington, DC: Government Printing Office).
Grossman, Gregory (1986) 'Inflationary, Political, and Social Implications of the Current Economic Slowdown', pp. 172–97 in Hans-Hermann

Höhmann *et al.* (eds), *Economics and Politics in the USSR: Problems of Interdependence* (Boulder, CO: Westview Press).

Katsenelinboigen, Aron (1977) *Studies in Soviet Economic Planning.* (White Plains, NY: M. E. Sharpe), esp. ch. 7, 'Market Colours and the Soviet Economy'.

Millar, James R. (1985) 'The Little Deal: Brezhnev's Contribution to Acquisitive Socialism', *Slavic Review*, 44, pp. 694–706.

O korennoi perestroike upravleniia ekonomikoi: Sbornik dokumentov, (Moscow, 1987).

Treml, Vladimir G. (1982) *Alcohol in the USSR: A Statistical Study*, (Durham, NC: Duke Press Policy Studies).

Treml, Vladimir G. (1985) 'Alcohol Underground in the USSR', *Berkeley-Duke Occasional Papers on the Second Economy in the USSR*, no. 5.

6 Soviet Restructuring in Relation to the Chinese Reform

Michael Kaser

THE GENESIS OF 'TAUT PLANNING'

In the early 1950s all states with a ruling Communist Party had adopted a homogeneous economic mechanism – that of the USSR. The Soviet 'command economy' had been constructed within a very short space of time – the single year 1930 embraces most of the essential changes – and responded to the political dictates of centralised authority. That authority was constituted by Stalin himself and it can be argued that, having assured political autocracy, he would not tolerate the persistence of economic forces which might gainsay him or undertake activities contrary to those embodied in a central plan. The forcible collectivisation of the peasantry and the elimination of private small-scale industry and trade removed from the economy all those whose performance was geared to the domestic market. Soon afterwards, the same exclusion was applied to those who responded to changes in foreign markets: by 1938 a deliberate policy of self-sufficiency had reduced exports to a mere half per cent of Soviet GNP (Holzman, 1963, p. 290). The political imperative did not render such exclusive centralisation irrational for economic development, for it could be contended that all resources were thereby mobilised to achieve a few crucial outputs, such as the expansion of capacity for engineering in order to provide capital equipment and defence goods, and for that new capacity to be supplied by energy, steel and other inputs and housing, food and clothing for the workers. Such concentration of economic activities on a narrow set of objectives was later characterised by a famous Polish economist as *'sui generis* a war economy' (Lange, 1961, p. 139).

That observation is relevant to the hostile external environment in which Stalin's form of central planning was adopted in Eastern Europe and China. By 1951 each of the seven states ruled by

Communist Parties in Europe* had adopted five- (or six-) year plans on the Soviet model with similar apparatus for their implementation, notably nationalisation of industry, transport and trade, compulsory procurement in farming (collectivisation had, however, only barely begun) and the monopolisation of foreign trade. Albania, Bulgaria, Czechoslovakia, the GDR, Hungary and Romania were in the early phases of such plans and were members with the USSR of their own economic group, the Council for Mutual Economic Assistance (Comecon); Yugoslavia was nominally within the period of a five-year plan, 1947–51, but was abandoning centralisation and nationalisation for worker self-management and a 'socialist market'. With the exception of Yugoslavia, the communist-governed states confronted the rest of Europe in the Cold War and were soon to respond to the North Atlantic Treaty by their own military pact, the Warsaw Treaty. The Chinese Communist Party, by its victory in 1949 over the Guimindung in all China save Taiwan, was in armed conflict on its borders – Korea and Taiwan – and under censure by the United Nations. Mongolia had started its first five-year plan in 1948; North Korea and North Vietnam began two-year plans in 1949 and 1955 respectively (see Kaser, 1967, p. 66). Even if Stalin had not pressed his system on his East European allies, Mao had not welcomed Soviet economic advisers and had other Asian Communist Parties not fallen into line, the hostile environment would have rendered rational the adoption of planning for a war economy.

The belligerence of the Cold War is now part of history, though relations between Communist-Party-ruled and non-communist states can still be tense. Conferring here in Seoul, one cannot but be aware of the closed frontier to our north and of the shooting down not so long ago of a Korean airline as it flew towards this city. There are indeed some in the armed forces and in defence industries who argue for the continuance of central planning as assuring their charges the priority in supply which they long enjoyed. But even they would accept that their governments' objectives in allocating economic resources cannot be exclusively military; moreover, for some years they have been told that a strong, broad-based economy is needed to underpin their material provision.

---

* Mostly as a consequence of mergers with socialist parties in 1948 or thereabouts, some Communist Parties had changed their names and the designation they collectively adopted was 'Communist and Workers' Parties'.

The widening of the economic objectives of a ruling Communist Party since the days of Stalin and Mao – notably to obtain the gains of international trade and to satisfy the diverse and growing demands of households – is one part of the indictment of 'taut' central planning. The other part is the waste of resources occasioned by the use of so unsophisticated an economic mechanism. Macroeconomic ranking by simple priority and the microeconomic maximisation of production are emanations of a supply-determined system. Although under capitalism the macroeconomy can be characterised as 'demand-determined' (at least within the Keynesian analysis), its microeconomic equilibrium is of course the outcome of both demand and supply conditions. In Eastern Europe and the USSR, 'extensive' development – that is, growth by the addition of manpower, capital assets and natural resources – is being forced out (by a stringency of labour and the moderation of a high investment propensity) in favour of 'intensive' development – that is, the improvement of the efficiency of currently exploited factors of production.

Mongolia and Cuba (which went through a period of extreme 'priority' planning in the 1960s) once had large rural manpower reserves upon which to draw for 'extensive' development, but in both countries the majority of the population is now urbanised (71 per cent in Cuba and 52 per cent in Mongolia). China can still foresee a wealth of human resources – the population of working age will rise from 585 million in 1980 to 760 million in 1990 and 850 million by the year 2000 (a rising proportion of the total population from 59.7 through 69.6 to 71.1 per cent) on estimates by the World Bank (1985, Tables 8.2 and 8.3, Projection B). Yugoslavia (with 600 000 workers abroad and nearly one-fifth of those at home unemployed) and Albania (with the highest demographic growth in Europe) are not yet faced with a labour shortage, but their ruling parties have chosen economic structures (extreme devolution in the one, extreme centralisation in the other) which are of little help in a comparative analysis of Soviet and Chinese reform. Soviet-type planning made large areas of economic activity irrelevant to the equilibrium analysis of market economies: Stalin's slogan to 'overfulfil the production plan' and Mao's maxim of 'self-reliance' were two sides of the same priority for supply conditions – the former maximised outputs, the latter minimised inputs.

A MARKET IN FARM PRODUCE

A first stage in reform is hence to moderate the effect of taut supply-side planning by applying the influence of demand conditions. Both China and the USSR began by fostering responsiveness to market-expressed demand in agriculture. In China the commune as an entity monopsonising the labour of its conscribed membership has been replaced by village councils and a 'contracted household responsibility system' which allows the farm household to be remunerated according to the output of the land, livestock or craft to which it applies its labours. Property rights remain limited in two ways. First, some obligatory procurement contracts are still imposed, but the average quota was reduced from 70 to 30 per cent of the expected crop in 1985. Secondly, the land is at its disposition (for as long as thirty years), not in its ownership but as a right to usufruct which is saleable, together with the value increment occasioned by any capital improvements it may have made. Farm output has flourished and the flow of produce to the towns has furnished backing for incentives among the non-farm population.

The collective and state farms in the USSR remain, but since 1981 the 'contract brigade' has spread among the former. Such a brigade is normally small and confined to a family-related group; unlike the brigades which have been units of collective farms since their creation, their membership is self-chosen and they select their own leader and work schedules (Gagnon, 1987). As in China they are remunerated by results, but their regular tenure of the same piece of land or herd of livestock is not as firmly guaranteed. Nor have they developed as rapidly as their potential demands.

At the June 1987 Central Committee meeting Gorbachev complained that 'the family contract system is insufficiently widespread, although the efficiency of these forms of organisation of, and payment for, labour is high enough' (Gorbachev, 1987). The Director of the Institute of Economics of the USSR Academy of Sciences has cited the success of Chinese agricultural reform in urging that, while retaining more of the collective framework than in China, 'we would energetically encourage the development of the family form of labour' (Abalkin, 1987a). Soviet families are being urged to till more intensively the plots around the farm homestead and to sell their produce on town markets (Shmelev, 1987). The collective and state farms for which they work have been instructed to sell the fodder and young livestock which such production requires.

Under a 'law on the enterprise (association)' enacted by the Supreme Soviet in June 1987, state farms will be able to sell some of their farm produce (and all their non-farm production) outside the state supply system; collective farms have recently been allowed to sell up to 30 per cent of their output on the free market.

Both China and the USSR have established 'agro-industrial' agencies which link farming with the production of its inputs and with the processing of its outputs. Each phase is thereby rendered more sensitive to derived demand. The opportunity for rural diversification has been opened further in China by the authorisation of 'township industry' – usually small-scale factories and workshops.

COMPETITION IN NON-FARM PRODUCTION

A penetration of market-generated transactions into the supply-determined state sector has been effected in both countries by allowing individuals to set up businesses (short of employing personnel outside the family) and production and service co-operatives. A marginal private sector had always been tolerated under the centralised system; that part which had been illicit has been legalised and is now subject to taxation. 'It is not accidental', observed Gorbachev (1987) to the Central Committee in June, 'that a "shadow economy" of sorts has emerged.' The private and co-operative sector is already substantial in China and in the USSR has gained impetus from laws of 1986 and 1987 which open twenty-nine crafts and services to private enterprise and allow co-operatives in public catering, services and the production of consumer goods. In China, the government has encouraged the general spread of non-farm individual activity, the township industries in rural areas and collective enterprises in urban areas; all help to absorb young people who cannot find state employment.

State enterprises in both countries are no longer guaranteed a supply of inputs and the purchase of outputs to the maximum of their productive capacity under an annual plan. The opening of part of their capacity to transactions negotiated by enterprises themselves is a notable relaxation of taut planning and patently introduces competition into the bulk of each country's economic activity. Autonomous management and self-financing are prominent in the Soviet 'law on the enterprise (association)' of June 1987 but they will continue to be subject to state orders [*goszakazy*] which guarantee the satisfaction of top-priority social requirements . . . which are necessary, first of all, for the solution of state social tasks, the implementation of scientific and technical programmes, the strengthening of the country's defence potential and for the delivery of farm produce to state stocks. . . . Enterprises must be assured broad independence in concluding agreements on the basis of economic norms and the orders of consumers.(Gorbachev, 1987)

The corresponding Chinese law on the enterprise was on the point of enactment at the People's Congress session of April 1987 but the combination of state orders and competitive transactions has been in operation since 1979. The present writer has characterised Chinese practice as 'dual track', because each enterprise uses its capacity either under state orders or in response to market demand – from other productive enterprises or from wholesale trade. The difference from the Soviet system, as it appears from the decisions of the June 1987 Central Committee, is that the prices at which the marketed quantities are sold may vary from the official price applicable to state orders (Kaser, 1987). The degree of price flexibility in China varies between branches of industry. Thus by February 1987 20 per cent of the production of consumer durables and foodstuffs was being sold at the official price under state orders, a further 40 per cent could be sold at a 'floating price' under state orders and the remaining 40 per cent was uncontrolled and saleable at any chosen price. The 'floating price' had to be within a range of 20 per cent above or below the official price.

Addressing the June Central Committee meeting, Gorbachev (1987) called for

all types of prices and tariffs to be reconsidered in their aggregate and the organic connection between wholesale procurement and retail prices and tariffs should be ensured during a radical reform of the price system. It is necessary consistently to reflect in them the socially-necessary expenditure on the production and marketing of output, its consumer-orientated properties, the quality of output and effective demand.

He went on to speak of a combination of 'stability and flexibility' and the law on the enterprise, enacted just afterwards, envisages centrally fixed, negotiated and free prices. The wholesale price reform, which will be effective from 1 January 1990, and the retail restructuring the next year will be extensive. The Director of the Research Institute under the USSR Committee on Prices [*Goskomtsen*] suggested that wholesale prices would have approximately to double, although engineering goods would not need much change, and that in retail pricing foodstuffs would increase significantly in price while turnover tax cuts might bring down the prices of manufactured consumer goods (Chaplanov, 1987, p. 1). Earlier a member of his staff, with one from *Goskomtsen* itself, had described the research that had been undertaken to calculate the wholesale prices that would stimulate technical innovation and diffusion (Goroberidze and Lakhov, 1986, pp. 88–94). The chairman of *Goskomtsen* spoke of existing 'prices playing little role in creating balance between supply and demand, leading to continual shortages both for retail and wholesale goods' (Pavlov, 1987). He added that food subsidies in 1987 would total 58 billion roubles.

China has already experienced moderate inflation consequent upon the liberalisation of pricing to competition: the official index in 1987 showed an annual rate of 6 per cent. The Soviet index, held almost constant over many years (whereas the Chinese index had been allowed to rise), will have to increase sharply as reform takes place in 1991.

The excessive Soviet retail price stability has accumulated a great deal of 'inflationary overhang'. At the June Central Committee, Gorbachev (1987) revealed the extent of repressed inflation in the Soviet Union. He reported that between 1971 and 1985 money in circulation had increased 3.1 times, whereas the output of consumer goods had only doubled. Retail prices for bread and many food staples have remained unchanged since 1954, while dairy products are still at prices set in 1962. A large inflationary gap opens every year, due to rises in money wages and in farm incomes, while output of goods to spend the money on rises more slowly and prices largely do not reflect the enhanced demand.

The promise of freer transactions between state enterprises, embodied in the economic reform, and the growing share of private production and trade make essential a rational price relationship between demand and supply. The immense inflationary overhang of unspent roubles is a threat to that part of the economic reform and it was therefore not surprising that rumours were reported that a currency reform was in prospect.

There has been no link between the external rouble – which is merely an accounting device, its rate of exchange into foreign currencies being entirely formal – and the purchasing power of the domestic rouble for international transactions, whether retail or wholesale. Gorbachev's promise, however, at the same Party Central Committee meeting, that the rouble would be made convertible 'stage by stage' may be linked to an internal reform so that the government may declare that the new rouble has a realistic purchasing-power parity with foreign currencies and thereby render it more acceptable for Soviet citizens to hold off spending their money during the fragile period of economic reform.

A possible timetable would start, as clearly it has done, with rumours of monetary reform along the lines of those which took place in the USSR in December 1947 and January 1961. In both those past cases, ten old roubles were exchanged for one new rouble, but in the first case only a small holding of roubles could be exchanged and the remainder were demonetised – that is, wholly lost to the holder. The present rumour confirms that roubles in savings accounts will not incur financial loss and must be directed towards Soviet citizens who have no qualms about putting roubles into their named bank accounts. Deposits in the savings bank will reveal to the authorities the true extent of the problem and they are likely to freeze deposits for a certain period while retail prices and the supply of consumer goods are being adjusted to the new market conditions.

COMPETITION FROM FOREIGN ENTERPRISES

It would give added credibility to that new domestic rouble if some element of convertibility were applied. Initially there might be some foreign currency for travel abroad or for enterprises and shops to buy a few Western consumer goods. Many aspects of the economic reform, including joint ventures with Western companies and freedom to trade abroad by state enterprises, require a realistic exchange rate.

The relationship of domestic to foreign price relativities in the USSR has already been the subject of a decree of the Central Committee and the Council of Ministers (19 August 1986) which defined 'differentiated exchange-rate coefficients' to link 'actual contract prices' with those in domestic prices. Citing the decree and the new practice of the DVK [*differentsirovanye valyutnye koeffitsienti*]

Zakharov, head of a sub-department of the USSR *Gosplan*, notes (1987) that the coefficients range from 0.3 to 6.0 – that is, for some transactions the domestic rouble is three times undervalued by purchasing-power parity; for others it is six times overvalued. He argues that it is logical for that range to be narrowed, but that a unified single rate could not be applied until three to five years hence.

China reached that point in 1985, when a unitary exchange rate superseded the multiple 'internal settlement rates' (as World Bank, 1985, p. 101, termed them), but it had the advantage of 'the current account surpluses of recent years, large reserves and the ready availability of foreign capital' (ibid.). By contrast, the USSR currently runs a large deficit in convertible currency trade, is heavily indebted to the West and would meet resistance from Western banks if it sought to raise much new money abroad.

Both China and the USSR require exchange rates which reflect comparative purchasing power if competition is to be activated from foreign enterprises. Both countries now accord substantial foreign trading rights to domestic enterprises (though China rescinded some in 1984) and admit joint ventures with foreign firms. In addition, each has a special relationship which allows wholly owned foreign enterprises to operate on domestic territory. For China it is the 'special economic zones' along the coast near territories whose political reunification the government expects in the future. Shantou and Shenzhen are near Hong Kong (to be incorporated in 1997), Zhuhai is near Macao (to be incorporated in 1999) and Xiamen is near Taiwan. This proximity is not irrelevant because the incorporatable territories are guaranteed their own separate economic systems for fifty years and will constitute enclaves with numerous foreign holdings. For the USSR the special relationship is with the member states of the Council for Mutual Economic Assistance (CMEA): laws of 1987 allow firms from those countries to have wholly owned enterprises in the USSR.

Gorbachev summarised the Party's expectations of competitiveness from abroad at the Central Committee in June:

> The reorganisation of economic management opens broad scope for enhancing the efficiency of our external economies ties and – particularly important – for enhancing the impact of the external market on the functioning of industries and enterprises, on the quality of their products and on scientific and technological progress.

COMPETITION IN BANKING AND FINANCE

In addition to the competitiveness among enterprises arising from the motivation of state enterprises to make profits to invest and allocate themselves, common now to both countries' reforms, each is authorising competition among banks, which will serve as adjudicator on a still-limited capital market. Enterprises can choose between ploughing back profits and earning interest on bank deposits; China has gone further in opening modest stock exchanges in Beijing, Shanghai, Shenyang, Tianjin and Wuhan. Banks with which deposits are made are seen under the reform as competing for those deposits and for borrowers. China has already abandoned its 'monobank' system: besides the People's Bank (and the Bank of China for foreign transactions) there are now specialist banks for agriculture, investment and working capital. A resolution of the Soviet Party Central Committee, 'Main Provisions for Fundamentally Reorganising Economic Management', in June resolved

> to consider it advisable to establish specialised banks with due account for the peculiarities of economic complexes and fuller satisfaction of the population's requirements for credit-and-settlements services, to turn the credit granting system into a highly qualified, reliable and interested partner of enterprises and organisations.

The Soviet special relationship with CMEA has a further dimension in the sphere of banking. The resolution just cited went on to say: 'Special attention should be devoted to raising the purchasing power of the rouble, and to ensuring its stage-by-stage convertibility, first and foremost, within the framework of the Council for Mutual Economic Assistance.' Rybalko, a deputy director of a Ministry of Finance department, foresees (1987) a role for the CMEA current-account bank, the International Bank for Economic Co-operation, in creating funds for multilateral settlements and in establishing realistic mutual exchange rates among members.

COMPETITION AND CONTRADICTIONS

A final word in this chapter must relate competition with controversy and contradictions. The days are patently long past when Stalin's 'genius' or Mao's *Thoughts* overrode all discussion. The emergence of non-antagonistic 'contradictions' was soon accepted in both countries, but the preparation and implementation of the economic reforms have raised many controversies and debates and engendered considerable differences among political and administrative groups at all levels. It is hence appropriate to conclude with the words used in a summary of a 'Round Table on Contradictions of the Socialist Economy at the Contemporary Stage' held in Moscow in November 1986, by Abalkin (1987b, p. 4): 'It is wholly natural that in the course of the discussion many interesting opinions were expounded and on many issues views were advanced which were divergent and often diametrically opposed.' It seems right to indicate that thirty years on, a 'hundred flowers' are blooming in China and in the USSR.

References

Abalkin, L. (1987a) Reported by P. Cockburn, 'Senior Soviet Economist Presses for Family Farms', *Financial Times* (London), 15 July.

Abalkin, L. (1987b) 'The Economic Contradictions of Socialism', *Voprosy ekonomiki*, no. 5 (May).

Chaplanov, V. I. (1987) Interview on Moscow Radio, *BBC Summary of World Broadcasts*, 15 July Part I, no. 8620, section B.

Gagnon, V. P. (1987) 'Gorbachev and the Collective Contract Brigade', *Soviet Studies*, vol. 39, no. 1.

Gorbachev, M. S. (1987) 'On the Party's Tasks in Fundamentally Restructuring the Economy', *Pravda*, 26 June.

Goroberidze, A. and B. Lakhov (1986) 'Price and the Effectiveness of Incentives', *Planovoe khozyaistvo*, no. 10, October.

Holzman, F. (1963) 'Foreign Trade', in A. Bergson and S. Kuznets (eds), *Economic Trends in the Soviet Union* (Cambridge, MA: Harvard University Press).

Kaser, M. (1967) *Comecon: Integration Problems of the Planned Economies* (London: Oxford University Press).

Kaser, M. (1987) 'One Economy, Two Systems': Parallels between Soviet and Chinese Reforms', *International Affairs*, Summer.

Lange, D. (1961) *Pisma ekonomiczne i spoteczne 1930–1960* (Warsaw).

Pavlov, V. (1987) Report by P. Cockburn of interview with Novosti Agency, reported: 'Soviet Prices Chief Calls for Overhaul', *Financial Times*, 14 July.

Rybalko, G. (1987) 'The Current Role of the Foreign-Exchange Mechanism', *Ekonomicheskaya gazeta*, no. 11, March.

Shmelev, N. (1987) 'On the Social Content of Private Subsidiary Production', *Ekonomicheskaya gazeta*, no. 9, February.

World Bank (1985) *China. Long-Term Development Issues and Options*, (Washington, DC: World Bank).

Zakharov, S. (1987) 'Through Foreign Exchange Coefficients', *Ekonomicheskaya gazeta*, no. 29, July.

7 The Soviet Communist Party and Economic Reform: a Case Study

Yong-Chool Ha

1 THE 1973–5 REFORM: BACKGROUND AND CONTENT

This chapter examines the attitudes of a sample of thirty *obkom* (provincial committee) first secretaries to the 1973 production association reform during the three years 1973 to 1975. Since the idea of production association had already been mentioned at the 24th Party Congress in 1971, speeches and articles from 1971 and 1972 are also added.

The 1973 reform may be viewed as an attempt to respond to deteriorating economic performance and, in effect, as an acknowledgement of the failure of the 1965 reform. Its main thrust was to counter the re-emergent centralised management system by establishing an intermediate level between ministries and enterprises. This was also a reflection of the lesson learnt from the experience of 1957 to 1969 in that it tried to avoid the supremacy of both local interests and central administration.[1]

Production associations were organised by vertically and horizontally incorporating several (two to five) enterprises which were related with respect to productive processes, materials or products. Special emphasis was laid on the inclusion of organisations which dealt with research and development (R&D). Depending upon the type of industry and technology, there were variations in the numbers of layers in the industrial management system.[2] The hope underlying the reform was to achieve an improvement in industrial performance through better co-ordination, specialisation, easier introduction of new processes and products – all leading to an improvement of quality and lowering of costs.

In the area of day-to-day operations, associations were given the rights which enterprises were supposed to have had under the 1965 reform. To ease the burden on central planning agencies and ministries, production associations were themselves to divide the planned tasks among constituent enterprises. Administrative details which the centre had previously handed down to enterprises were now to be largely taken care of by associations. By cutting the number of operating units for which the centre was to plan, a more efficient information exchange and better communication were to be achieved. In many cases associations included also the design and R&D organisations, and were supposed to help them to introduce new technologies into production. The rationale for this was to make the application of new technologies easier by putting research closer to production. At the same time it was hoped that creating larger economic units would spread the risk of failure in industrial innovation more widely.

Associations were also given the right to set up various funds to cover R&D activity, the introduction of new technology and the development of export production, by providing financial assistance to member enterprises and organisations. Old enterprises were to lose their legal status as autonomous economic units and associations were to operate on the *khozraschet* principle: that is, on profit–loss accountability.

The 1973 reform also had a distinctive political context. Since 1965 the collective leadership had been through several stages of power and authority building. The 1965 reform was largely sponsored by Kosygin, and as his reform did not bring about the desired results, Brezhnev used this failure in an effort to build his own authority. By 1971 the ascendancy of Brezhnev was clear and the idea of production associations was first proposed by him at the 24th Party Congress. The clear purpose of the proposal was to correct what was acknowledged to be an overcentralised management system. While it is not clear whether the proposal also aimed explicitly at increasing the role of the Party, it is clear that it represented an attack on central government bureaucracy. Such an anti-centre theme might have been welcomed by many local party officials.[3]

However, after 1971, when the reform idea was proposed, it took two years to prepare and enact the necessary legislation. Unlike the earlier reforms of 1957 and 1965, the attention given to this reform was not intense. To begin with it was never called a reform and was never accorded large-scale public discussion and mass-media highlighting. This may be partly due to the fact that the idea had been developed for some time before 1971. In some parts of the Ukraine and Leningrad, it had already been tried in the 1960s. The more subdued tone might also be due to the reform being launched at a time when the succession problem was already solved and stability had set in, while the other two reforms were launched at earlier stages in the life of the respective regimes. The original plan for implementing the 1973 reform called for starting operations according to the new mode by 1975. This date was later postponed until 1980.[4] There was also significant unevenness in the transition to the new system among different sectors. The higher the need felt for ministerial power, the more gradual was the progress, as seen in the slow transformation of the heavy and machine-building industries.[5]

But who precisely stood in the way of a faster transition to the new system? That is, who were the losers under this new system? These questions are relevant when we look at the responses of the *obkom* first secretaries to the reform. First, ministries and *glavki* (the specialised commodity bureaux within ministries) were clear losers in having to relinquish their traditional powers of control over enterprises. Indeed, many of the *glavki* were to be abolished. Secondly, many enterprise directors also lost power and status, since enterprises lost their independent legal status. At the same time, the evaluation of enterprise performance under the new system was to be made in terms of the contribution to net outputs of the association, excluding goods used by other members of the same association.

This situation of enterprises *vis-à-vis* their associations was to some extent shared by local party organs, especially by *raikoms* (regional committees). What was profitable for a *raion* (region) might not be so profitable for its association. This is a situation that might be called 'localism on a small scale', analogous to the relationship between *oblasts* (provinces) and the centre in the 1957 reform. Furthermore, the association reform might give rise to the old issue of the nature of party leadership, of parallelism versus the territorial principle. Parallelism refers to bringing the Party close to the government and the economy in order to facilitate its intervention in industrial and other matters, while the territorial principle advocates a role for the Party that is basically complementary to that of the state. If an association covers enterprises scattered over more than two *raions*, the question arises as to which *raikom* the enterprises should report: to the *raikom* of the main enterprise within the association, or to the *raikom* of its location.

It seems that the production association reform did not imply any immediate power changes for the *obkom*. If anything, it made it easier for the *obkom* to exercise control because of the larger size of the association. It also meant an increase of power at a local level. However, as suggested above, the *obkom* had to deal with many obstacles to the implementation of the reform. There are several questions to consider with regard to the *obkom* first secretaries. To what extent did they pay attention to the reform? What was the relationship between the implications of the reform for the power of these officials and their level of attention to it? If they paid attention, which aspects received most attention? How did they view the issue of parallelism versus the territorial principle? Did they sympathise with the *raikoms* which stood to lose power due to the reform? Did leadership politics at the top affect their responses to the reform? To answer these questions, we shall first review perceptions of the reform by our sample of Soviet first secretaries.

2   PERCEPTION OF THE 1973–5 REFORMS

2.1   Goal perception

In contrast to the heavy-industry orientation of the 1957 reform, and in addition to the stress on quality of the 1965 reform, *obkom* first secretaries paid, in 1973, more attention to quality and variety. Their orientation towards consumer satisfaction became much stronger than before. In line with this, the importance of light industry became more visible in their speeches and articles. There was virtually no secretary in the sample who emphasised heavy industry as a priority item, although some spoke about the need for heavy industry to help produce consumer goods, a government policy at that time. [6] *Obkom* first secretaries clearly understood that consumer satisfaction may not rise simply by putting out goods without considering consumer tastes.

Also important was their recognition that the old system of sporadic and formalistic quality control would no longer suffice.[7] They realised that improving quality is a complex matter involving not only well-qualified people and the right technology, but also proper incentives for workers.[8] Particularly important for this was the so-called intensification of production, now that reliance on extensive growth was no longer considered an option.

In their discussions of incentives, it seems that the younger secretaries gave priority to material incentives, while the older generation stressed moral incentives. The following quotations illustrate this difference in emphasis:

> From our point of view, the question of material incentives should be considered seriously, and additional incentives which would help increase productivity of work faster should be put into effect. Perhaps, the portion of bonus for the overfulfilment of plan has to be increased, if that overfulfilment means higher quality. The payment of reward for the results of the past year should be closely tied with the level of productivity of labour achieved, not simply with the stage of work.[9]

> The problem of quality is not only economic but also related to important psychological and moral factors of the education of a communist relation to work. . . . No less valuable, from our point of view, is the moral aspect of the matter. The application of the moral incentives opens up unlimited possibilities for creativity, initiative and the discipline of cadres.[10]

2.2 Environmental change

The perceptions of adverse changes in the environment were quite extensive and serious; consequently concern about natural resources and the protection of natural environment became more salient than before. For example, the *obkom* first secretary of Buriat, Modogoev, showed his concern about protecting the Baikal region:

> The problem of efficient use of natural resources is closely related to the tasks of conserving the natural riches of Baikal – a marvellous creature of nature . . . Baikal is dear to every one of us, and our sacred duty is to fully protect its invaluable wealth, use that wealth reasonably, not bringing any loss to nature in the region.[11]

2.3 Perception of complexity and the political environment

The perception of increasing complexity of various tasks could be detected in the emphasis on the importance of information. The secretaries wanted to have information on what to produce, when, where and to whom to sell products, or when to remove products as people's tastes change. In this regard, it is interesting to note that one secretary argued that shops should be allowed to reject goods that cannot be sold.[12] This is significant in that these officials began to recognise the need for a better feedback mechanism operating directly between producers and consumers. However, no secretary went so far as to call for consumer sovereignty.

In their perception of the political environment at home, almost all the officials recognised that by 1971 Brezhnev had consolidated his power. Brezhnev's name was frequently invoked, and his policies were duly mentioned. The fact that the 1973 reform was launched at the time of the consolidation of power by one leader, after the collective leadership stage had ended, provided an incentive for the *obkom* first secretaries to respond to it. The fact that power was consolidated in the hands of a single leader put pressure on them – not so much by the need to identify politically with the leader as by the duty to implement his policies. In other words, showing political and symbolic support probably became less important than fulfilling given tasks, in this case contributing to the demonstration of the effectiveness of the reform programme.

2.4 Party domain and role

It is interesting that in 1971–3, no *obkom* first secretary articulated a systematic review of the 1965 reform. That is perhaps understandable, for it would have been politically dangerous. However, the lingering impact of the 1965 reform was visible. Most secretaries emphasised the importance of sales and profits as success indicators. In line with the 1965 reform, the concept of inter-brigade contracts was also mentioned.[13]

In terms of the role of the Party, two discernible orientations appeared. The first represented a very cautious approach to economic problems whereby the party supervisory activity was to be predictable and steady. Its directives were dialogue-orientated rather than resembling orders. The Party was also viewed as providing a micro-environment favourable to bold innovations.[14] The second orientation stressed ideological tempering and the moral education of people, along with increasing labour discipline. As one secretary said: 'Increasing labour discipline is a real reserve for increasing social wealth, one which does not require capital investment and yet can yield big and quick results.'[15] This orientation also emphasised a strict control and watchdog function for the Party *vis-à-vis* enterprises, along with intense pressure on solving economic problems.

3 RESPONSES TO THE 1973 REFORM

The party officials under survey mentioned production associations as such relatively infrequently, yet three groups of responses to them can be identified. The first group engaged in rather detailed discussions. The second avoided detailed or sophisticated discussion, and took the reform in a matter-of-fact manner. The third did not mention associations at all. However, this does not mean that the third group necessarily opposed the reform. After all, production associations did not adversely affect the power of regional party secretaries. The background characteristics of each of the last two groups, in terms of age and education, do not display any discernible pattern. Nevertheless, if we combine these two groups the picture becomes slightly clearer in that seven out of twelve secretaries were born before 1920, as compared with five out of sixteen secretaries in the first group, indicating that the support of the reform by younger officials was probably greater.

3.1 The first group

The responses of this group were noteworthy for their comparatively detailed discussion of the reform. However, apart from the fact that they were younger, there is no clear common personal factor that might explain this response. If we divide associations between industrial and agro-industrial associations (or complexes), it becomes clear that secretaries of the latter group in rural regions were mainly concerned with the agro-industrial complexes, while secretaries of industrial regions were more concerned with production associations.

Statements on production associations and agro-industrial complexes were different in content, but in both cases the support for the idea of association was overwhelming. Responses to production associations may be grouped into several categories. To the *obkom* first secretaries, associations meant above all an increase of power at the local level *vis-à-vis* the centre. Associations, they argued, should be given more autonomy or even the status of ministry. For these party secretaries, associations meant an increase in local bargaining power. The rights of their financial autonomy and greater local participation in planning were accordingly identified as important.[16]

Various positive economic effects were expected by these officials. The reform would solve the shortage of resources through more rational use, to be effected by closer co-operation of similar enterprises. It would also bring about increased productivity through

Table 7.1   *The First Group*

Name	Year of birth	Party entry	Education	Area (UA)*
I. Bondarenko	1926	1950	agriculture	66:34
V. Degtyarev	1920	1945	mining	87:13
V. Dobrik	1927	1954	rail trans.	51:49
P. Fedirko	1932	1957	rail trans.	66:34
Yu. Khristoradnov	1929	1951	economics	69:31
F. Knyazev	1916	1940	pedagogy	48:52
V. Konotop	1916	1944	machine-bldg	71:29
P. Kozyr	1913	1939	HPS †	59:49
E. Ligachev	1920	1944	aircraft cons.	64:36
T. Lisovoi	1923	1946	economics	31:69
F. Medunov	1915	1942	agriculture	49:54
G. Romanov	1923	1944	shipbldg	66:34
F. Tabeev	1928	1951	economic	58:42
A. Vatchenko	1914	1940	physics-maths	78:22
I. Yarkovoi	1927	1957	husbandry	27:63
I. Yunak	1918	1944	agriculture	76:24

* UA refers to the ratio between urban and rural population of a region. Here this ratio is taken as an indicator of a region's level of industrialisation. The ratios are from *Narodnoe Khoziaistro, RSFSR*, 1973.
† HPS stands for Higher Party School.

SOURCE   *Ezhegonik*, 1982; *Narodronoe, Khoziaistvo, RSFSR*, 1973.

Table 7.2   *The Second and Third Groups*

Name	Year of birth	Party entry	Education	Area (UA)
A. Drygin	1914	1935	agriculture	54:46
A. Eshtokin	1913	1943	mining	85:15
P. Fedirko	1932	1957	HPS & transp.	66:34
P. Leonov	1918	1944	tech. inst.	82:18
A. Modogoev	1915	1940	HPS	52:48
G. Pavlov	1913	1940	agriculture	50:50
B. Popov	1909	1931	HPS	70:30
V. Ptitsyn	1925	1946	industry	89:11
S. Shaidurov	1926	1952	mining	76:24
N. Shibaev	1915	1957	agriculture	69:31
V. Taratuta	1930	1957	agriculture	31:69
M. Trunov	1931	1955	agriculture	43:57

SOURCE   *Ezhegodnik*, 1982; *Narodnoe Khoziaistvo, RSDSR*, 1973 specialisation and economies of scale. The larger size would also make it safer to take risks in introducing new technology.[17]

Some first secretaries came out in support of parallelism. One said that 'the logical outcome of the policy of concentration and specialisation of production is the establishment of large party organisations.'[18] The party organisation, according to this official, should be able to deal with the most complex technological issues. The association's party committee should be granted the rights of a *raikom* of the Party.[19] Along with this preference for strong power of associations over individual enterprises, his emphasis on raising the rights of party committees would most probably mean parallelism.

If production associations were concerned primarily with managerial aspects, the agro-industrial association entailed in addition political aspects.[20] The main goal was of course to improve the rural standard of living by introducing industrial methods into agriculture. Specifically, the association members constituted enterprises and state farms, as well as state farms and collective farms. In terms of specific responses, these were basically the same as those towards industrial associations. The autonomy and rights of the association director were defended and it was argued that he or she should take full responsibility for the association's operations. Some also strongly emphasised financial autonomy:

> It is important to expand its financial and economic autonomy. It is necessary for it to be granted the rights to decide the question of distribution and redistribution of profits, formation and use of funds for incentives for all the workers of all branches of the association.[21]

So far there is not much evidence of support for either the territorial principle or parallelism. This was also the case with the issue of localism at the level below the *obkom* (the *raion*). One plausible reason for the lack of commentary on these issues might be that it was quite rare to see situations in which they arose.

Generally, the level of discussion on issues related to the reform on the part of *obkom* first secretaries was disappointingly low. The fact that the reform provided new tasks for these officials was important, since it involved organisational reshufflings. Further, in the case of the agro-industrial complexes it provided a sense of ideological satisfaction from upgrading the status of villages. A simple answer would therefore be that the secretaries saw the reform to be in their interest and thus must have supported it. But this is not a sufficient answer, for in 1957 they displayed conflicting responses, even though the reform increased their power much more than did the 1973 reform.

Answers may be found in several different areas. First, the 1973 reform did not change the rules of the game from the perspective of *obkom* first secretaries. It certainly did not take away the rights of *obkoms*. It actually made it easier for them to deal with enterprises through associations, because for one thing, the number of enterprises which *obkoms* had to deal with was greatly reduced. For another, the change made it easier for *obkoms* to deal with the centre, because of the transfer of rights of the *glavki* to the associations. But these changes did not bring about any fundamental shifts in the power of the *obkom*, and thus did not necessitate as much detailed discussion as the 1957 or 1965 reforms.

Secondly, by 1971–3 policy came to be less intertwined with the power struggle at the top than it had been in 1957 or 1965. From the perspective of the *obkom* first secretaries, this meant that they were not called upon to support the 1971–5 reform as a mark of support for the leader. The reform was primarily billed as an effort to improve efficiency. As such, it was viewed mainly from bureaucratic rather than political perspectives. Since the reform did not change the rules of the game in management, there was also no great need to discuss it from that bureaucratic perspective.

As the 9th Five-Year Plan drew to a close, attention to the reform dropped sharply. More mobilisational themes re-emerged instead. The interventionist role of the Party was again stressed. At the same time, complaints against the centre became more visible. The low level of attention among these officials can be explained by several factors: the nature of the reform, the degree of need for a political role depending on the state of high politics, and the demands of bureaucratic role expectations.

3.2 Responses of political clients

The following two cases illustrate the working of patron–client ties. One was Khristoradnov, first secretary of the city party committee for Gorky, but promoted to first secretary of the Gorky region in 1974. He must have been closely associated with Katushev, with whom he worked in Gorky during the 1960s. And Katushev was a client of Brezhnev. In his speech as first secretary of the Gorky city committee, Khristoradnov did not mention the association issue, although he touched on the importance of moral incentives and of the Party's active role in production.[22] After the promotion in 1974, however, he immediately endorsed Brezhnev's agricultural policy. He even went so far as to recall the agricultural policies adopted at the March plenum in 1965, which is known to have been Brezhnev's agricultural initiative. He also praised the agro-industrial complex, another Brezhnev policy, as 'proof of the increasing economic, scientific, and technological potential of our state' and as a 'new path to socialist reconstruction of the countryside'.[23] This change of attitude may in part reflect different positions and thus different responsibilities. However, strong support for Brezhnev's agricultural policies may also reflect Khristoradnov's education in finance and economics, and his leadership of a heavily industrial *oblast*.

The second case is Klyuev, first secretary of the Ivanovo region. He was appointed to this position in 1972. Before that, when he was second secretary of the same region, his writings heavily reflected the spirit of the 1965 reform. He strongly supported material incentives and acknowledged the positive results of the reform. At the same time, he complained about the central ministry's interference in local affairs. While not denying the role of *Gosplan* for purposes of national planning, he urged central planners to consider more seriously the points of view of local parties on the grounds of their better familiarity with local issues. However, after becoming first secretary of the Ivanovo region in 1972, he attributed the association reform to Brezhnev, addressed in detail the process of establishing associations, and emphasised the successes that the reform had brought about. It is not certain that Klyuev, in fact, owed his job politically to Brezhnev, since traditionally the region has been regarded as a stronghold of Kosygin, as evidenced by the case of Smirnov in the 1965 reform. Admitting the limitations on identifying definite patron–client ties, however, what is important is that apparently anyone who had just become a regional first secretary, regardless of his or her immediate political ties, had to play an expected political role in relation to the top party leader, especially so at the stage of power consolidation at the top.

4 CONCLUDING REMARKS

In terms of scope of structural change and changes in the rules of operation of the Soviet economy the 1973 reform was not as serious as the earlier two reforms. The extent of discussion by *obkom* first secretaries was accordingly modest. The authority-building stage of the top leader, once his power had been consolidated, put greater stress on actual plan fulfilment. This factor further drew the attention of party officials away from the reform, especially since Brezhnev's own references to associations were drastically reduced after 1973. Among the responses of first secretaries, the difficulties noted were often the usual problems of planning and central bureaucracy. Localism, and the territorial principle versus parallelism, were not regarded as serious issues. The reform, however, was welcomed by the *obkom* apparatus since it enhanced its power and appeared to facilitate plan fulfilment.

Notes

1. For the literature on which the following discussion of the 1973 reform was based, see Conyngham, *The Modernization of Soviet Industrial Management*, ch. 6.(Cambridge University Press, 1982), Timothy Dunmore, 'Local Party Organs in Industrial Administration: The Case of Obedinennie Reform', *Soviet Studies*, vol. XXVI, no. 1 (April 1980), pp. 3–34; Alice Gorlin, 'The Soviet Economic Association', *Soviet Studies*, vol. XXVI, no. 1 (January 1974), pp. 3–27; idem, 'Industrial Reorganization: The Association', in US Congress, Joint Economic Committee, *Soviet Economy in a New Perspective* (Washington, DC: Government Printing Office, 1976), pp. 345–90; Leon Smolenski, 'Towards a Socialist Corporation: Soviet Industrial Reorganization of 1973', *Survey*, vol. 20, no. 1 (Winter 1974), pp. 24–35.
2. Gorlin, 'Industrial Reorganization: The Association', p. 165.
3. George W. Breslauer, *Khrushchev and Brezhnev as Leaders*, ch. 11, pp. 183 ff (George Allen and Unwin, 1982).
4. Gorlin, 'Industrial Reorganization', p. 164.
5. Ibid.
6. Brezhnev's speech at the 23rd Party Congress, *Pravda*, 30 March 1971.
7. Yunak, *Izvestia*, 13 December 1974. Konotop also said: 'Every day the demand of buyers grows for quality of goods which are widely consumed. Enterprises which produce them must always be prepared not only for changing production in accordance with such demands; they should also be interested in improving quality and assortment of goods'. *Izvestia*, 16 June 1972; Romanov, *Leningradskaia Pravda* (*LP*), 10 September 1973; Degtyarev, *Izvestia*, 15 August 1972; Taratuta, *Sotsialisticheskaia industriia* (*SI*), 26 October 1974.
8. Konotop, *SI*, 19 February 1974.
9. Taratuta, *Pravda*, 14 December 1974; Ligachev, Izvestia, 20 July 1972.
10. Shibaev, *Pravda*, 7 April 1971; Eshitokin, Izvestia, 13 June 1972; Riabov, *Ekonomicheskaia Gazeta*, (*EG*), no. 23 (June 1973), p. 5.
11. Modogoev, *EG*, no. 37 (September 1971), p. 6.

12. Yunak, *Izvestia*, 13 December 1974.
13. Tabeev, *EG*, no. 14 (April 1972), p. 3.
14. Bondarenko, *EG*, no. 20 (May 1975), p. 8; Konotop, *SI*, 19 February 1974.
15. Eshtokin, *Izvestia*, 13 June 1972; also Drygin, *EG*, no. 12 (March 1971), p. 4; Yarkovoi, *EG*, no. 23 (June 1973), p. 5; Ptitsin, *SI*, 16 September 1973.
16. Romanov, *Pravda*, 19 April 1973; Konotop, *Pravda*, 24 November 1972; Ligachev, *EG*, no. 29 (July 1974), p. 5.
17. Bondarenko, *EG*, no. 10 (March 1971), p. 4; Kozyr, *EG*, no. 19 (May 1971), p. 7; Tabeev, *EG*, no. 14, p. 26.
18. Romanov, *LP*, 20 March 1975.
19. Ibid.
20. Bondarenko, *Pravda*, 30 August 1971; Kristoradnov, nechernozemlio", *Oktiabr'*, 1975, no. 7, p. 169; Kozyr, *EG*, no. 19 (May 1970), p. 7; *Pravda*, 14 November 1971.
21. Bondarenko, *EG*, no. 10 (March 1971), p. 4.
22. *SI*, 14 April 1974.
23. Khristoradnov, 'Shaginechevnozemia', *Oktiabr*, 1975, no. 7, p. 168.

Part III
Eastern European Countries

8 Economic and Political Reforms in Socialist Countries of Eastern Europe: a Comparative Analysis

Jerzy J. Wiatr

In the second half of the 1980s the movement towards socioeconomic reforms in socialist countries has increased in force. Three main factors are involved:

(i) At the end of the 1970s and in the early 1980s, after the death of Mao Zedong and the arrest of the so-called Gang of Four, the new Chinese authorities gathered around Deng Xsiaoping introduced widely understood economic reforms and, to a certain extent, liberalised the country's political life. The Chinese experience, particularly the evident economic progress achieved as a result of the reform, has become for other socialist countries an important argument in favour of reform.

(ii) The Polish crisis at the beginning of the 1980s made forcefully clear the magnitude of the threat caused by maintaining unreformed economic and political structures. In conditions of crisis, the Polish United Workers' Party had made a critical evaluation of its policy and, in its Extraordinary Congress in July 1981, declared itself to be in favour of reform. This declaration was reaffirmed during the next Congress in 1986. In spite of the fact that Polish reforms have encountered serious difficulties and resistance, they are important because the leadership continues to maintain that there is no policy option other than economic and political reforms.

(iii) The present Soviet leadership appointed in 1985 has begun a struggle against the conservative heritage and clearly declared itself to be in favour of the policy of 'restructuring' and 'acceleration'. Such is the position of the USSR in the world socialist community that this new policy must be at present the most important element in the process of socialist reforms.

The three circumstances mentioned above have ensured that for the first time in the history of the world socialist community, the tendency towards reform encompasses several of the largest socialist countries. Even though conservative tendencies remain in all the socialist countries, and are either openly antagonistic towards reform or are in secret opposition, the chances for reform have never been as great as they are at present. The historical need for reform in these countries is expressed by the fact that their development processes are not realised spontaneously, but call for and require conscious leadership. Given this fact, socialism is standing at a crossroads: either progressive reform or stagnation, the latter implying a relative regress. The ability to comprehend this alternative is a characteristic of an ever-increasing part of the leadership of socialist states.

Under these new conditions, the experience of past reform is of the greatest importance for appreciating the mechanisms to which they gave rise, as well as their setbacks and resistance. Such a historical comparative analysis does not, of course, assume that a simple rerun of past events is likely. History never repeats itself exactly. Nevertheless, experiences found in history may still be useful today.

In my comparative analysis I shall concentrate on three countries in which reforms were introduced with differing results: Yugoslavia, Czechoslovakia and Hungary. In choosing these three countries I am not suggesting that no reforms were undertaken in the remaining countries of Eastern Europe, but I feel that apart from Poland and now the Soviet Union and China, the reforms in these three countries have been deeper than anywhere else. Since the reform experiences of Yugoslavia, Czechoslovakia and Hungary have a long history, they are particularly well suited to such a comparative historical analysis.

1   YUGOSLAV SELF-MANAGEMENT REFORM

The Yugoslav revolution was undertaken and carried out by a Party which, in its ideological orientation, did not differ in any significant way from other parties of the communist movement. The peculiarity of the Yugoslav situation did not stem from the particular orientation of the Communist Party of Yugoslavia (CPY) but from the fact that this Party, to a much greater extent than the Communist Parties of other Eastern European countries, had its roots in the masses, and that in the liberation war it managed to win the support of the majority of Yugoslavia's nations. As a consequence, the newly created socialist state had in itself from the start more revolutionary force than did other states in Eastern Europe, and the revolutionary elite of Yugoslavia felt more self-confident about its inner strength. These characteristics of the Yugoslavian revolution created a situation in which, in the conditions of Stalinisation of the European socialist countries, the conflict between Stalin, as well as his Information Bureau of Communist and Workers' Parties, Kominform, and the leadership of the CPY became inevitable. This was a conflict not between separate ideological conceptions but around the matter of Yugoslavia's independence and the right of its communist leadership to independent decisions regarding the path of the Yugoslav revolution.[1] Only as a result of this conflict was the need to develop Yugoslavia's own conception of building socialism born.[2] The development of this conception was the starting point for reform of the political system, the first of its kind in the history of the socialist countries. Its aim was to move away from the model of the state and economy formed and implemented during the rule of Joseph Stalin in the USSR and other socialist countries.

The new political doctrine of Yugoslav communists was born from the need to justify theoretically the divergence between Yugoslavia and the USSR. The doctrine was formulated for the first time at the Fifth Congress of the CPY in July 1948 and developed and enriched in the resolutions of the subsequent Congresses of the CPY (the League of Yugoslav Communists from the 6th Congress in 1952) as well as in the works of its leading theoreticians, in particular Edvard Kardelj[3] and Boris Kidric.[4] This doctrine encompassed the following ideas:

(i) The Soviet model is not a universal formula for all the socialist countries, since (a) the various countries develop in different conditions and (b) Stalinism is a bureaucratic distortion of socialism.[5]

(ii) The socialist state, after fulfilling the basic revolutionary tasks, should progressively prepare its own extinction. With this aim in mind, the institutions of self-management should be developed. If this perspective is not adopted, it will lead to the state's bureaucratisation (statism), which Yugoslav theoreticians see as the basic source of Stalinism.

(iii) The socialist state must abstain from managing the whole economy, although Yugoslav theoreticians do not postulate total withdrawal from influencing the economy. Kidric, for example, spoke of decentralisation, but not of the liquidation of the 'administrative-operational management of the economy'.

(iv) The workers should take over direct control of the production process. With this in mind, workers' councils were introduced in 1950. The first official formulation of the workers' self-management doctrine occurred in the speech by Joseph Broz-Tito during the meeting of the Parliament of Yugoslavia on 26 July 1950. Alongside the workers' councils, the trade unions were to be an element of socialist democracy, a major purpose of which was to educate the workers so that they would be capable of directing the self-managed economy.

(v) The development of socialist farming must not be based on the Soviet model of kolkhoz farming but may combine collective farming with individual farming. The acceptance of this part of the new doctrine occurred relatively late, in 1953, and was the result of the serious failures of Yugoslav collective farming.

(vi) The role of the Communist Party should be different from that of the Party in the Stalinist USSR. Although the Party, as well as the state, would die out in the future, for the present phase of building socialism the Party should emphasise its new character by concentrating on the ideological and political education of the masses and not by exercising direct power.[6]

These basic elements of the doctrines of Yugoslav socialism were the result of the collective work of the Party, in which an outstanding role was played by its leaders-theoreticians: Kardelj, Kidric, Pijade and Bakaric. Even though this doctrine was often called 'Titoism' in the West, Joseph Broz-Tito participated to a relatively small degree in formulating it. Nevertheless, it is beyond doubt that its development proceeded with his political support and that in the long run the authority of the Yugoslav leader was crucial in determining the final shape of the new doctrine of building socialism.

The doctrine of Yugoslav socialism developed progressively, but its major assumptions were formulated at the beginning of the 1950s. In later years the doctrine was attacked by those demanding a more radical political liberalisation, in particular by Milovan Djilas and the intellectuals gathered around the philosophical paper *Praxis*.[7] Essentially, it has remained as the theoretical basis of the Yugoslav economic and political reform.

This reform has developed in several phases. In the first phase, at the beginning of the 1950s, workers' councils were introduced, the decentralisation of the economy was carried out, the powers of communes and republics were increased, the legal conditions enabling the functioning of the private sector were created. The second phase began at the plenary session of the party's Central Committee in Brionia in July 1966, when an open confrontation took place between the reformist wing and the more conservative orientation, whose leading representative was the vice-president of Yugoslavia, Aleksander Rankovic. The removal of Rankovic from all his state and party posts and the discarding of the 'centralist' position opened the road to further reforms. Economic reforms went in the direction of subjecting the economy fully to the rigours of the market mechanism. In the political sphere, the reforms of the late 1960s brought about the democratisation of the election law by introducing the possibility of two candidates running for office,[8] increased autonomy for the republics, and the reorganisation of the parliamentary system by introducing several separate chambers.

The final phase was the reaction of the central authorities to calls for national separation in Croatia in 1971. Tito reacted to this evident crisis of the federation by calling for unity and strengthening the role of the Party, and also by condemning nationalism and the 'anarchistic-liberal' tendency. In the aftermath of the 1971/2 crisis Yugoslav reforms were not withdrawn, but their boundaries were defined more precisely (in particular, in the new constitution of 1974). At the same time, President Tito initiated steps to ensure continuity of the political system after his death. The principle of collective management of the Party and the Federation was introduced and the principle of rotation in all state and party posts (apart from the army) was reimposed. After the death of Marshal Tito (in May 1980) this new arrangement passed the test and, despite economic difficulties in the 1980s, has ensured the stable functioning of the Yugoslav state.

In my view, Yugoslav reforms are an example of a successful

process of directed socialist change. In saying this, I do not maintain that Yugoslavia is not experiencing any difficulties. Its serious economic and political problems (see the next chapter by Ivo Bićanić for details) are widely known and openly discussed in Yugoslavia. There is also increasing pressure for deeper democratisation of political life by many communities, particularly in Croatia and Slovenia. All this will pose serious problems for Yugoslavia and will lead to a call for further reforms. Nevertheless, the past experience of Yugoslav reforms must, I suggest, be evaluated positively. They have, in my view, given Yugoslavia a consumption growth that is faster and more harmonious than in other socialist countries with their centralised, command-type economic system. They have also allowed the Yugoslav economy to survive an exceptionally difficult period of isolation from other socialist countries (1948–55). In the political sphere, the Yugoslav reforms brought a serious strengthening of socialist democracy, through a real increase in the working people's participation in the governing process. Most importantly, the reforms have created the conditions for the functioning of a multinational federation, not without disturbances and tensions but, on the whole, more successfully than might have been predicted on the basis of the dramatic history of mutual relations between the nations and peoples of the present Yugoslavia. Without idealising the Yugoslav experience, I am convinced of its historical significance for the prospects of building socialism.

The Yugoslav model, however, evolved from particular historical conditions and does not serve as an automatic copy for countries in different conditions. That being said, it is still an extremely interesting example of a process of successful socialist reforms and therefore, deserves careful analysis by reformers in other socialist countries.

2 THE CZECHOSLOVAK ATTEMPT AT SOCIALIST PLURALISM

In the mid-1950s, when most other socialist countries began to liquidate what was euphemistically called 'the consequences of the cult of the individual', Czechoslovakia seemed to remain outside this process. The great monument to Joseph Stalin stood over the Veltava River until 1962, and the victims of the great trials were still not fully vindicated. But even though the reason why the then Czechoslovak authorities could for so many years oppose de-Stalinisation remains unclear, the consequences of this policy are obvious. De-Stalinisation in Czechoslovakia, which had been delayed and suppressed for more than a decade, erupted as a result with a greater force and adopted a more radical form than it would otherwise have done. In this delay and eruption, I suggest, lies also the basic internal source of the failure of the subsequent Czechoslovak reforms.

The reforms were undertaken late, in the mid-1960s, and at first only in the form of modest economic changes.[19] The drafts of economic reforms, developed under the intellectual leadership of Professor Oto Sik before 1968, encompassed moderate decentralisation and market moves, modelled partly on the economic ideas developed in Poland in 1957 by the Economic Council under Professor Oskar Lange and partly on the Yugoslav experience. Implementing these reforms met with difficulties and resistance. By the mid-1960s in Czechoslovakia there was growing tension in the intellectual community and increasingly strong postulates of reform were voiced. In 1967 these postulates began to reach the directing organs of the Party, as reflected, among others, in the speech made by Alexander Dubček at the plenary meeting of the Party's Central Committee in September 1967.[10] In the autumn of that year, student demonstrations increased the political tension. To diffuse it, the meeting of the Central Committee in January 1968 removed Antonin Novotny and elected Alexander Dubček as the Party's First Secretary. The meeting set off the process of fast and deep-reaching political and economic reforms.

In the economic sphere, the reformers demanded the creation of competitive markets and limits to state intervention. But, significantly, they postulated no increase of the private economy. In the political sphere, they called for the democratisation of the state and the Party, law-abidance, reforms of the election law, and political pluralism. In the sphere of relations between the nations of Czechoslovakia, they called for an end to the Czech domination over Slovakia.[11]

These reform ideas gained support very quickly among the party intellectuals who articulated them in the 'Action Programme' on 5 April 1968.[12] This programme covered the following areas of importance:

(i)   It was argued that the correct road to socialism for Czechoslovakia was different from the road embarked upon by other socialist countries.

(ii)   Stalinism, sectarianism, and limiting democratic rights were condemned.

(iii)   The economic system was criticised as outdated, backward and, as a consequence, the cause of economic stagnation in Czechoslovakia. A decentralisation and democratisation of the management of the economy was postulated.

(iv)   The need for co-operation by all classes, social strata, groups and nationalities was emphasised, and the principle that the various interests of these groups should find an institutional expression was advanced. In this context the programme redefined the role of the Party in social and political life, making its leading or hegemonic role dependent on the support of the masses.

(v)   Relations between Czechs and Slovaks were to be based on the principle of equality in a federal state.

(vi)   In the economic sphere the programme called for industrial democracy and the scientific management of the economy. It predicted the breaking away from egalitarianism, and the strict application of the principle of wages depending on the quality and results of work.

(vii)   The programme predicted the introduction of a new political system of managing society, breaking away from excessive centralisation and creating conditions for the articulation of group interests. It predicted the drafting of a new constitution. All the political parties forming the National Front were to acquire greater independence, but the programme did not make it clear how this was to be co-ordinated with the leading role of the Communist Party.

(viii)   The programme predicted the introduction of legal norms which would guarantee freedom of speech, foreign travel, and law-abidance.

(ix)   It foresaw an increase in the role of representative bodies and a change in the election law to ensure that they reflected the will of the citizen.

(x)   It also advanced the principle of separating party offices from state offices and the principle of effective control by the people over those in authority.

(xi)   It stressed the need to give science, education and culture a higher rank, and to ensure freedom for creative work.

Alongside the Action Programme, pronouncements postulating even more radical changes were voiced in Czechoslovakia, including the restitution of the right to form political parties and to hold contested elections. Even though these postulates were not included in the Action Programme, the absence of a decisive rejection of them by the leading party reformers created the impression of a certain lack of precision on the limits to proposed political changes.

Czechoslovak reforms were undertaken from the top, on the initiative and under the leadership of the Party's Central Committee, but in the course of 1968 the postulates of reform started to outgrow what was initially the common platform of the Czechoslovak leadership. Internal divergences among the leaders deepened while at the same time popular pressure for more radical changes grew, in particular among the intellectuals, students, and the majority of the mass media. From spring 1968 onwards the divergences between the Communist Party of Czechoslovakia and the Communist Parties of other Warsaw Pact countries also deepened, and this was expressed in publicly formed polemics.

The turning point for the reform movement was the invasion of Czechoslovakia by the armies of the five states of the Warsaw Pact on 21 August 1968. The Czechoslovak leadership was taken to Moscow, and on 28 August the Soviet–Czechoslovak communiqué was issued by the two leaderships.[13] The direct consequence of the August events was not the withdrawal of Czechoslovak reforms, but a clear definition of their boundaries. Soon after August 1968 constitutional regulations of the relations between the Czechs and the Slovaks on the basis of an equal federation were implemented, yet other intended changes were either impeded or partially withdrawn. The struggle against radical socialist reformers and 'anti-socialist forces' was increased. In the Party itself the process of eliminating some of the particularly active leaders in the pre-August reform movement had begun. In April 1969, Dubček himself was removed from the post of First Secretary of the Party. Later events went towards the total elimination, not only from the leadership but also from the ranks of the Party, of representatives of the reformatory trend, a mass purge of the party ranks, and the wholesale condemnation of the policy of 1968. With the exception of federational solutions, all the reform proposals were discarded and recognised as indications of revisionism. Czechoslovakia returned to the model of a centralised state and an order-based economy.

The failure of the Czechoslovak reform had its internal and external causes. The basic external cause was the fact that the reforms were conducted in a way which created the impression that the integrity of the Warsaw Pact was being weakened. All this occurred in conditions of a deterioration in East–West relations at a time when the Vietnam War had reached its most ferocious point. This was also the period when conservative tendencies began to dominate in the USSR, after the dismissal of Khrushchev in 1964. The new Soviet leadership was ideologically opposed to any far-reaching changes. I believe that the internal causes were no less significant. The Czechoslovak reforms were introduced hastily, without preparation. Neither society nor the Party had undergone the necessary process of gradual development of the reform programme and the social forces acting for reform did not have enough time to consolidate their influence. The delayed de-Stalinisation resulted in the eruption of radical projects and uncontrolled activity, in part directed not only against the distortions of socialism but also against Communist Party rule. The Party itself, accustomed to Stalin-type discipline, was unable to develop a political struggle against these tendencies. Its leadership, it appears, did not take fully into consideration the stand and the interests of other socialist countries, in particular the USSR, and entered the path of international conflict without developing its own strategy should such a conflict occur. As a result, Czechoslovakia was unable both to avoid the escalation of the conflict, as Poland did in October 1956, and to resist effectively external pressure, as Yugoslavia did after 1948. In the difficult conditions after August 1968 the Czechoslovak leadership did not maintain its unity either; this fact decisively contributed to the deepening of the political consequences of the Warsaw Pact military intervention.

The failure of the Czechoslovak reforms was a bitter lesson for other socialist countries. I believe that the memory of these experiences was of no small significance for the events which followed in Poland in 1980–1, particularly for the policy of the country's leadership.

3   THE HUNGARIAN NEW ECONOMIC MECHANISM

The introduction of the economic reform in Hungary took place on 1 January 1968, and thus coincided with the beginning of the reform movement in Czechoslovakia, but both the substance of the reform and the method of its implementation were totally different. The Hungarian economic reform was a move fully controlled by the political leadership, undertaken from above and within the boundaries described by the Party and the state authorities. Its effect was also different. The Hungarian reform has survived and, in many respects, become an example to be followed by other socialist countries in their process of reform.

The Hungarian reform evolved from the experience of the great political crisis which encompassed Hungary in 1956, leading to military intervention by the USSR. The government of János Kádár stressed from the beginning that it would not return to the road of Stalinism. The new Hungarian leadership led a struggle 'on two fronts': against the rightist-revisionist threat and against the dogmatic-sectarian threat, blamed for creating the situation leading to crisis. This struggle on both fronts prepared the Hungarian Communist Party to undertake, after the stabilisation of the political situation, a well-thought-out and feasible economic reform.

The party and state leadership of Hungary gathered around János Kádár drew conclusions from the 1956 experience. In the political sphere the more radical reform proposals were not implemented (apart from allowing two or three candidates to run for one office in contested elections). Nevertheless a new style of government was introduced, law-abidance was re-established, the policy towards political opposition was gradually liberalised. The new climate was well expressed by Kádár's often-quoted statement that 'all those not against us are with us'. The political liberalisation of the 1960s created favourable conditions for launching the economic reform, but unlike Yugoslavia and Czechoslovakia, the reform was not tied to significant political democratisation.

The Hungarian reform was based on two fundamental principles: increasing the role of the market mechanism and decentralising economic decision-making. In the 1970s it brought the unquestioned benefits of market equilibrium, an increased standard of living, an openness to new technologies and an increase in economic contacts with other countries, in particular with the West. Against the background of the great difficulties experienced by the majority of socialist countries in the 1980s, Hungary stood out clearly, at least for the Polish observers, as an economically successful country.

This does not mean to say that the Hungarian reform was radical. In a recently published assessment of the Hungarian reform a prominent Hungarian economist, János Kornai, described its results as a hybrid, where elements of a centralised order-based system coexist with elements of a market system. Such a 'mixed' economic system has the faults and the virtues of these two distinct types, but both appear in a subdued form.[14] Kornai also points to the social consequences of the Hungarian reform, in particular to the overlapping of the two types of social inequalities: those generated by the order-distributive system and those created by the market. As a consequence, Kornai believes, 'Hungary is a mixture of distributive consequences of both the bureaucracy and the market', which in his opinion have been ignored for a long time by the technocratically disposed supporters of the reform.[15]

Kornai's study also encompasses an interesting review of the basic stands concerning the future of the Hungarian reform. He distinguishes the following directions:

(i) 'market socialism', as understood by Oscar Lange; Kornai holds serious objections to this model, pointing in particular to the 'built-in, in a centrally controlled system based on state ownership, tendencies to generate chronic overbalance of demand in different spheres of the economy';[16]

(ii) the 'naively reformatory' direction which he at one stage advocated and which is based on dismissing a conflict between bureaucratic control and the demands of the market;

(iii) 'Galbraith socialism', placing its hopes in large socialist corporations coexisting with the market-organised sector of small and medium manufacturers; Kornai believes this direction (which he himself coined) to be the 'legitimisation of the *status quo*';[17]

(iv) 'radical reformism' with which the author is at present sympathising, and which lies in demanding the removal of all restrictions to enable the free functioning of market mechanisms; in Kornai's opinion the adoption of this position would call for radical changes in the system of ownership.[18]

I have presented in slightly more detail the position held by János Kornai, since it is at present the fullest analysis of the effects and tendencies of the Hungarian reform. It clearly shows that this reform has given rise to its own contradictions and that the process of change initiated by it has not yet been finished. This does not change my view that the Hungarian reform was successful.

The success of the Hungarian reform was its political base. The fact that the dogmatic-sectarian wing had been discredited and defeated enabled the Hungarian leadership to proceed with it in the first place. In the second place we must mention the consistency with which the leadership has kept the reforms on course. The painful experience of 1956 made it decide to embark on a path of moderate reform, and it has not left this path despite difficulties encountered on the way. The reform owes its success also to the attitude of Hungarian society, formed by the experiences of 1956. For in Eastern Europe, socialist reforms are threatened not only by conservatism, but also excessive – as judged by what is feasible – radicalisation of the masses, which may place the reformers in a situation whereby pressure from below forces them to make moves which prove suicidal, as in Czechoslovakia in 1968.

Finally, the third reason for the survival of the reform is the careful consideration by its architects of the political reasons stemming from the position of Hungary in the socialist community. In reforming the economy, Hungary has moved far away from the compulsory models of the other CMEA countries in the 1970s. At the same time, the Hungarian leadership has remained totally loyal to the socialist community politically, signalling clearly in advance the boundaries of the conducted reforms. Due to this policy, even in the period when conservative tendencies were evident in the USSR and other CMEA countries, the Hungarian reform did not lead to a conflict between Hungary and the other socialist states. It may even be assumed that for the supporters of reform in the USSR, the Hungarian experience formed a certain testing-ground, observed by them with benign interest.

4 CONCLUSIONS

The experience of past reforms, both successful and unsuccessful, in the European socialist countries allow us to come to several general conclusions.

First, the success of the reform has depended on whether its course was under the control of the political leadership of the state. The Yugoslav self-management reform and the Hungarian New Economic Mechanism were introduced by the party and state leadership, without pressure from the masses. During the process of implementation of these two reforms the pressure from below for more radical changes was not significant. In Poland the political reforms of 1956 were introduced under conditions of social pressure and in a climate of developing crisis, but the decisions of the Central Committee of the PUWP in October 1956 created the political conditions for the new leadership to take the situation under control and realise the planned changes. But in Czechoslovakia in 1968, as well as in Poland in 1980–1, social pressure was such that the political leadership had lost, to a greater or lesser extent, control over the course of events, in particular over the contents and timing of the proposed changes. In Poland, in my view, only the imposition of martial law created the conditions for the implementation of reforms under the leadership of party and state authorities.

Secondly, the success of the reforms in countries other than the USSR depended on the attitude towards the reforms of other socialist countries, in particular the USSR, and on the manner in which the political leadership of the country undertaking reforms could solve the international problems stemming from that attitude. The situations of *conflict* and *co-operation* may be distinguished here. An example of co-operation significantly contributing to the reform's success is, in the first place, Hungary. An example of extreme conflict leading to the reform's defeat is Czechoslovakia. Yugoslavia is an example of a conflict carried out by the country conducting the reform in a victorious way. The conflict carried out in this way was the source of strength for the reformatory process, as it was also supported for patriotic reasons. The Poland of 1956 was an example of a conflict solved peacefully as a result of talks (in Warsaw in October and in Moscow in November 1956). In this way the initial fears of the Soviet Union as to the direction of changes in Poland were dispersed, but at the same time fairly precise boundaries of the intended reforms were established.

Thirdly, the success of a major systemic reform depends on the ability of the political leadership to overcome the dogmatic-conservative resistance and, simultaneously, to remain in control over the process of change. Yugoslavia and Hungary are good examples of the internal struggle for the reform conducted in this way. The Poland of 1956 (as well as that of 1980–1) is an example of a struggle of tendencies in which the dogmatic-conservative tendency was defeated, but not without the ability to mount a counter-offensive in the future.

Fourthly, all the reforms, with the exception of Hungary, witnessed a co-operation of economic and political changes. The reform's success lies in the leadership's ability to withstand changes and succeed in conducting a policy of reforms. The reformers' dilemma is based on the fact that their programme presupposes the democratisation of the centre of authority, which in conditions of political struggle between reformatory and anti-reformatory tendencies may act towards weakening the reformatory power of the leadership. A counterbalance for this threat is the reliance by the leadership's reformatory wing on the support of the population at large.

The experiences of past reforms are not a good guide for the situation today, mainly because the policy of reforms has now been undertaken by the Soviet leadership gathered around Gorbachev. This opens up entirely new possibilities, but also new problems. Reform in a great socialist power, a multinational Soviet state, will need to be of a totally different kind from the reforms initiated in the smaller socialist countries of Eastern Europe. In the first place, the international context which matters is the state of East–West relations rather than the relationship of the reforming country and the Soviet Union. The scale of the problems also differs, as well as the scope of the struggle for the future of the reform. The result of this struggle will clearly have a decisive influence on the course of reformatory processes in the European socialist countries. Earlier reforms, as well as those under way at present in other countries, have prepared the ground and supplied the experience for the Soviet reform, thereby strengthening the forces acting for it in the USSR. Without doubt, the process of reforming socialism has gained strength in the last few years and has become an international process in the full sense of the word.

Notes

1. This is how the well-known Yugoslav author and politician Vladimir Dedijer puts it. See V. Dedijer, *Izgubljena bitka J. V. Stalina* (Sarajevo, 1969) and, by the same author, *Tito* (New York, 1953).
2. Compare on this topic: Fred Warner Neal, *Titoism in Action: The Reforms in Yugoslavia after 1948* (Berkeley, Los Angeles, 1958) and A. Ross Johnson, *The Transformation of Communist Ideology: The Yugoslav Case, 1945–1953* (Cambridge, MA, 1972).
3. Edvard Kardelj, *Integration of Labour in a Society of Self-Management* (Belgrade, 1981). A series of articles on Kardelj's contribution, with a wide selection of his writings, is included in a special edition of the Slovenian paper *Teorija in Praksa* (No. 7–9, 1979).
4. Boris Kidric, *Sabrana dela* (Belgrade, 1959–60, 3 vols).
5. The former vice-president of Yugoslavia, Milovan Djilas, went furthest in negating the Soviet system. In 1954 he was removed from all party and state posts. Djilas, from criticising the Stalinist system, went on to a total criticism of communism; see M. Djilas, *The New Class: An Analysis of the Communist System* (New York, 1957).
6. Josip Broz-Tito, *Govori i clanci* (Zagreb, 1959, vol. 6, p. 265; interview given on 9 November 1951).

7. See Svetozar Stojanovic, *Between Ideals and Reality: A Critique of Socialism and Its Future* (New York, 1973; Yugoslav edition under the title 'Izmedju ideala i stvarnosti' appeared in Belgrade in 1969). See also Miloslav Zhivkovic, 'Mit i dogma u jugosloveskoj ideologiji', *Sociologija*, vol. 27, no. 1–2, 1985, pp. 159–72.

8. The best analysis of Yugoslav elections was given by Lenard Cohen and Paul Warvick, *Political Cohesion in a Fragile Mosaic: The Yugoslav Experience* (Boulder, Co, 1983).

9. From amongst Western works on the topic of Czechoslovak reforms the most valuable, albeit controversial, are the works of Galia Golan: *The Czechoslovak Reform Movement* (Cambridge, 1971) and *Reform Rule in Czechoslovakia: The Dubček Era, 1968–1969* (Cambridge, 1973); and H. Gordon Skilling, *Czechoslovakia's Interrupted Revolution* (Princeton, NJ, 1976). From the perspective of his own experience, this period was discussed by Zdenek Mlinaz, a former Secretary of the Central Committee of the Czechoslovak Communist Party, now a political scientist, in *Ceskoslovensky pokus o reformu 1968: analysa jeho teorie a praxe* (Cologne, 1975). In Czechoslovakia, after 1969, works have appeared criticising the 1968 policy and its ideological justifications.

10. *Rude Pravo*, 29 September 1967.

11. See the discussion of national relationships and their repercussions in the work of Viktor Pavlenda: *Ekonomicke zaklady socialistickeho riesenia narodnostnje otazki w*, Ceskoslovensku (Bratislava, 1968).

12. *Rude Pravo*, 10 April 1968.

13. *Pravda*, 28 August 1968.

14. János Kornai, 'The Hungarian Reform Process: Visions, Hopes and Reality', *Journal of Economic Literature*, XXIV, no. 4, 1986, pp. 1687–1737.

15. Ibid., p. 1724.

16. Ibid., p. 1728.

17. Ibid., p. 1731.

18. Ibid., p. 1733.

9 Systemic Aspects of the Social Crisis in Yugoslavia

Ivan Bićanić

1 INTRODUCTION

This paper deals with the economic and social crisis in Yugoslavia which started in 1979. This crisis was triggered off by the world recession, but has since continued unabated and without relation to events in the world economy. By the middle of 1988 it had not yet reached its lowest point. Thus it has become an internally sustained crisis, one that is part of the long-term growth path of the economy, but at the same time one that has evolved into the longest, deepest and harshest crisis in nearly seventy years of Yugoslav history (Bićanić, 1986b).

This chapter concentrates on only two aspects of the crisis: its systemic, particularly bureaucratic causes and the welfare implications for the population. The administration's mismanagement of the economy has, I shall claim, contributed a great deal both to the severity of the crisis and to its length. The second aspect is related to the incentive to supply the labour input necessary for production. I shall argue that without substantial changes, of both management methods and the incentive system, even the best-intentioned policies cannot succeed.

2 THE ADMINISTRATIVE BIAS IN THE YUGOSLAV ECONOMY

The Yugoslav economy of the 1980s can best be described as a 'neither plan nor market, *ad hoc* reflexively administered economy'. In other words, we are dealing with an economy in which all the major economic decisions are taken by an unaccountable administration of top politicians, businessmen and government officials. Their decisions are taken on an *ad hoc* basis – that is, they are of a stopgap nature, taken on a case-to-case basis and with no necessary link to a coherent overall policy. These decisions are reflexive, meaning that they are taken after the event and hence are frequently counterproductive due to policy lags. They are also taken in an economic environment in which markets determine neither prices nor flows of commodities and services and therefore do not motivate transactors, in which central plans are not only unimplementable but also nonbinding. For brevity, this kind of economy will be called an 'overlord economy', a term used first, but with a different meaning, in 'How not to Develop a Country: An Essay in Economic Pathology' (in Bićanić, 1972).

Even though the overlord economy has become more visible and prominent during the present crisis, it has in varied forms been the dominant type of organisation of the Yugoslav economy since 1929, the year in which King Alexander introduced his 'personal dictatorship'. Thus great care should be taken when deciding what part of the blame for the present crisis is to be put on socialism, self-management or the recently chosen form of self-managing socialism, the 'associated labour paradigm', implemented since the early 1970s. Many Yugoslav economists – in my view, mistakenly – tend to put all the blame on the 'associated labour paradigm'.

Undoubtedly this paradigm, best described by its most prominent proponent, Korać (1977, 1980 and 1982) and the famous critics Bajt (1986), Horvat (1985) and Pjanić (1983), cannot be a good foundation for organising an economy. Its deficiencies have been well known since it was expounded in the early 1960s as a way of implementing the 'Marxian Law of Value' in a socialist self-managed economy. An economy with no public price on capital or labour necessarily leads to allocative inefficiencies and very low factor mobility. Attempts to 'economise through agreements' eliminate the values necessary for sound economic calculation and make the budget constraint soft, to the point of nonexistence. Unclear ownership relations do not locate risk-takers and lead instead to many inefficiencies. The list of defects could go on to include every aspect of the economy, but most of these criticisms share one common characteristic with the paradigm itself: they are theoretical, deductive, ideologically charged and very rarely based on sound econometric, empirical evidence. For while the secular slowing-down of the economy has been demonstrated (see Mencinger, 1986b, for an econometric analysis, but most of the numerous books on the crisis also deal with the issue), not much research has been done to establish the extent to which the paradigm was actually implemented. Perhaps its introduction was merely a reflection of the syndrome whereby 'when the Yugoslav economy runs into difficulties it tends to change the institutional framework' (Horvat, 1970, p. 5), while at the same time leaving the overlord economy unchanged and unchecked.

The rest of this section of the chapter will analyse the 'track record' of the overlord economy. Three aspects of administrative decisions will be dealt with: (i) economic mismanagement as a cause of the crisis, (ii) economic mismanagement during the crisis, and (iii) adaptations to the overlord economy.

(i) Economic mismanagement as a cause of the crisis

Two aspects of economic mismanagement prior to the crisis must be distinguished. The first is related to the quality of the administrators, the second to the quality of the decisions which were taken.

Understandably enough, there is little information about the quality of the administrators. Apart from anecdotal evidence and folklore about their intelligence, only one serious study stands out, together with the statements of top administrators. The study (Kregar *et al.*, 1985) shows that before their appointment the top civil servants in Croatia (those elected and vetted by the Croatian Parliament) who were studying law studied longer, took more exams, and got worse grades than the average student. They also had the typical value system of bureaucrats, respecting hierarchy and rules and disliking initiative and decisions. Even though the study was based on a small sample, its findings are quite in accordance with statements by top administrators. Thus, the President of the Federal Executive Council was appalled by the poor level of administration when she began her term of office (as she admitted in an interview after her mandate was over); the Minister of Foreign Affairs stated, again after his mandate had run out, that half the ambassadors were not up to the job; the present Minister of Finance also claims not to have the personnel for writing good laws, and so forth.

The employment of administrators without the required expertise and the subsequent practice of negative selection leads to two phenomena. One is the much-discussed 'dominance of politics over economics' (Maksimović, ed., 1985), the principle by which all issues are reduced to the political. The other is an increasing dependence on unofficial economic activities, which offer an overlord economy the most efficient way of muddling through.

The poor quality of the administrators is best reflected in the kind of decisions they take. For example, they did not react to the oil shock of the early 1970s with an appropriate energy policy, but resorted to increasing foreign indebtedness (Drpić, 1985). In the early 1980s, neither the National Bank nor the government bothered to find out the size of the debt. The domestic currency was administratively kept overvalued (Potić, 1985), requiring an elaborate system of export subsidies and import barriers (Čičin-Šain, ed., 1986). The excess of domestic consumption over domestic production kept rising (Miljković, ed., 1986). During this period, the import-led policy did not achieve its goals. Thus the export sector was put into a disadvantaged position (Korošič and Mates, 1981), monetary policy played a passive role (Rogić, 1985), as did fiscal policy (Jurković, 1985), while national planning had become meaningless (Mencinger, 1986a).

This kind of economic policy has led, over the last ten years, to inefficient growth. The capital coefficient grew increasingly very high (Stipetić, 1986), the differences in regional development increased (Bogunović, 1985), relative prices did not follow world trends (Popov, 1983), major redistributions of income between sectors continued (Korošić, 1984), and import dependence increased, especially in the export sector (Babić, 1980). Throughout the whole of the 1970s, while development was showing these negative characteristics, the real purchasing power of the population kept rising (Šefer, 1981), and the rate of inflation was, as a result, increasing (Korošić, 1986). The national income lost through such inefficient development was consequently immense (Bajt, 1986) and the national economy was going through a process of increased peripheralisation in the world economy (Bićanić, 1986a).

By the end of the 1970s, and with another change of international circumstances, the 'import-led growth' bubble burst. The rises in oil prices and interest rates triggered off a world recession. In the case of the Yugoslav economy, they also triggered off an internally generated crisis whose lowest point has not yet been reached.

(ii) Economic mismanagement during the crisis

The economic crisis of the 1980s caught the administrators by surprise, but its severity (shortages of basic consumer products, rationing, a fall in real incomes by more than 10 per cent, zero growth, debt repayment problems, and so on) made ignoring it impossible. From the beginning the crisis incited two types of reaction. The first was stopgap policies targeted at maintaining international liquidity and domestic production. The second was the writing of a consensus blueprint for survival (a consensus of politicians representing as they see fit their various regions and with their varied ideological biases). The stopgap policies were largely unrelated to the blueprint. Three phases of such policies may be distinguished. The first lasted from the beginning of the crisis in 1979 to the 16th Plenary Session of the Central Committee of the League of Communists of Yugoslavia (CC LCY) in 1985. The second phase followed, and lasted until the adoption of the Intervention Law on Personal Incomes at the end of 1986. The third phase started at the beginning of 1987 and is still running. The *éminence grise* of the first phase was the most prominent Yugoslav economist, Aleksandar Bajt, the director of the Institute of Economics of the Ljubljana Faculty of Law, in my view the only centre of organised and serious empirical research in Yugoslavia. The major constraint on policy decisions was the government's letter of intent submitted to the International Monetary Fund (IMF). Its targets were to maintain external liquidity (which was achieved), to reduce domestic consumption (which was not achieved in the state sector, thus redistributing an increasing share of national income to the administrators), to increase exports (achieved at a lower level than planned), and to maintain production levels. These targets were to be attained through a phased increase in domestic interest rates, to 1 per cent above the inflation rate, exchange rate floating at a 'realistic level', price controls for major products, and an incomes policy based largely on persuasion. Even such sceptical observers as the prominent Yugoslav economist Branko Horvat thought that these second-best policies could go a long way in dealing with the crisis.

When by 1985 many of the targets were either achieved or were close to being achieved, there was a major turnaround in economic policy. The change also coincided with somewhat more lax IMF conditions, a Congress of the LCY and the last days of the mandate of the prime minister. The economist who supplied the theoretical explanation and justification for the political decision to change course was Milutin Ćirović, a professor at Belgrade University, drawing on the work done by economists in the National Bank of Yugoslavia. Targets for inflation rates were set and the levels of interest rates and exchange rates were linked to these targets, which meant lowering the former and revaluating the latter. It was thought that these measures, together with wage controls, would give the economy a sufficient stimulus and that the actual inflation rate would fall. However, the administrative control over prices, foreign exchange and enterprise income distribution remained. This policy package was called 'programmed inflation' and was immediately criticised by the professional economists – criticism which in no way hindered its implementation.

The effects of the policy were the opposite of those intended. Inflation rose, exports fell, productivity growth fell and when the wage policy was loosened towards the end of 1986, there were major wage increases in anticipation of a policy change. The last phase, which started at the end of 1986, involved a wage freeze for some and a reduction of money wages for other enterprises; a return to a policy of positive real interest rates and a downward-floating exchange rate; and a pledge to introduce markets and ease direct foreign investments. But a rising rate of inflation, social unrest and defaulting on debt payments have increased administration in the field of price control and tabled suggestions of further administration in foreign currency earnings.

The stopgap policies of the third phase are, at least in rhetoric, linked to an economic reform. Major new laws have been passed or are before Parliament. These involve changes in the Constitution, the Law of Associated Labour, laws on enterprise income distribution, banking, bankruptcy, and so forth (Mates, 1987). According to the government timetable, the Constitution and Law of Associated Labour should be changed during 1988. The other laws have already been missed. If implemented, these laws would amount to a major reform of the economy. However, implementation has been postponed indefinitely.

Thus, since the start of the crisis three blueprints for survival have been offered, and a fourth is to be offered by mid-1988. The first was the Long-Term Programme of Economic Stabilisation, frequently referred to as the Kreigher Report or the Long-Term Programme, published in 1982. The second was the Critical Analysis of the Functioning of the Political System, referred to as the Critical Analysis or the Vrhovec Report, published in 1984. The third was published in 1987 and is called the Thesis for the Further Development of the Economic System, while the fourth is being prepared by the Mikulić Commission.

The Long-Term Programme (LTP) and the Critical Analysis (CA) were written by two different groups of politicians (and of social scientists chosen by the politicians). They also represent two different blueprints whose visions of the economic system make them mutually exclusive. The differences concern markets, the LTP stressing their all-encompassing nature and the CA their historical temporality; the calculation of factor costs, the LTP using prices and the CA no *a priori* valuation; the role of banks, the LTP seeing them as independent businesses while the CA stresses their role of providing financial services; the micro-organisation, the LTP stressing the role of the whole enterprise and the CA the basic unit of associated labour, and so forth. To a great extent the CA programme implied a return to the deductive principles on which the associated labour paradigm was built, the same principles which the LTP has avoided incorporating. The third blueprint, the Thesis, has a much narrower scope and implies a return to the LTP. This narrow approach means that many vital issues which are divisive have been sidestepped. The Thesis is clearest on the issue of attracting foreign capital, introducing money markets and allowing more than one type of ownership.

The economic policy-makers, both in their stopgap capacity and as authors of blueprints for survival, have not been successful. Each change in economic policy has led to a further deterioration of the economy. The only unchanging characteristic has been the increased reliance on the economics of overlord, for indeed there has been an increasing rigidity in the control of prices, wages, foreign currency earnings, and so on. Obviously, the administrators must have had a deep belief that rules, regulations, laws and limitations can represent a viable policy to deal with the crisis – in any case a policy less dangerous than any of the unimplemented reforms currently on offer.

(iii)   Adaptations to an overlord economy

The economy had to adapt to the above-described type of economic (mis)management. There have been two main forms of this adaptation, both of which have had a very important influence on the economic structure. The first is the 'bias to bigness', the second an increased reliance on 'unofficial economic activities'.

The bias to bigness reflects a structural adaptation of the economy to the economics of overlord. Over time the size distribution of Yugoslav enterprises (excluding the private sector) has become asymmetric, with few small firms, a large number of big ones and, by international standards, very few really large enterprises. The average size seems to be somewhat smaller than that in comparable socialist economies, but larger than in capitalist economies. Studying the size distribution of firms in the Yugoslav economy is difficult for institutional and statistical reasons. The definition of the enterprise is unclear due to the complex relationship between constituent, basic organisations, while the published data do not distinguish sufficiently between enterprises and plants. The results of research concerning the large-scale bias by Petrin (1986) indicate a similar distribution, while Ocić (1983) and Miljković (1986) point to the existence of few enterprises with plants in more than one region. Anecdotal evidence also seems to indicate the described size distribution of firms.

The asymmetric size distribution now in place is the long-term result of two interconnected influences: the efforts of economic policy and the rational reactions of enterprises.

There are four dominant reasons why enterprises should react to the economics of overlord with a bias to bigness. First, it helps to internalise markets. In an economy which sets no price on capital, inter-enterprise mobility of capital is very low, so that large enterprises and intra-enterprise mobility provide a degree of flexibility. Also administratively regulated prices lead to scarcities which, however, can be avoided in intra-enterprise transactions. Secondly, large enterprises provide protection. There are internal funds to cover losses, there are greater resources to deal with administratively created shortages, there is greater bargaining power and lobbying power *vis-à-vis* the administrators and, lastly, there is a greater probability of 'socialising the enterprise losses'. Thirdly, the bias can be explained by the mania for prestige present in any developing country, for it is often easier to obtain finance for grand, status-enhancing projects which are supposed to revolutionise life in a region, than for small projects whose openings and backers pass unnoticed.

Lastly, as in any other economy, the size of the enterprise is connected to managerial prestige and status. The manager of a large enterprise thus appears more successful as a negotiator with the administrators when bargaining over terms of business. While the above represents an *ex post* reaction, there are also definitive reasons for the bias in the way the administrators have organised the economy. Social overheads are independent of firm size, thus representing a lower average fixed cost for larger enterprises. The vision of administrators involves a notion of 'large is beautiful', so that many mergers are pushed through by politicians as a means of rationalising and streamlining the economy. The constraints placed on the private sector, both by law and by fiscal policy, have limited its size and prevented the rapid growth of private firms of all sizes.

An increasing reliance on unofficial economic activities has been an equally important adaptation. In an economy with so many rules and regulations (Pusić, 1986), many of which may be contradictory, unofficial activities serve to cut through red tape. Keeping to the letter of the law would cause major disruptions in production, close many factories and put many managers in goal. But the great reliance on unofficial activities as a way of operating an overlord economy has another important consequence: it devalues the civil aspect of society and the credibility of the legal system. The term 'useful lawbreaking and dealing' has gained usage.

Of course, even administrators enter into unofficial activities. Many do so for direct personal gain, but the activities I have in mind are entered into for other reasons. Managers wish to show their skill as negotiators and successful operators, politicians to gain points as good defenders and champions of their constituents' interests, and civil servants to claim success for their rules. All these activities are primarily designed to maintain and operate an overlord economy in the common knowledge that if one stuck to the rules, the economy would simply cease to function.

Four areas are especially important for unofficial economic activities by the administrators. These are foreign trade, bank loans, solving shortages and bottlenecks, and negotiating prices and new rules. With an overvalued currency, debt problem, import controls and export subsidies in a highly import-dependent economy, foreign trade is the natural area for unofficial activities. Foreign currency is traded in 'grey markets' and at 'grey rates' among enterprises, import licences are traded, foreign currency earnings of enterprises are not repatriated in time and spare parts are smuggled in by businessmen to avoid red tape.

With a negative real rate of interest, there are excess demands for investment and bank loans, so that these have to be distributed by non-market means. The loans for new investment are used to cover investment overdrafts, and short-term loans to finance wage increases are intended to reduce worker discontent and stop strikes. While the former can be negotiated over a longer period, the latter are needed quickly and at short notice. Apart from the excess demand for loans, the economic system which envisages banks merely as centres of 'financial services', and not as business enterprises, gives great impetus to the unofficial distribution of loans. Shortages and bottlenecks other than those related to importing raw materials and spare parts are not solved by markets and prices but by telephone and distribution. This is an area where the bias to bigness becomes especially important.

The negotiation of prices and favourable rules is a very complex area which cannot be dealt with in this chapter. The scope of unofficial activities is wide, from creating artificial shortages of basic consumer products to appealing to national interests. The importance of all can be best summed up in two often-quoted statements: it is not important what your job is but where you work, and it is not important to produce but to have favourable 'conditions of production'.

3 THE WELFARE IMPACT OF THE CRISIS

In the last resort the success of any economic system depends on its ability to provide the population with a satisfying level of present and future economic welfare. This goal cannot be achieved unless the population has the incentive and ability to supply an efficient labour input. Without this, even the best 'grand design' constructions of economic systems and policies cannot succeed. This section deals with the extent to which the economy has mobilised the only abundant resource – labour – and with the even more important issue of whether there are grounds to expect that the labour supplied will pull the economy out of its present crisis. In other words, this section deals with the question of how the economy has evolved into a 'low-labour-performance economy', and with the possibility of raising labour efficiency.

Before analysing the topic, one introductory remark is necessary: the welfare impact of forty years of building socialism and thirty-five years of self-management has, with one exception, not been on the agenda of the 'research programme' of economists, Yugoslav or other. Serious research, both theoretical and empirical, on the welfare of the population is minute and has mainly been undertaken by mathematicians, statisticians and national account specialists. The exception is the personal income of the employed in the socialised sector, but even this topic entered the research programme by virtue of its relation to other topics which have been in the limelight for over twenty years. When analysing the 'operation of the Marxian Law of Value in a self-managed, market socialist economy' some issues relating to wage incomes were studied, such as the statistical dispersion of sectoral average wages weighted in various ways, the transformation of capital income into labour income, the income distribution according to labour input and according to the results of labour, and so on. On a more mundane level, the issue of whether 'workers eat their machines' and the ways of determining the enterprise wage fund were discussed at such length in the 1970s that the decade could be called the era of 'wage fund self-management'. A much-discussed issue was also whether workers, through their self-managing decisions, induce a wage-push inflation. But this and the other issues were not approached from the point of view of their effects on economic inequality, welfare, labour supply or incentives to work efficiently.

This state of affairs has meant that economic policies dealing with or affecting these aspects did not have a sound basis. These policies have had to be based on anecdotal remarks, often inspiring but rarely correct; ideological and deductive biases, accumulated over a long period; and stylised facts, which were often not supported by serious empirical research. The following section attempts to show the importance of this omission. Three issues are discussed: (i) the falling expectations of the population, (ii) populist egalitarianism, and (iii) unofficial economic activities designed to allow the population to 'muddle through'.

(i) The falling expectations of the population

It is impossible to measure expectations directly. Questionnaires, unless they are supported by indirect evidence, are also highly unreliable. Economic theory nevertheless attaches great importance to people's economic expectations. It is argued in this section that the questionnaires and other data quite definitely point to a fall in expectations of an improvement and indicate that the economy has adapted to this by becoming a 'low-labour-efficiency economy'.

Questionnaires with data on expected living standards have been conducted since 1977, the last being published in Sirotić (1986). There had been a major shift during that period. Until 1980 just over 10 per cent of the adult population expected a fall in the coming year (just over half no change and the rest an improvement). The shifts occurred in 1981 and 1982; from 1983 over half the polled group expected a fall in living standards, and less than 10 per cent an improvement (Sirotić, 1986, p. 3). The same survey shows that in 1985, 61 per cent of the polled households did not consider their regular household income sufficient, while 57 per cent did not consider total household income sufficient. When asked to evaluate their own living standards, 85 per cent of the households thought it was average or below average (Šrajer, 1984b, p. 38).

The perceived fall corresponds with the statistics. During the crisis real incomes and wages have been falling (in one year, by as much as 10 per cent) and from their 1979 high they are back to the levels of the late 1960s (Miljković, 1986). The importance of labour incomes in household budgets has also fallen (Božović, 1985), and unemployment has increased, especially among the young, women and educated (Miljković, 1986), thereby significantly reducing the probability of employment. The demoralisation of the labour force can also be seen from the widespread stealing reported by enterprises (*NIN*, no. Vejnović, 1984); from the fact that only 6 per cent of the employed considered that they worked the full eight-hour day while 44 per cent estimated that they worked less than four hours (Djukić-Srdar, 1986, p. 54); and given that intra-firm differentials were not considered stimulating by 68 per cent of the employed, of which 41 per cent considered the differentials to be unrelated to labour input (Šrajer, 1984a, p. 14). Understandably enough, the preservation of living standards is sought through incomes earned elsewhere.

There is another aspect of falling expectations which must be mentioned, for despite the rhetoric of political meetings, the scope for self-management in enterprises has been reduced during the crisis. The share of enterprise income left to the enterprise has been falling (Miljković, 1986). Although most investment decisions had already been taken outside enterprises before 1979 (Long-Term Programme), workers' councils at least had a major part to play in distributing the wage fund. During the crisis, even this has been significantly eroded.

(ii) Populist egalitarianism

Studies of economic inequality always stress that falling living standards bring distributional issues into focus. This has been true of Yugoslavia in all three types of distribution: interregional, intersectoral and interpersonal. It is interesting that in each of the three areas a 'stylised fact' has emerged. The three stylised facts are not proved conclusively by empirical research, and indeed seem to me to be at odds with reality. This section discusses only the stylised fact related to interpersonal inequality.

It has been suggested that since the crisis, social inequality has been increasing while intra-enterprise differentials have been decreasing; that the former has attained socially unacceptable proportions, while the latter are completely destimulating; and that the rising inequality is not based on labour incomes and is hence unjustified by the ruling principle of economic justice. This stylised fact is expounded by politicians, supported by the research of some economists and apparently accepted by a large section of the population (at least as far as population surveys show; see Marković, 1984, or Šrajer, 1984a). As for the research of economists, this is found wanting in many respects (Bićanić, 1986a). Data unsuitable for studying inequality are used; they are recalculated along unwarranted lines; dispersion and inequality measures are mixed up, and so on. The research of the author (Bićanić, 1984a, b) definitely does not support this populist egalitarian stylised fact in any aspect but one – the fall in intra-enterprise differentials.

Since 1963, when the first household survey was compiled by the Statistical Office, income inequality has gone through two phases: one phase of large changes, a major rise from 1965 to 1970 and a fall with a minimum in 1973; the other of small changes, a rise until 1979 and a small fall since then. Since the mid-70s the inequality level has remained almost unchanged, at a magnitude similar to the pre-1965 one. This is the case with the income inequality of all households as well as urban households with only the inequality of wages. Qualitatively the same changes have taken place for the various regions. The more developed regions had lower values of inequality measures during the whole period for all major types of household.

Comparing the inequality for various types of household, certain patterns emerge on the national level and on the level of all regions, except the most developed. Inequality levels of urban households follow, in terms of magnitude and the direction of change, the overall inequality. Rural inequalities are significantly smaller and show very small changes. Among the rural households, mixed (urban and agricultural) ones show the same direction of change as the urban ones, but the changes are of a smaller magnitude. The agricultural households have inequality levels somewhat above those of mixed ones, but with an opposite direction of change. In international comparisons, inequality levels in Yugoslavia since the mid-70s are low. This is also the case for interoccupational differences. The only valid element of the stylised fact above is that the intra-firm differentials are low (Šefer, 1982) and are quite correctly perceived as such (Šrajer, 1984a). The above-described changes in economic equality do point to the successful, if misorientated, influence of economic policy and what I would call the egalitarian bias. The one increase of inequality in the late 1960s was quickly and efficiently reduced in the early 1970s and regular agreements on incomes policy, together with campaigns against inequality, have successfully kept the levels low. Equally, the egalitarian policy towards private agriculture is reflected in the inequality measures, which are low and show small changes. Thus, while being incorrect in its view of economic inequality, populist egalitarianism has been successful at keeping social inequality low by both national and international standards.

(iii)   The stabilising effect of unofficial economic activities

As has been noted in section (i), the population has been subjected to great economic difficulties since the crisis. Falling real incomes have eroded twenty years of development, bringing rising unemployment and a falling share of labour incomes. Insufficient regular and labour incomes underlie falling expectations and the lack of both incentive and opportunity to work efficiently. The crisis has also sustained populist egalitarianism. The only valve open for 'muddling through' the crisis, and decreasing the welfare loss of the population, is the unofficial economy.

But unofficial activities which have become important during the crisis have created employment not in industry and services, but in agriculture, and in that sense reflect a backtracking of development. The unofficial activities involved are related to the increased importance of mixed households and their agricultural incomes, and the increased reliance of urban households on occasional work in rural areas, part-time gardening, and direct purchases from the villages. Mixed households are now an important feature of the Yugoslav economy: they possess about 30 to 40 per cent of arable land (*Ekonomska politika*, no. 1734) and represent one in three households. Depending on relative prices, they can change the area under cultivation from year to year, as well as shift labour between the urban sector and agriculture. They are also irregular surplus producers and tend not to specialise (Cvjetićanin and Dilić, 1978). Their activities are part of the unofficial economy because they retail through unofficial channels and take sick leave or are absent from work during the top agricultural season, disrupting urban activities during these times (Bićanić, 1986a). Only 35 per cent of households do not produce any food of their own (Maroević, 1985, p. 30).

It is therefore obvious that unofficial economic activities have greatly eased the fall in living standards. In relation to this and other unofficial economic activities an interesting thesis was presented by a sociologist, who suggested that the crisis has formed a *détente* between the administrators and the administrated (Županov, 1984). The latter are permitted to enter unofficial activities and muddle through the crisis as best they can, provided they do not question the exclusive power of the former. The continuing social stability, despite the severest crisis the country has so far experienced, seems to indicate that the thesis should not be dismissed immediately; indeed, it may even help to explain the cause of the rising number of strikes in 1987 and 1988 and the fact that they are no longer related to issues of money wages and intra-enterprise differentials.

References

Babić, M. (1980) 'Analiza uvozne zavisnosti jugoslavenske privrede', *Ekonomski pregled*, vol. xxxi, no. 9–10, pp. 419–40.

Bajt, A. (1986) *Alternativna ekonomska politika* (Zagreb: Globus).

Bićanić, I. (1984a): 'Kako mjeriti nejednakosti', *Naše teme*, vol. xxviii, pp. 855–64.

Bićanić, I. (1984b) 'Analiza raspodjela i raspona .asobnih primanja stanovništva u Jugoslaviji od 1963 do 1981 godine', unpublished PhD thesis, Zagreb University.

Bićanić, I. (1985) 'Nejednakosti i Rični Sohoci', *Ekonomska politika*, no. 1718.

Bićanić, I. (1986a): 'O nemoći naše ekonomske znanosti', *Kulturni radnik*, vol. xxxix, no. 6, pp. 59–67.

Bićanić, I. (1986b): 'Some General Comparisons of the Impact of the Two World Crises on the Yugoslav Economy', in Berend, I. and Borchardt, K. (eds) (1986) *The Impact of the Depression of the 1930s and its Relevance for the Contemporary World* (Budapest: Academy Research Centre).

Bićanić, R. (1972) *Turning Points in Economic Development*, (The Hague: Mouton).

Bogunović, A. (1985) *Regionalni razvoj SFR Jugoslavija i SR Hrvatske* (Zagreb: Liber).

Bozovic, P. (1985) 'Privredni Cilansi Jugoslavija u uslovima finansijske konsolidacije privrede i Canaka u 1984 godini', *Finansije*, vol. 40, no. 5–6, pp. 451–70.

Čičin-Šain, A. (ed.) (1986) *Doing Business with Yugoslavia*, (Belgrade: Privredna komora Jugoslavija).

Cvjetičanin, V. and E. Dilić (1978) 'Csnovna obeležja mešovitih domaćinstva, *Jugoslavenski pregled*, vol. xxii, no. 4, pp. 135–44.

Djukić-Srdar, M. (1986) 'Kakva je stvarna potrošnja stanovništva', *TRIN*, No. 4, 1986, pp. 51–8.

Drpić, I. (1985) *Energetika i privredni razvoj*, (Zagreb: CKD).

Horvat, B. (1970) *Privredni sistem i ekonomska politika Jugoslavije* (Belgrade: IEN).

Horvat, B. (1985) *Jugoslavensko društvo u jrizi*, (Zagreb: Globus).

Jerovšek, J., S. Maričić, J. Mencinger, T. Petrin, E. Pusić, V. Rus and J. Zupanov (1986) *Kriza, Blokade i Perspective*, (Zagreb: Globus).

Jurković, P. (1985) 'Analiza ekonomskog položaja društvenih djelatnosti u razdoblju od 1977 do 1982. godine', *Ekonomski pregled*, vol. xxxvi, no. 34, pp. 101–18.

Korać, M. (1977–82): *Socijalistički samoupravni način proizvodnje*, vol. i (1977), vol. ii (1980), vol. iii (1982), (Belgrade: Kumunist).

Korošić, M. (1986) *Inflacija i mogućnost suzbijanja* (Belgrade: Naucna knjiga).

Korošić, M. and N. Mates (1981) 'Ekonomski položaj izvozne privredne', *Ekonomski pregled*, vol. xxxii, no. 1–2, pp. 33–44.

Kregar, J., E. Pusić and I. Šimonović (1985) 'Kadrovi u upravi', *Naša zakonitost*, vol. xxxix, no. 7 pp. 761–76.

Maksimovik, I. (ed.) (1985) *Ekonomija i politika*, (Belgrade: Odeljenje drustvenih nauka SANU, vol. vi).

Marković, M. (1984) 'Pogled na socijalne razlike-što ih uvjetuje i koliko smetaju', *TRIN* no. 2, 1984, pp. 3–10.

Maroević, T. (1985) 'Koliko smo u prosjeku prosječni', *TRIN*, no. 1–2, 1985, pp. 19–34.

Mates, N. (1987) 'Uz nove mjeve ekonomske politike', *Naše teme*, vol. xxxi, no. 1–3, pp. 3–16.

Mencinger, J. (1986a) 'Društvenoplaniranje-utvara i realnost ovladanja budućnošću, in Jerovšek *et al.* (1986).

Mencinger, J. (1986b) 'Granice razvoja, "dogovorne ekonomije" ili determinante uspješnosti u-sljedećim godinama', in Jerovšek *et al.* (1986).

Miljković, D. (ed.) (1986) *Jugoslavija 1945–1986, Statistički prikaz*, Savezni zavod za statistiku (Belgrade).

Ocić, Č. (1983) 'Integracioni i dezintegracioni procesi u privredi Jugoslavija, mimeo (Belgrade).

Perišin, M. (1980) 'Statistička kretanja investicija u osnovna sredstva po socialistićkim republikama i pokrajinama za razdoblje 1952–1977', *Ekonomski pregled* vol. XXXI, no. 1–2, pp. 39–56.

Petrin, T. (1986) 'Kriza male privrede', in Jerovšek et al. (1986).

Pjanić, Z. (1983) *Samouprivni privredni sistem*, (Belgrade: Radnička stampa).

Popov, S. (1983) *Ličnidohoci i inflacija troškova*, (Belgrade: Ekonomika).

Potić, M. (1985) 'Politika deviznog kursa i realizacija naših platnobilančnih ciljeva', *Jugoslavensko bankarstvo*, vol. xv, no. 5, pp. 27–37.

Prica, M. (1983) 'Obim i raspored inostranih kredita za investicija', *Jugoslovenski pregled*, vol. xxvii, no. 12, pp. 475–8.

Pusić, E. (1986) 'Kriza pravnog sistema', in Jerovšek *et al.* (1986).

Rogić, Z. (1985) 'Analiza uzročno-posljedičnih veza izmedu novčne mase i privredne aktivnosti u Jusgoslaviji', *Jugoslovensko bankarstvo*, vol. xv, no. 9, pp. 9–17.

Šefer, B. (1981) *Socijalna politika* (Zagreb: Informator).

Sirotić, Š. (1986) 'Što ove godine kazuju ocjene uvjeta života', *TRIN*, no. 3 1986, pp. 3–10.

Šrajer, K. (1984a) 'Utjecaj prihoda na socijalne razlike', *TRIN*, no. 2, 1984, pp. 11–20.

Šrajer, K. (1984b) 'Doživljaj vlastitog standarda', *TRIN*, no. 3, 1984, pp. 31–9.

Stipetić, V. (1986) 'Ekonomska znanost i opadajuća efikasnost investiranja u Jugoslaviji od šezdesetih godina naovamo', *Ekonomski pregled*, vol. xxxvi, no. 5–6, pp. 167–96.

Vejnović, M. (1984) 'Kradja kao oblik protesta', *Privreda*, no. 6, 1984.

Zupanov, J. (1984) 'Opadenje standarda i drustvena stabilnost', *TRIN*, no. 3, 1984, pp. 7–18.

10 Ideological Features Yet to be Overcome in Soviet-Type Economies

László Szamuely

INTRODUCTION

The question of reform in Hungary has been debated for over three decades now. This debate necessarily, and by conscious self-constraint, has concentrated on the reform of the economic mechanism and has resulted in some established positive changes in the Hungarian economy. Yet we cannot be satisfied with the pace of progress in finding solutions to specific domestic problems. Recently those who closely follow the hesitant development of the economic reform came to the conclusion that changes in the economic sphere alone were not sufficient for a major leap forward. Public attitudes, the mechanism and criteria of political decision-making, the functioning of mass media, formal and informal rules of public life must necessarily change as well.

If such an all-embracing reform in a socialist country tries to change social practice seriously, it must first clarify its relation to the concept of socialism. Otherwise it will be doomed to groping about in the darkness of pragmatism, or be engaged in constant infighting with ideology legitimising the old social system and the value judgements of its leading social strata. However simple and comfortable it may seem to ignore the discrepancies between pragmatic economic policy and ideology, this comfort may exact a high price in the long run: lack of social and political support, and a general confusion of social values.

Hungary is not alone in recognising that the ideological image of socialism needs to be updated in accordance with the reforms aiming at the modernisation of economy and society. Gorbachev (1987), in his speech at the important January session of the Central Committee of the CPSU, said that one of the causes of the slowing-down of economic and social development and the postponement of necessary changes was that 'theoretical concepts of socialism remained to a large extent those of the 1930s–40s, when the society had been tackling entirely different tasks.'

In this chapter I shall make an attempt to investigate some of the characteristic elements of the official concept of socialism in the socialist countries which, while emerging under the singular circumstances of socialist practice in the Soviet Union, have acquired the status of general validity on the ideological level. I have in mind not only the example of the Soviet Union in the 1930s and the 1940s but also those peculiarities in the post-World War II development of Eastern Europe which have become an indispensable part of the ideology and image of socialism.

THE MERGER OF POLITICS, IDEOLOGY AND ECONOMIC MANAGEMENT

The Soviet model of socialism was heavily influenced by the fact that the socialist transformation was to be carried out at the same time as the abolition of economic backwardness. The coincidence of these two processes has provided the state with an extraordinary importance in the economy. Another historic feature of the Soviet model has been the accumulation of all political power in the hands of one party, thereby making it virtually inseparable from the state. A broad consequence of this inseparability was that the political and ideological spheres became and were seen as the almighty demiurge of the economy. Of the many further implications of this state of affairs, I am going to discuss only those affecting the ideology and the image of socialism.

It is an old axiom of the literature on the functioning of socialist economies that as a consequence of overcentralisation decisions are referred to the upper levels of the hierarchy, with numerous adverse effects. But in a Soviet-type economy the top level is tantamount to the *political* level. Hence the illusion that in a socialist economy politics is not only almighty, but also an integrating force within the economy. Some Hungarian sociologists and political scientists still hold this view (Bihari, 1982), but this is only an illusion, the primordial role of politics notwithstanding. Politics cannot invalidate economic laws and constraints, and it would necessarily fail if it tried to do so. The illusion that it is politics that integrates and runs the economy is also deceptive. Let me refer in this context to the distinction made by János Kornai (1971, pp. 176–87) between the autonomous and the higher functions and their controlling systems within the economy, an analogy he drew from biology. According to this analogy, the autonomous functioning of a modern economic system is more or less the same all over the world. Such autonomous functioning keeps the economy together and provides for human existence without recourse to commands or high-level decisions. The area of higher functioning *par excellence* is economic development, with characteristics such as capacity enlargement, the change of production structure and macroeconomic decisions, the introduction of major new technologies, and so on. In a Soviet-type economy the sphere of politics merges with and subsumes these higher economic functions. This merger/interwovenness, caused by the objective nature of the system rather than any arbitrary decisions, has many adverse consequences. The gravest and most researched is the blending of two totally different systems of criteria and logic of decision-making: political and economic.

The sole and most important criterion of economic decisions is efficiency. Political decision-making, however, aims at the establishment, maintenance, and strengthening of power. Of course, the two criteria are not necessarily in conflict and may even reinforce one another. Nothing can serve better the stability of political power than an efficient, dynamic economy, and vice versa, structural change in the economy enforced by political power can accelerate economic growth and may further the attainment of a higher level of efficiency. But all this notwithstanding, the two criteria are different. In the history of socialist economies there have been some radical structural changes implemented at the initiative of the political and ideological spheres, but the main driving force behind such restructuring has been the creation of a social and economic base for the new political power, not efficiency criteria at all. That is why Stalin had to invent the economically unintelligible concept of 'higher-order efficiency' (Stalin, 1952, p. 59). The most telling example is the collectivisation of agriculture based on political and ideological motives, a move from whose dismal effects many socialist countries could not recover for several decades. But the two kinds of logic can also diverge in another sense. Politics aims at maintaining the stability of power; it may therefore oppose and slow down economic restructuring necessary for reasons of efficiency. The experience of socialist countries suggests that those in power may recoil from the risk of social tension and choose instead the preservation of the old, obsolete structure.

But of prime importance for our theme is another, much less investigated consequence of the merging of political, ideological and economic decision-making – that the political and ideological sphere interprets economic problems within its own value system and gives reasons for its economic decisions expressed in terms of its own language. That is why *economic decisions acquire an ideological and political meaning*. Georg Lukács, the outstanding Marxist philosopher, used to say, in my view correctly, that Stalin was quick to create ideology out of short-term interests, to motivate actual political decisions. Due to the operation of the preserved institutional system, policy decisions, forms of corporate organisation, and so on are presented even today as inherent features of socialism from the very moment of their introduction. In the following sections I shall deal with some 'features' of socialism which are, in effect, no more than ideological interpretations of individual decisions, rational only in the actual setting of the time, but irrational under changed circumstances. If, due to the peculiarities of the Soviet-type system, economic rationality must acquire an acceptable ideological interpretation before being adopted, then once rational but now obsolete solutions would take on ideological value, acquire an almost social character. This is why the concept of socialism itself, encompassing many incongruous and accidental elements, often conflicts with today's drive for progress and economic rationality.

No new concept, however diligently propagated and inculcated into the minds of individuals forming the masses, can solve this conflict. For if praxis does not live up to ideals, the result is a confused social consciousness and the relativisation of values instead of a new value system. To solve this conflict, the root of its cause – that is, the fusion of the economic decision-making sphere with the political and ideological spheres – must be eliminated.

Closed economy as an ideal

Socialist economy envisaged as a closed economy, its preference for reduced international relations, was also the logical consequence of the actual circumstances of emerging socialist societies. Soviet Russia, surrounded by a hostile environment, had no other choice. Seclusion in any case was not irrational for a huge country with enormous human and natural resources. Both political necessity and economic rationality were amalgamated in the all-embracing Stalinist theory of 'socialism in one country' which became the ideological justification for eliminating opponents within the Party.

It is interesting that this political-economic-ideological peculiarity of Soviet development was in accordance with a possible interpretation of Marxian economics. I have in mind the contradiction originating in the well-known Marxian thesis of the withering away of commodity production under socialism. Marx and Engels were true internationalists and thought of socialism as full internationalisation of the economic and spiritual activity of mankind. Even in a work as early as *The Communist Manifesto*, they enthusiastically greeted the multiple contacts, even the 'universal interdependence of nations', that would replace, as a result of capitalist industrialisation, the previous local and national seclusion (Marx and Engels, 1848, p. 39). At the same time, the Marxian–Engelsian vision of socialist economy with a central body assessing needs in physical terms, and distributing goods and factors of production accordingly, would appear to rest on the implicit assumption that such an economy is both closed and self-supporting.

The assumption of closed economy, of course, was only an implicit consequence of the thesis on the termination of commodity production. Marx and Engels never came (nor could they possibly come) to this conclusion, as it would have totally contradicted their *Weltanschauung*. But it is quite symptomatic that their disciples, the German Democrats of the late nineteenth century, declared a programme to this effect.[1] National seclusion, condemned by Marx and Engels, thus became part of the Marxist tradition or its offshoots. It can also be found in the different trends of many Western socialist parties (for example the British Labour Party, the French Socialist Party and the New Left).

Marx's own method of economic analysis has also contributed to the conception of socialist economy as a closed one. When analysing the reproduction of social capital he used several simplifying assumptions, and one of these was to neglect foreign trade. The famous schemes of simple and extended reproduction in the second volume of *Das Kapital* describe reproduction in a closed economy. Marx's original idea was to eliminate this restriction later and to deal with foreign trade and the world market in subsequent parts of his work. However, these parts were never written. Nevertheless, for Marx the closed economy is only an abstraction to ease the exposition of his argument. Later, however, Marx's schemes of reproduction became the theoretical basis on which macroeconomic planning and balances were built. Material balances in physical terms, which are the main pillars of this system, have the task of balancing domestic supply and demand. Foreign trade has traditionally played a subordinate role in these balances – imports are a *supplementary* source to ease shortages, and the only role of export earnings is in financing imports. The Marxian methodological principle thus corresponded to the concept of a closed socialist economy in which no commodity production takes place. This principle also influenced implicitly the development strategy of socialist countries, in that it insulated planning and management from the outside world. Today, however, it is first of all a petrified social and economic practice, and interests connected within, that maintain and strengthen this idea of inward-looking socialism, since the original political and military considerations are no longer valid.

Nevertheless, in the official ideology and propaganda as well as in long-term policy objectives of socialist countries, separation and isolation from the world economy remain of a positive *value*. References are made to the necessity of defending 'economic independence' and even scientific and technological 'invulnerability'. Translated into the language of economics, these notions suggest restrictions on participation in the worldwide division of labour. This process – the loss of market share and the effective ousting of socialist countries from world markets – has already been going on for many years due to the inertia of the old development strategies and economic practices.

From Table 10.1 one can discern that foreign trade expanded fairly rapidly after the destruction wrought by World War II and the isolationist period of the Cold War. The share of European CMEA countries in world trade peaked in the mid-1960s. Since that time, however, a slow but steady loss of market share has been under way, though held up for some time in the early 1980s by high Soviet oil prices (but this had no impact on the position of the six small CMEA countries). The share of the six trade-dependent small CMEA countries (dubbed in the table – inaccurately – 'Eastern Europe' for the sake of brevity) went back to the trough of 1950. Within this, the share of Hungary in world trade, which had been 0.65 per cent in 1938 and 0.7 in 1970, fell to 0.5 in 1982 and was 0.43 in 1986.[2]

When evaluating these figures we have to bear in mind that they also include the intra-CMEA trade. If we consider trade between CMEA and the industrialised (OECD) countries only, the share of

Table 10.1   *The Share of European CMEA Countries in World Trade*
(per cent)

	1950	1960	1965	1970	1975	1980	1982	1983	1984	1985	1986
Export											
CMEA TOTAL	6.8	10.1	10.5	9.8	8.9	7.8	9.1	9.7	9.4	9.0	8.8
of this											
Soviet Union	3.0	4.3	4.4	4.1	3.8	3.8	4.7	5.0	4.8	4.5	4.5
Eastern Europe	3.8	5.8	6.1	5.7	5.1	4.0	4.4	4.7	4.6	4.5	4.3
Import											
CMEA TOTAL	6.3	10.3	10.5	9.6	10.1	7.5	8.1	8.5	8.0	8.0	7.9
of this											
Soviet Union	2.3	4.2	4.1	3.6	4.1	3.3	4.1	4.3	4.0	4.0	4.0
Eastern Europe	4.0	6.1	6.4	6.0	6.0	4.2	4.0	4.2	4.0	4.0	3.9

SOURCE   Data before 1975: László Csaba's calculations based on the *UN Monthly Bulletin of Statistics* (Csaba, 1986, p. 220); from 1980 the author's calculations, based on *UN Monthly Bulletin of Statistics*, July 1987.

that trade in world trade is between 2 and 3 per cent. Even in the trade of two neutral European countries which traditionally have close links with socialist countries, and where discrimination is out of the question, the CMEA share is modest: 10 per cent in Austria and 20 per cent in Finland.

The public in the socialist countries is unaware of these facts because the 'success propaganda' uses mainly growth or production data as well as the socialist countries' share of world industrial output. Even if we disregard the fact that these production statistics are largely inflated, it remains true to say that *socialist countries play a small and diminishing role in world trade*. This has serious consequences in at least two respects.

First, with regard to production, science and technology, socialist countries profit less from the international division of labour than the rest of the world, and this trend is worsening. Partly as a result of this, socialist countries need much more material and human inputs in order to obtain the same final demand goods. Low efficiency damages international competitiveness, thus increasing the lag behind the world level and further reducing the possibility of participating in the international division of labour. A vicious circle arises, and this circle can be broken only if economic policy, economic management and the contrived system of values, falsely believed to be socialist, are all changed at about the same time.

Secondly, if a decline in the CMEA's market share cannot be halted, socialism has to face the prospect of worldwide erosion. In the era of a global military balance, and a nuclear stalemate flowing from the threat of mutual destruction, the outcome of the competition between the two major world systems is being increasingly determined by economic factors: the ability to provide goods, aid, credit, technology, and so forth.

To sum up: isolating the economy from the outside world can no longer be regarded – either explicitly, as it was formerly, or implicitly, as it is today – as an inherent trait of socialism and a value in itself. Such a policy contradicts both the modernising character of Marxist theory and the very goals the theory was originally intended to further – 'economic independence', 'rapid growth', 'economic invulnerability', and so on. One of the major objectives of reform in socialist countries over the last three decades has been exactly to change this situation by opening up to the world economy. This opening does not mean that exports should be increased at any cost: it is the whole economic system that must be changed. But the long history of experiments with reform indicates that all reforms are necessarily doomed to failure as long as their implementation is attempted in the conditions of orthodoxy bequeathed from another historical period. In my view, unless this situation changes, the vicious circle cannot be broken.

The development of heavy industry as a politico-ideological value

In Eastern Europe socialism was, in the public mind, identified with rapid industrialisation. Inevitably, this rapid industrialisation became tantamount to 'socialist construction' in the social psychology, and thereby a characteristic trait of socialism with a political and ideological value attached to it.

But this socialist industrialisation was a rather peculiar one. I have in mind not the differences between socialist and capitalist industrialisation with regard to their financial sources, methods of implementation and social objectives, but some other traits. First, this industrialisation has been autarkic, its central goal being the satisfaction of domestic needs. Secondly, it has placed much emphasis on heavy industry, and within it on the arms industry. Whether this military motive has been justified or not, efficiency criteria became secondary. Modernisation as a goal was pushed into the background, or made dependent on military considerations. The elimination of economic backwardness *per se* and the aim of successfully catching up with the developed capitalist world was replaced by the desire to establish equal or superior military capability.[3]

As a consequence of these two peculiarities, the ultimate objective of development became the establishment of all raw and basic material capabilities necessary to operate a heavy (defence) industry, independent of the outside world. It is not surprising that Stalin, in his February 1946 speech which was treated as a fundamental programme document not only in the Soviet Union but in all Eastern European countries for the following decade, reduced the long-term development strategy to the production of certain quantities of four basic raw materials: iron, steel, coal and oil. This programme, operating exclusively in terms of physical quantities, made no mention of a product of such political importance as grain.

In Hungary, the slogan of the first five-year plan which started in 1950 was to build up a 'country of iron and steel'. This slogan was a telling symbol of the Stalinist industrialisation model. It also brought out its irrationality in a country where, apart from labour, all the necessary conditions for such a project were lacking. But however powerful military, social and political justification of this programme was at the time and place of its original inception, the establishment and perpetuation of such a production structure in post-World War II Central and Eastern Europe has clearly been a blunder.

The problem is not only that all internal and external sources of extensive (quantitative) development are exhausted, but that the character of economic growth has changed all over the world. Modern technologies and goods with low material and energy intensity devalue extraction and basic materials production, as well as low skilled labour. Newly industrialising countries have become the main providers of the mass products of medium technology (textiles, footwear, household appliances, chemicals, steel products, cars), invading and winning the relevant markets from Central and Eastern European countries. In such circumstances, to maintain and enlarge so-called smokestack industries means stagnation, marginalisation and the squandering of national income and wealth without any hope of things turning for the better.

All this notwithstanding, in Hungary and other Eastern and Central European socialist countries, a large (in Hungary the preponderant) part of investment resources are spent on basic materials and the energy sectors. What is behind this unbelievable stubbornness in economic policy? Certainly not ignorance or unawareness of developments in the world economy (this latter was possibly true for the new leaders and managers of the late 1940s and early 1950s). There can only be two possible reasons, which I discuss below in turn.

1 A certain stratum of society has a stake in perpetuating the established economic structure.

This is a natural and understandable phenomenon. It is also common in Western countries when workers in the so-called crisis industries join forces with their employers to obtain government subsidies, tax relief, and protection against foreign competition. They also employ attractive political and ideological arguments in defence of their jobs. The real purpose of their 'class-militant' behaviour is to make their tax-paying fellow-workers pay for the maintenance of their endangered workplaces. It is true that with the large-scale unemployment of the last decade it has become impossible to distinguish structural from cyclical (transitional) unemployment, and therefore every claim for the maintenance of employment may seem to be rational and well justified.

But here the parallel ends. In countries of 'real socialism', labour shortage, not unemployment, is the rule and this will not change within a reasonable period of time, despite rumours to the contrary. Therefore full employment does not figure high on the list of arguments of the Hungarian and other Eastern European 'protectors of industry'. Rather, they refer to quasi-economic interests and ideological considerations. Quasi-economic arguments can consist of stability of provision, international obligations, capacity utilisation, and so on. I call them quasi-economic because what is at stake is usually some artificially created monopoly position, the abolition of which would benefit consumers. Alternatively, it could be the consequence of some previously incorrect investment decision, in which case society would profit – or lose less – by the quick withdrawal and redeployment of capital instead of dragging old burdens on. The list of ideological arguments is even longer: from the 'glorious revolutionary traditions', through the advantages of large-scale enterprises, to outright political demagogy in defence of the 'achievements of socialism'.

In reality the only 'achievements' under threat are the positions of high- and medium-level economic managers, government officials and political leaders. Through past social and economic development, heavy industry has gained priority both in finance and status; its executives have great personal power and social prestige. For decades this sector has also been the source of new cadres for government and party leadership, and vice versa. The heavy-industry 'lobby' therefore has resources as well as formal and informal power unmatched by any other sector. This has been one of the main, self-generating reasons for the priority development of heavy industry for four decades. The amazing inflexibility of development strategy is caused not simply by the inertia of the decision-making machinery but also by strong interest groups that were successful in presenting themselves as national, macroeconomic interests and even as the interests of the worldwide socialist community.

2 *The perpetuation of the old image of socialism as a legitimation factor*

This also has its role in the prolonged development of heavy industry and, within it, in the defence and materials sectors.

Paradoxically, these sectors are the most 'successful' in Soviet-type economies. This can be explained by their small product range, the homogeneity of product quality and great volumes, all of which made these sectors relatively suited to central planning and management in physical terms. Secondly, products of the material sector could comply relatively easily with the quality and other delivery requirements of the world market. Thirdly, these products are relatively far away from the consumer; the controversy over quality can thus be kept from the public. Finally, the direct and indirect military output of these sectors is more or less of the same quality as that of industrial capitalist countries, due to the special attention given to the military sector.

For reasons already discussed, heavy industrialisation in socialist countries was identified with the construction of socialism. The strategy of this industrialisation in most cases was not based on economic rationality. Economic decisions in all these countries were hotly debated – as a rule – in ideological disguise. Therefore in order to change the role of heavy industry, the involvement of the highest authorities and a revision of the underlying ideology is needed. Such a move involves inherent risks; hence it requires tremendous effort, determination, courage and united willingness on the part of the leadership.

That is why a reform which promotes economic rationality cannot be successful unless the ideology of socialism is revised, however risky such a revision may be.

SOME LESSONS FROM THE HUNGARIAN ECONOMIC AND SOCIAL POLICY

Hungarian economic and social history of the four decades after liberation of 1945 may broadly be divided into two periods. The first twenty years were those of radical socioeconomic change, with the sphere of politics (and the value system on which it relied) as its driving force. This period of revolutionary change in Hungarian society ended at some point in the mid-1960s. The economic reform started at that time was motivated by efficiency goals, and the leadership intended to direct Hungarian society towards a performance-based value system. Looking back one can see that the political and ideological spheres have nevertheless continued to insist on the socialist image of the former period, while the functioning of social institutions was not in accord with developments in the economic sphere. This caused confusion and a standstill in the reform process. The final result was an odd compromise: extensive development further pursued in big industry, isolation from the world market, the policy goal of 'CMEA-wide autarky' maintained and the structure of industry reflecting the objectives of the previous era.

The world market changes of the 1970s found Hungary unprepared. In the second period (up to the end of the 1980s) the determining impulses are coming from the world market and the Hungarian economy's reactions are merely defensive. Social stability has as a result been preserved, but at the expense of modernising the economic structure. Inappropriate adjustment to rapid structural changes in the world economy and the subsequent slowdown of economic growth have probably led to the widening of the gap between Hungary and industrialised capitalist countries. It is an unequivocal statistical fact, however, that Hungary's share of the world market has shrunk, along with that of other CMEA countries.

From the analysis it necessarily follows that the main driving force of future social development in Hungary must be the concern to revive its economy. This follows not only from the ominous signs of falling behind in terms of world economic performance but also from an increased 'sensitivity to economy' in a society where living standards will have stagnated, if not fallen, for at least a decade. The economy will function to an increasing extent in an environment of international competition, but it has to obtain the assistance of other social spheres in order to survive. In the light of this situation, the objectives of the political and ideological spheres, international political activity, opinion-makers, the education and social policy – all have to be reconsidered and subordinated to the above-mentioned concern. In order to reach accord, the whole of society must realise that we cannot preserve our socialist values, social achievements and the stability of the socialist system if we cannot modernise the economy in line with the criteria of world market competitiveness. Naturally, we should first of all decide which socialist values ought to be preserved. In this chapter I have noted the elements of the socialist image which are of dubious value and should be discarded in order to move ahead. My treatment of such elements was not exhaustive. I chose those which tend to be overlooked by social scientists or about which the judgement is not uniform in socialist countries.

A further task is to add new values and elements to our socialist image which were either missing before or were lost, worn away in the process of history. They include social and economic self-government; the right of different property forms (private property included) to coexist on an equal legal and actual basis; the autonomy of the individual in the collectivist economy; performance principle versus solidarity; and social care, and so forth.

Notes

1. In one of my earlier studies (Szamuely, 1974, pp. 24–7) I gave a detailed account of how Karly Kautsky, the orthodox Marxist, author of the Erfurt party programme of 1891, explained in his commentary on the programme that trade, even international contacts in general, between countries have to 'shrink considerably' under socialism as national economies become self-sufficient.
2. According to figures by Béla Kádár (1986, p. 89).
3. This can be best demonstrated by Stalin's famous and widely quoted statement on the reasons for forced industrialisation. This statement was made at the 4 February 1931 national session of economic managers: 'To slow down the rate of growth means falling behind. And who falls behind is beaten. . . . The history of old Russia is . . . full of such beatings due to backwardness. She was beaten by the Mongol khans. She was beaten by the Turkish beys. The Swedish feudals. The Polish and Lithuanian noblemen. The British and French capitalists. The Japanese barons. Everybody beat her because of her backwardness. Military backwardness, cultural backwardness, industrial backwardness, agricultural backwardness. . . . We are 50–100 years behind the developed countries and have to catch up within ten years. Either we do that or we will be crushed' (Stalin, 1951, pp. 39–40). Fifteen years later, looking back in his electoral speech, he

could declare with satisfaction that the Soviet Union turned into an industrial country in the thirteen pre-war years. The sense and objective of industrialisation was formulated in the same way as before: 'The Party knew that the war was imminent and the country cannot be defended if it has no heavy industry. Therefore we had to start to build up heavy industry immediately. Any hesitation in this matter was equivalent to defeat. The Party did not forget the words of Lenin, who had said that without heavy industry the country's independence, the Soviet system, cannot be defended' (Stalin, 1946, p. 15). In the same speech after outlining the long-term (fifteen-year) development programme of heavy industry, which provided for a tripling of industrial production, he justified the programme with one small sentence: 'This is the precondition to be sure that our country is secured against anything unexpected' (Stalin, 1946, p. 19).

References

Bihari, M. (1982) 'Politikai mechanizmus és demokrácia' (Political mechanism and democracy), pp. 276–94 in *Válság és megujulás* (Crisis and renewal) (Budapest: Kossuth Könyvkiadó).
Csaba, L. (1986) 'CMEA in a Changing World', *Osteuropa-Wirtschaft*, no. 3.
Gorbachev, M. S. (1987) 'O perestroike i kadrovoi politike partii' (On reconstruction and the Party's personnel policy), *Pravda*, 28 January.
Kádár, B. (1986) 'Hungary's External Economic Strategy in the Second Half of the 1980s', *Külpolitika* (a special issue of the Hungarian journal *Foreign Policy, Budapest)*.
Kornai, J. (1971) *Anti-Equilibrium* (Amsterdam/London: North Holland).
Marx, K. and F. Engels (1848) (1970) 'Manifesto of the Communist Party', in *K. Marx, F. Engels, Selected Works*. (Moscow: Progress Publishers).
Stalin, J. (1946) '*Rech na predvybornom sobranii izbiratelei stalinskogo izbiratelnogo okruga g. Moskvy 9 fevralia 1946 goda*' (Address to the electorate of the Stalin district in Moscow, 9 February 1946) (Moscow: Gospolitizdat).
Stalin, J. (1951) 'O zadachakh khoziaistvennikov' (On the tasks of managers), *Sochineniya*, vol. 13 (Moscow: Gospolitizdat).
Stalin, J. (1952) *Ekonomicheskiye problemy sotsializma v SSSR* (Economic problems of socialism in the Soviet Union) (Moscow: Gospolitizdat).
Szamuely, L. (1974) *First Models of the Socialist Economic Systems* (Budapest: Akadémiai Kiadó).

11 Revaluation of the Past Experience and the Future of Economic Reform in Poland

Józef Pajestka

The socialist economy, society and socialist central planning in particular have developed so much over the past decades that some revaluation of the underlying concepts and premisses now seems desirable. Such a revaluation is called for not only because of the accumulation of ideas and evidence, but also because the socialist socioeconomic reality is showing important new directions of change, both within national boundaries and worldwide. Patterns of thought have to be adapted to this changing reality. Man should not become a servant of his creations, and this holds true for ideas as well. Thus these new directions of change call for a new conceptualisation in the field of the socialist economy with a view to elaborating the most desirable institutions and policies for the future. This conceptualisation is the main subject of this chapter.

Although my argument is based largely on the Polish experience, the chapter is not limited to the 'Polish case'. My intention is rather to raise issues of relevance to all countries under 'really existing socialism'.

The progress of human civilisation has been shaped by our growing capabilities as individuals to act consciously – that is, to base our behaviour on purposeful and deliberate activity. To act consciously individually is not tantamount, however, to the conscious shaping of socioeconomic processes within a wider societal framework. The latter concerns a pattern of human interactions, of relations and institutions, which may – but not always – be conducive to integrated societal guidance.

The conscious shaping of socioeconomic processes is also a desirable model of human behaviour, one based on a praxeological principle and widely acknowledged nowadays. Within European culture the age of Enlightenment ushered in an understanding of reality in terms of rational behaviour. This idea was only one step away from the paradigm of the conscious shaping of socioeconomic processes. It is by taking this step that the socialist theory of planning came about. The paradigm has found ever wider acceptance, and recently there has been a tendency to apply it even to global economic processes. Formulation of the new international economic order and international development strategy would, if successfully implemented, be a further step in this direction.

Seen as a praxeological principle, the conscious shaping of processes is based on cognisance of the present, utilising all available knowledge and experience, and on anticipation of the future which, although necessarily formed on the basis of past experience, nevertheless reflects the unique capability of the human mind. It is also based on value judgements – that is, on judgements of what is just and rational. Both comprehension (including anticipation) and value judgements involve aims and objectives, as well as ways and means. Thus one can state that to act consciously is tantamount to acting with cognisance of what one wants to attain and how best to achieve it. The last point can be subdivided by discerning: (a) with what material means and (b) in what ways. In the context of economic reforms the ways relate particularly to institutions and policies.

The praxeological principle of the conscious shaping of socioeconomic processes, as explained above, seems a worthy general directive to adopt in development planning. It has not, however, taken this form in Eastern Europe. The concept of planning, as developed in theory and applied in practice, has in fact narrowed down the sphere of the conscious shaping of reality.

According to the initial theoretical premises, planning was conceived as operating mainly in the sphere of the 'exchange system', by being a substitute for markets in solving the problem of the allocation of resources. This allocative function of planning, still emphasised by the bureaucratic mode of thinking, has overshadowed other functions and has led to the neglect of some of the most important aspects of the development process and socioeconomic change. National planning in socialist countries has in fact been so overburdened with allocative functions, which it was anyway incapable of performing properly, that the other, sometimes more crucial, development problems were neglected or sent into oblivion.

For a long time the problems connected with societal values and aims were largely forgotten. After major changes of socialist character in the socio-institutional sphere, further changes have been on the agenda of development planning only to a very limited extent. They have reappeared in recent years, though sometimes with great pain and difficulty. This experience demonstrates that concern for continuous socio-institutional change is indispensable in development planning.

It can be seen that although the social, moral and institutional issues have been somewhat neglected in the past, their significance is growing in line with the development process and historical change. This growing significance reflects new tendencies in societal behaviour. Planning has to adapt to cope with these tendencies.

The primary theoretical element of socialist planning can be seen in the concept of macroeconomic rationality, as opposed to the economic efficiency of an individual firm. This theoretical orientation came from a critical appraisal of the capitalist economy in which microeconomic efficiency paralleled great macroeconomic irrationality; the latter could be seen in periodic crises, mass unemployment, great social discrepancies, and lack of purposeful long-term orientation. It was the concept of macroeconomic purposefulness and rationality, viewed as a corollary of social ownership of the means of production, which was the central idea of political organisation in socialist society, in the national planning system, and in the socialist management system. Looking at the development process historically, it can be stated that this theoretical orientation initially helped to overcome the inherited structural and social disproportions, and to frame new structures favourable for self-sustained development. But further on in the development process, this central idea, with all its implied institutional solutions, has been showing ever greater deficiencies.

It is my view that it is now necessary for the socialist countries to attain a new balance between macro-rationality and micro-rationality. Institutionalisation of macroeconomic rationality is indispensable, but the point is that it should not be carried out in a way that eliminates the necessary conditions for rational behaviour at the micro-level. One cannot have sound general development unless it is based on rational and dynamic behaviour of firms and other social and economic organisms.

The core of the problem does not lie in a theoretical acceptance of the indicated proposition, which may even sound like a cliché. It lies in its institutional implications. Creating the conditions for micro-rationality requires appropriate institutional change. Without going into sophisticated arguments here, a somewhat simplified conclusion can be presented as acknowledging the need for three basic institutions: real money, the market mechanism, and the independent firm. Although this again may sound to many like a cliché, it must be appreciated that the creation of these institutions really involves a radical change of the initial institutional premisses.

Economic reforms carried out today in a number of socialist countries can be characterised by the following elements: firm installation of the above three institutions; their marriage with central, strategic planning; and observance of the principle of social justice in guiding the economy. It is to be noted, however, that the necessary institutional changes encounter serious obstacles, both theoretically and in practice. The socialist countries do not, as is sometimes claimed, possess an 'automatic' facility in undertaking institutional change; such change seems to be as difficult to implement in those countries as elsewhere.

DETERMINANTS OF INSTITUTIONAL CHANGE IN POLAND

The identification of factors and forces operating in the field of institutional change is difficult and subject to uncertainty. Still, some analytical insights into future conditions and tendencies may be attempted from which, in turn, conclusions allowing for more rational policies may be deduced.

Hypotheses and expectations of future tendencies must be continually verified. This type of verification is necessary in every area of science; it is also indispensable in economic policy. For we have here an exceptionally difficult process of cognition where we find not only highly diversified causal factors but also characteristics of behaviour which may undergo changes in the process of time.

Notwithstanding the difficulties and uncertainties, there appears to be a great need for scientific analysis and anticipation of the future. This is necessary if we aim at increasing rationality in current policy. We cannot act rationally in investment projects unless we consider future conditions. Myopia is no less harmful in undertakings related to the mode of functioning of the economy and society.

In anticipating future tendencies in Poland, I assume that a certain number of determinants of change in the economic system can be identified. By 'determinants' I mean features of the development process which operate as causal reasons for progress, with strong implications for institutional solutions. Some such determinants of change in the Polish economic system are the following:

(i) Societal aspirations and the political system can be expected to continue to exercise a strong drive for economic progress. It can be anticipated that, against the background of historical experience, this drive will strengthen the position of rational pragmatism, which will mean a very open attitude in the search for institutional solutions aimed at maximising economic efficiency.

(ii) Educational and cultural advancement of the people has already been the main driving force of institutional and political change. In addition, the human factor is of growing importance in the economic process. Thus both operating societal forces and the logic of the development process will continue to demand adequate solutions. Conclusions should be drawn from this for shaping the enterprise culture of the nation and the political system of the country. The creativity of the people cannot be limited to economic management only. Those who are creative in the economy demand active participation in all aspects of decision-making, including the political.

(iii) The growing importance of scientific-technological advance and worldwide high innovative dynamism are commonly acknowledged. Both have important implications for Polish internal development as well as the country's ability to participate in international exchange. Compared with the initial, somewhat autarkic policies, far-reaching change should be expected. In the past, the creation of basic conditions for self-engineered growth was considered to be the right policy, while nowadays the inclusion of the economy in an international division of labour has become a cardinal requirement for prosperous development. This requirement necessitates adequate – indeed, radical – institutional and policy changes.

(iv) The development process leads to growing economic interdependence; it increases the need for flexibility in economic relations and brings forth diversified and complex features of human needs. All these changes require adequate measures in the area of co-ordinating economic activities. Experience shows that this cannot be accomplished by any administrative method, and that the only way out is the establishment of a market mechanism. It should be expected that the organisation and guidance of the market mechanism, adapted to various internal requirements as well as in response to external factors, will be of crucial importance for improving efficiency.

(v) The growing need of the people to participate in shaping the course of socioeconomic development demands adequate institutional and political solutions. There are no grounds for expecting that aspirations to participate in self-management and on various public platforms will decrease or vanish. On the contrary, one should expect further limitation of the various elitist institutions and procedures and strengthening of the pressure for democratic solutions. The corresponding line of institutional change should be advanced.

TECHNOCRATIC-CONSERVATIVE OPPOSITION

In any analysis of factors that determine socioeconomic processes, the forces which oppose the institutional changes outlined above are an important feature. They are referred to here as the technocratic-conservative groups. These groups have a mechanistic understanding of the development process; they fail to comprehend the complicated and changing nature of development interrelations and display ignorance, partisan interests and an emotional stand inimical to change. It seems worth observing that these opposing forces voice no theory of a counter-reformatory type. They operate more like a blind force of resistance to change.

In reviewing the odds of success for technocratic-conservatism it is useful to recall a recent historical experience. There is a close similarity between the opposing forces appearing at present and those which managed to check the reforms in the mid-1970s. If such a negative action proved effective in the past, why can it not be so now? There seems to be a clear answer to this question. Changed historical conditions make a recurrence of the earlier experience unlikely. In the mid-1970s the reform was killed by an influential section of the bureaucratic elite. This was achieved thanks to the favourable opportunity offered by foreign credits which became a substitute for both the reform and the necessary structural adjustments. But this substitute policy had no prospects in the long run. A prominent feature of the conservative position is, therefore, lack of shrewd foresight. This feature of conservative forces can be found in different forms all over the world. Today the country cannot incur more debts or draw on other resources which would provide the mainstay for the survival of technocratic conservatism. The role it played in the past cannot be repeated. The only way out for the country now is to raise efficiency, to be innovative and to undertake sound structural changes. All this calls for the institutional changes outlined above, not for continuation of old methods.

Conservatism is basing its faith in strong central pressure and stringent controls over all socioeconomic processes, but the Polish state is no longer capable of mobilising this type of force. Neither the superior authorities nor the lower ranks are capable of restoring the system of relations and the institutions of the initial stages of industrialisation.

Conservative communist technocracy has, I think, no chance of survival in the long term, for it proposes no solutions to the problems which determine the country's progress. From the perspective of today it would appear that, for the first time since 1945 the odds are, in Poland, against such technocratic conservatism in the field of economic reform with its associated institutional and political change.

EGALITARIANISM, WELFARE STATE AND MOTIVATIONS FOR PROGRESS

Socialism has brought with it the promise of economic superiority and social justice. These two ideas have been deeply rooted in the social consciousness and exercised a profound impact on real processes. The functioning of the socialist economy has also been under their influence. The institutional set-up and all the economic mechanisms should be seen to be strongly linked with these ideological premisses.

Due to these initial premisses and the policies inspired by them (for example in the field of employment, education, and so on), socialism gave rise to particular expectations, leading to strong egalitarian tendencies among a wide social stratum. Egalitarianism has deep roots in socialist society. Historically exploited groups, people from the social margin, handicapped people, and others perceived that socialism was offering them a great new opportunity and pressed for its realisation in the name of equality – in my view, the dominating idea.

It is nowadays possible to evaluate *ex post*, on the basis of real historical experience, the effects of the revolution of aspirations under socialism.

It seems worth observing that unleashing wide societal aspirations has become, first of all, a most powerful factor in socioeconomic progress. It has lain behind the strong drive aimed at fast economic growth, shared by both societal forces and the state. A nation without aspirations can never become dynamic. Imparting aspirations to society can therefore be considered an initial step in development policy.

In the course of development, however, this element of socioeconomic mechanism can change. In Poland a wide gap developed between aspirations and their realisation. This led to great social frustration and discontent, sociopolitical manifestations of disapproval and conflict, and the weakening of the state in performing the function of protecting long-run societal interests. As a result, the rate of progress slowed down. This historical experience gives grounds for an observation that the economic policy of the central authorities was evidently incapable of converting aspirations for change into strong motivations for progress. It was, of course, not the policy alone which was responsible for the final outcome, but the ideology and the institutional mechanism themselves also influenced the policy.

This deterioration was taking place with increasing intensity throughout most of post-war Poland. It was neither clearly perceived nor understood by analysts or policy-makers. Its impact on the social consciousness and on patterns of economic behaviour is, however, evident today. It is like a social disease in need of a cure. The search for a cure should indeed be one of the long-term aims of the economic reform. The reform should bring about changes that would prevent egalitarianism from undermining the motivation for economic advance; it should not allow human aspirations to undermine social discipline and the capability of the state to carry out long-term policy goals but should make them instead a strong motivation for progress.

These changes cannot be realised in a short period of time, so they must remain a long-term aim of the reform, to be supported by appropriate ideological premises. Polish reform has only started to acquire this orientation. The reformers are still fighting against initial obstacles and difficulties, attempting to overcome hostile forces and unfavourable external conditions. There does, however, exist an understanding that reforming the laws and institutions can be effective only if it leads to a change in patterns of human behaviour. Since this requires time, it has to be a long-term aim.

This long-term aim of the reform should be achieved through practical policies, of which the most important are the following:

(a) The policy of employment, bearing in mind that economic pressure through large-scale unemployment must be ruled out. A solution must therefore be found that would prevent the labour market from undermining the motivation for good work. If such a solution does not exist or is not found for other reasons, a conflict between the principle of full employment and the efficiency aim of the reform will have to be faced.

(b) The financial arrangements, including pricing, and other antiquated policies which allow every firm to survive irrespective of whether or not it brings losses to society. The Polish reform promises to start a radical change in this field. A law on bankruptcy has been adopted by the Polish *Sejm*, but although it has been applied in a few cases, it falls far short of the widespread implementation demanded by the iron logic of economic efficiency. Although justice is usually referred to in human relationships, it has long been applied to economic organisations as well. It would be too problematic to try to rescind this extended application now.

(c) The incomes and wages policy has been changed to ensure stronger motivation for good work, but it is very doubtful whether the changes are sufficient. There still seems to be a long way to go before a real improvement of the remuneration system is achieved.

It should be clear from the above that in an attempt to install a new linkage between social justice and the motivation for good work, economic reform is only a beginning. Human expectations still operate along old patterns. They appear in the form of social and political pressures to redistribute what is produced rather than as motivations for dynamic enterprise, fast innovation and high productivity. The conviction still prevails in national psychology that the success of an individual is determined more by the state than by his or her own activity. This paternalistic view is perhaps most strongly felt in this particular area of policy.

Developing strong motivations for economic progress in Poland appears only on the banner of future intentions. To delude oneself that 'the reform has already been introduced', that the matter is already settled, is to embark on the road of ineffective activity. Without an orientation towards new types of social relations, new value systems, there is no chance for effective action. Polish reform has so far touched only the surface of institutions and regulations, leaving the substance of human values and attitudes almost unchanged.

A system of relations, called the welfare state, has taken form in the struggle for social justice. The struggle for justice and the functions of the socialist state have by their nature led to the state becoming the main enforcer of this justice. Justice has many aspects, but one of them is equality of opportunity in education, care for handicapped people, good living conditions in old age, and so on. All these can be embraced by the concept of the welfare state. There seem to be no grounds for radical criticism of these functions and of this aspect of the nature of the socialist state.

Historical experience shows, however, that a certain critical attitude to the social (welfare) functions of the state is justified. Two problems emerge in this context. We have already discussed the first: that in performing the social functions, the state takes care not to undermine the motivations for good work. The second is an appropriate division of duties between the state and the family.

At one time the view was advanced that the socialist state should take over many functions of the family. In the light of historical experience, this does not seem feasible in the foreseeable future. In Poland it has been rejected strongly. We can and must, therefore, take a new systematic look at the division of responsibility between the state and the family, with a view to studying its motivational implications. New solutions are sought in this field, but it is not in this area that I wish to raise an issue of importance.

A major problem for the institutional set-up is the development of features of the welfare state not so much in relations between the state and the citizen as between the state and enterprises as well as other economic organisations. No justification of the existing relations of the latter type can be found in the principles of socialism. Socialist ideology used to put great emphasis on social justice, but it has never demanded justice for enterprises. Much can be said about the rise of state patronage over firms. In my opinion, its origin lies in a specific syndrome of institutionalised interests. In Poland, one important role has been a peculiar institutional development in which the alignment of the so-called branch ministries directly defending specific interests has gained in strength, while the institutions supposed to defend the general societal interests grew weak.

Leaving the historical evaluations aside, I would like to conclude the above analysis as follows:

(a) There can be no strong motivation for economic progress in economic organisations if their relations with the state continue to be shaped along the pattern of a 'welfare state'. This old institutional pattern tends to direct the efforts of enterprises not towards the struggle for efficiency but instead towards gaining income through various methods of influencing the state authorities.

(b) A welfare state for firms is essentially a very soft state, and as long as it remains such in relations with the people as workers, it is hard on the people as consumers. In such a system a lasting sociopolitical balance cannot be ensured.

(c) Experience shows that when taking this position, the state does not exert enough economic pressure on firms to be efficient and therefore is not in a position to programme and to implement necessary structural changes. These phenomena are clearly visible in the working of the Polish reform, precisely thanks to the circumstances by which it not only failed to change the paternalistic attitudes of the state apparatus to enterprises, but may even have strengthened them.

(d) Institutional transformations must be considered from the point of view of maintaining a proper balance of power between, on the one hand, the central government, which is supposed to protect long-term national interests, and, on the other, industries and regions. There is evidence to show that the wrong balance may seriously upset the prosperous development of the country.

While many aspects of institutional change have to be watched carefully, the crucial objective of the Polish reform is to change the economic relations between the state apparatus and enterprises, by departing from the paternalistic, welfare-state pattern. Without achieving this objective, not much benefit can be expected from the reform.

Part IV
Developing Countries

12 Testing the Soviet-Type Industrialisation Model in Socialist-Orientated Developing Countries

Wladimir Andreff

The so-called planned industrialisation model, one geared towards economic development based on state ownership and heavy industry, had spread to several Third World countries in the 1960s and 1970s. Its adoption was generally considered a symbol of political liberation and the best hope for economic self-sufficiency. Between 1960 and 1976, 1369 affiliates of transnational corporations were nationalised in the Third World, mainly in those countries which were implementing a socialist-orientated strategy of development.

In the 1980s planning and building of heavy industry no longer remain fashionable in most of the Third World, including some socialist-orientated developing countries. More policy U-turns might well appear in the future, as has already been the case in Ghana, Egypt and Somalia, and today the traditional socialist avenue is no longer seen as clearly the best. It has even been suggested that socialist-orientated developing countries (SODCs) have lost their illusions about, and their faith in, Soviet-type development (Laidi, 1984).

However, we must be careful about today's preoccupation with a simple-minded anti-Soviet or anti-socialist trend of thought. For this reason we intend, in this chapter, to assess – data permitting – the economic performance of the SODCs on more objective grounds.

1 THE MODEL OF SOCIALIST DEVELOPMENT

Our definition of the model in question is in terms of six economic features and one political characteristic. These are as follows:

(i) Agrarian reform, amounting more or less to land collectivisation and the setting up of co-operatives or even state farms;

(ii)   Nationalisation of the major part of industry and the whole banking system;

(iii) Economic development through centralisation and directive planning;

(iv)   Highest priority in medium-term plans to industry, and within industry to the production of investment goods and heavy intermediate inputs (Andreff and Hayab, 1978);

(v)   A decrease in the amount, or at least in the share, of foreign trade with the former parent state, linked with a diversion of trade to new partners, including Comecon countries and perhaps China;

(vi)   Legal obstacles to new direct foreign investment, which may go as far as the prohibition of new ventures and the renegotiation of existing agreements between the state and the transnational corporations, affiliates of which are allowed to operate;

(vii) A socialist or Marxist–Leninist political ideology, resting on a single-party system; a centralised system of power trying to control each individual is often a major outcome of this system.

These seven systemic features enable us to distinguish the SODCs from all the developing countries. In some countries one or more of the features may be at the level of wishful thinking rather than real fact. I include these countries in my sample of SODCs if their leaders are able to push them sufficiently close to the model of socialist industrialisation development. This remains true whatever differences may exist among the SODCs with respect to their resource endowments or level of economic development. Indeed, there are similarities in the economic organisation of a poor socialist-orientated country, such as Ethiopia, and a semi-industrialised country, such as Algeria, or even most Comecon countries. Thus the word 'model' is used here not to mean something exemplary but to specify the common pattern of SODCs, whose economic performance is to be appraised.

2   THE SAMPLE OF SOCIALIST-ORIENTATED DEVELOPING COUNTRIES

The Hungarian economist Jańos Kornai has suggested that 'in the world, twenty-seven countries are headed by a Marxist–Leninist

Party, are based on a state sector in industry, transport and banking , and are economies subjected to centralised planning and management' (Kornai and Richet, 1986). If we exclude the USSR and the six European members of the Comecon, which are the remaining countries that Kornai had in mind? No precise answer can be found in his writings, nor in the economic literature dealing with the Third World.

In an attempt to determine the boundaries of the so-called 'New Communist Third World', Wiles (1982) has divided all socialist countries into four groups. The first group comprises Comecon members: the USSR, six countries of Eastern Europe, Cuba, Mongolia and Vietnam. The second group includes countries which are clearly socialist, but not Comecon members: Albania, China, North Korea and Yugoslavia. To the third belongs the true 'New Communist Third World': Afghanistan, Angola, Ethiopia, Mozambique and South Yemen. Here Wiles's criterion is political: voting in favour of the Soviet motion on Afghanistan at the United Nations in January 1980 (notice that Grenada and Laos also voted in favour, but were not included). The fourth group comprises the supposed socialist countries such as Benin, Congo, Guyana and Madagascar, as well as Somalia, which has since changed its political system and policy. Wiles's classification is now outdated. Tiraspolsky (1983) added to the countries listed above Nicaragua and Seychelles as having moved close to the socialist model of development.

With a glance at the Soviet ranking of developing countries, as analysed by Lavigne (1986a), we can update the sample. The Soviet Union regards as socialist, and not just developing, the following countries: Cuba, Mongolia and Vietnam in the Comecon group, and also Albania, China, Kampuchea, Laos, North Korea and Yugoslavia. The Soviets then distinguish six developing countries with a 'confirmed' socialist orientation and nine with an 'asserted' socialist orientation. The six happen to be countries which are all observers at Comecon sessions. In countries of the 'asserted' category, the political party in power is not Marxist–Leninist in the Soviet view.

Given this Soviet classification, the SODCs which I am going to study are the following:

(1) Comecon members: Cuba, Mongolia and Vietnam.
(2) Developing countries outside Comecon, but considered by the Soviet Union as socialist. Of the six such countries, I shall include in my sample only Kampuchea, Laos and North Korea. The

other three, Albania, China and Yugoslavia, have specific characteristics which make them special cases.

(3) Developing countries with a confirmed socialist orientation: Afghanistan, Angola, Ethiopia, Mozambique, Nicaragua (since 1984) and South Yemen.

(4) Developing countries with an asserted socialist orientation: Algeria, Benin, Burma, Congo, Guinea (up to 1984), Iraq, Madagascar, Syria and Tanzania.

There are twenty-one countries in the four groups listed above.

It may be argued that other countries, such as the Cape Verde Islands, Grenada, Guinea-Bissau, Guyana, Libya, São Tomé e Principe, Seychelles, Zambia or Zimbabwe, should be included as well. Almost all these countries also claim to be on the path of planned industrialisation development and to be building a socialist economy, albeit in a pragmatic way. I exclude them from the sample of SODCs on the grounds of their being too heterogeneous, small and insular.

The twenty-one selected SODCs are a highly diversified lot. Ranked by GNP *per capita*, they are of three categories: the least-developed, middle-income and newly industrialised countries. To the least-developed category belong Kampuchea, Laos, Ethiopia, Burma, Afghanistan, Tanzania,Vietnam, Guinea, Benin, Madagascar and Mozambique, all with less than US $400 *per capita* in 1981 (in 1981 prices). To the middle-income category belong South Yemen, Angola, Nicaragua, Cuba, Congo, Mongolia, North Korea and Syria, with GNP *per capita* between US $400 and $1600 (1981 prices) in 1981. Only Iraq and Algeria can be regarded as newly industrialised, with GNP *per capita* standing at more than US $1600 (1981 prices).

3   AN ASSESSMENT OF ECONOMIC PERFORMANCE IN SOCIALIST-ORIENTATED DEVELOPING COUNTRIES

Table 12.1 contains data for an overall assessment of economic performance of nine SODCs for the years 1983 to 1985. It should be noted that Cuba's Total Social Product (TSP) may not be a good measure of the country's real value added, and that the Burmese data are of poor quality. Given this, the rates of economic growth are only moderate, when they are not actually negative. As for the rate of inflation, it is on a par with the rest of the Third World. The only

Table 12.1   *The Economic Growth in Nine Socialist-Orientated Developing Countries*

	Rate of growth of the national product (in constant prices)			GNP *per capita**		Rate of inflation	
	Index	1983	1984	1985	1984	1983	1984	1985
Algeria	GNP	0.1	0	6.0	2 410	5.7	6.6	8.5
Burma	GDP	5.6	6.1	6.6	180	7.1	8.5	4.2
Congo PR	GDP	n.a	−3.0	n.a	1 140	9.2	14.7	n.a
Cuba	TSP	5.2	7.4	4.8	2 930†	1.1	−0.7	n.a
Ethiopia	GDP	7.4	−7.0	n.a	110	−2.3	8.4	19.0
Madagascar	GDP	0.9	1.6	−1.5	260	14.2	11.8	14.0
Nicaragua	GDP	5.1	0.5	−2.5	860	32.9	53.2	334.4
Syria	GDP	5.8	n.a	−1.0	1 620	8.2	16.6	22.2
Tanzania	GDP	−1.2	2.5	n.a	210	26.5	38.4	6.5

NOTE   * In US dollars
      † TSP *per capita* GNP: Gross National Product; GDP: Gross Domestic Product; TSP: Total Social Product

SOURCES   World Bank and United Nations.

exception is Cuba, where the price index may, however, not reveal total inflationary pressure.

A longer-term and more comprehensive assessment may be obtained by noting how the ranking of our twenty-one countries, according to the World Bank estimates of GNP *per capita*, has changed over time. If the growth of the GNP *per capita* in a given country is faster than it is in neighbouring countries, its rank may improve. Bearing this in mind, let us look at the changes in rank between 1976 and 1983. Eight of our twenty-one SODCs did improve their ranking, another eight regressed and three remained steady. To the first group belong Algeria, Angola, Benin, Burma, Congo, Ethiopia, Guinea, Mozambique, Syria and, above all, North Korea, which overtook twenty countries within these eight years. Growth was below average in Afghanistan, Cuba, Iraq, Kampuchea, Laos, Mongolia, Nicaragua and Tanzania (Nicaragua has been implementing the model only since 1979). Growth was around the average in Madagascar, Vietnam and South Yemen.

A further general assessment of SODCs' performance may be based on the foreign trade balance and external indebtedness (Table

Table 12.2 *Foreign Trade Balance and Foreign Debt of the Socialist-Orientated Developing Countries* (million dollars)

	Foreign Trade Balance		Gross Foreign Debt (GFD)	Estimated ratio of the GFD to National Product[1]
	1982	1985	1985	
Afghanistan	−407	−410	1 434	47[2]
Algeria	+2 400	+2 700	24 013	44
Angola	+ 840	n.a.	1 403	55[2]
Benin	−855	−338	777	61
Burma	+132	+21	3 873	46
Congo PR	+260	+482	2 756	110
Cuba	−800	−2 160	7 035	20[2]
Ethiopia	−458	−550	2 008	37
Guinea	+143	+95	1 432	65
Iraq	−10 151	+2 007	11 632	19[2]
Kampuchea	−264	−190	522	n.a.
Korea DR	−272	−771	1 128	5[2]
Laos PDR	−180	−120	528	n.a.
Madagascar	−184	−83	2 590	104
Mongolia	− 47	−327	4 397	n.a.
Mozambique	−498	−573	1 442	62[2]
Nicaragua	−320	−515	5 405	165
Syria	−1 500	−2 085	4 201	22
Tanzania	−409	−744	3 374	67
Viet Nam	−1 490	n.a.	5 477	n.a.
Yemen PDR'	−559	−446	1 708	111

[1] The last year available, either 1984 or 1985; usually the ratio is GFD/GNP, in per cent.

[2] The ratio is GFD/GDP.

NOTES For Iraq, figures do not include trade and debt for military purposes. The data are 1982 instead of 1983 in the case of the trade balance of Benin, Guinea, Iraq and Nicaragua; n.a. = not available.

SOURCES IMF International Financial Statistics for trade balances; OECD Foreign Debt Statistics for debts.

12. 2). From 1983 to 1985 the trade balance was negative in all the SODCs except the following: oil-exporting countries (Algeria, Angola and Congo), an exporter of bauxite, gold and diamonds (Guinea), and Burma. In fact, for Burma the International Monetary Fund estimated that in 1982 only one-half of Burmese imports was

registered by customs. Its exports are also uncertain, given that opium is a major export item.

Given the data, it is not surprising to see foreign debt increasing in all the SODCs. The oil-exporting countries Algeria and Iraq[1] are two of the main world debtors. The position of many SODCs, in terms of the ratio of the gross foreign debt to national product, might be regarded as even worse than that of major debtors. Indeed, this ratio ranges from moderate levels for North Korea, Cuba and Syria to a very high level of about 100 per cent in Congo, Madagascar and South Yemen and an incredible 165 per cent in Nicaragua. Needless to say, these four countries survive today by refusing to service the debt.

In the post-1973 period, phenomena such as slowdown in economic growth, high inflation, growing foreign debt and a high level of indebtedness are all quite common in the Third World. Nevertheless, the data show that the model of planned socialist development has failed to protect the socialist countries from these ills, especially from slow development and foreign debt.[2] To these common problems the model seems to have added specific gross failures of its own, connected with overcentralisation of economic power, poor incentives for producers in the state sector, peasant opposition to collectivisation, and the 'gigantomania' arising from the priority given to heavy industry. These additional problems emerge clearly from case studies (Andreff, 1987). The experience of the various countries with the model can be summarised as follows:

(a) Unworkable applications of the model

In some countries, this may be due to a low endowment of natural resources or the small size of the economy, or a lack of manpower. It appears particularly difficult to turn the model into reality in economies which are too poor and too agrarian. This is our first conclusion. The examples of such countries are Benin, Ethiopia, Kampuchea, Laos, Madagascar and Tanzania.

Let us elaborate on the case of Tanzania, which has sometimes been taken as a 'perfect failure' of the model (Weaver and Kronemer, 1981). Even Julius Nyerere, the former Tanzanian leader, admitted the failure of his strategy of development when he gave up power voluntarily in 1985 (a rare occurrence in the Third World). This strategy was based on creating *ujamaa* villages, in which villagers would be allowed to farm private plots but would also be expected to work together on communal farms to produce a marketable crop. The second aim of the strategy, which was a special feature of the third plan (1976–81), was to create an industry producing basic goods. Although the share of the state sector increased in Tanzanian industry, the weight of industrial output in GNP decreased from 10 per cent in 1974 to less than 8 per cent in 1980 (Tiberghien, 1983). This occurred despite the building of new factories after 1976 (such as those preparing cashew nuts), cement plants, and industrial units in textiles, steel, chemical products, wood and paper (Kuuya, 1983). In 1980 all these units were working below their capacity: at 70 per cent in the tobacco industry, 50 per cent in the steel industry, 45 per cent in cement plants and 15 per cent in the bicycle factory. In 1984 all the factories were working at between 20 and 40 per cent of their capacity. Low productivity and mismanagement of state enterprises led to large deficits in the state budget. In spite of *ujamaa* villages, the growth of food was not much higher than the growth of the population. After so much hope, the Tanzanian experience had already clearly disappointed its supporters some years ago (Hirschbein, 1981).

(b) Diluted applications of the model

In those countries in which the model was implemented in a highly diluted form there is no convincing proof it was unworkable as such, since it was altered almost from the beginning. The relevant cases are Burma (Fenichel and Azfar Khan, 1981), Iraq, Mozambique, Nicaragua and Syria (Gottheil, 1981). A short glance at Mozambique will illustrate this. In 1977 Mozambican leaders decided that 'agriculture comes first to service local food requirements and industrial development, and that industry is to become the dynamising factor' (Saul, 1979). Between 1977 and 1980 heavy industry, however, regressed in the priorities of the government, the share of industrial output in GNP falling from 9.4 per cent in 1975 to 8.8 per cent in 1981. Communal villages were created very quickly after 1977, but the agricultural output steadily decreased until 1984. Food shortages, rationing, black market and price increases of food products made life more difficult for the people. This was exacerbated by the 1984 drought and cyclone. The situation was so difficult that as early as 1980 Mozambique embarked on economic reform by privatising some industrial plants. A monetary reform replaced the overvalued escudo by the low-valued metical. Mozambique seemed to be set on a course towards a mixed economy, with the coexistence of plan and market as its permanent feature (Kofi, 1981). The share of Comecon countries in Mozambican foreign trade has since remained low. Mozambique's application to join Comecon was rejected in July 1981. Under the pressure of its growing foreign debt, Mozambique finally joined the World Bank and the International Monetary Fund, signed the Lomé agreement with the EEC and obtained economic aid from the United States. The Club de Paris rescheduled the Mozambican debt in June 1987.

(c) Unsuccessful applications of the model

The model has been unsuccessfully implemented in some countries, usually those obtaining a large 'rent' by extracting and selling unprocessed minerals or crude oil in a period when world prices for these products were high. Here an exogenous factor has boosted economic performance. The SODCs which have enjoyed such a rent are Algeria, Angola, Congo, Guinea, Iraq and Syria. Apart from Iraq, all these countries have grown fairly fast, the best-known example probably being Algeria. In Algeria, the share of industry in GNP has increased steadily. Oil and gas form 98.5 per cent of total exports and other mineral products account for 1.1 per cent. Since the downturn of world oil prices in 1982, Algeria has striven to prepare itself for the post-oil era by changing the usual priorities of medium-term plans. The 1985–9 plan no longer gives priority to heavy industries. Instead, high priority is given to agriculture, self-reliance in food, health and other social activities, as well as to decentralising the economy. State trusts were dismantled by 1980. The private sector has increasingly enjoyed official support. In the 1986 budget incentives to export were voted in, and in December 1986 an austerity programme was passed. Hence it appears that the model did work in Algeria so long as oil prices and the associated rent were high. After the turning point on the world market, Algeria abandoned much of the substance of the original model.

(d) Aid-dependent countries for a successful model

The aid in question flows from Comecon countries. This aid plays the same role as does the rent in cases of category (c). Four countries are involved: Cuba, Mongolia, Vietnam, and Afghanistan. In 1981

Vietnam was given 35 per cent of total Comecon aid allocated to
Third World countries, with Cuba obtaining 26 per cent and Afghanistan 10 per cent. Moreover, their foreign trade is concentrated on
exchanges with Comecon countries. A good share of this trade is
subsidised by the Soviet Union and the six European Comecon
countries. Cuba sells sugar and nickel to Comecon countries at prices
above their world levels and buys oil at a price below the world level.[3]
From 1961 to 1978, such subsidies reached 21 per cent of total
Comecon aid to Cuba. The same degree of subsidisation is in evidence
in the case of Soviet–Vietnamese trade (Theriot and Matheson,
1979). Comecon aid is complemented by a certain measure of direct
investment within the four countries. In 1981, more than 50 per cent
of the Afghan national product was accounted for by factories built
with Soviet assistance. Until 1982 the Soviet Union co-operated in
565 Cuban plants, of which 264 were industrial. In Mongolia, 100 per
cent of wood production, 90 per cent of copper mining, 70 per cent of
energy production are provided by factories built with Soviet aid
(Kahn, 1984). Such factories account for some 35 per cent of the
Mongolian GNP. The Soviet Union financed 60 per cent of all
investment in Vietnam between 1976 and 1980. In Afghanistan,
Soviet funds reached 91 per cent of all foreign finance between 1980
and 1982 (Mathonnat, 1985).

In spite of Comecon aid, these four countries are heavily indebted
to Western countries as well. Cuban debt to the Soviet Union was
rescheduled several times, but Cuba also accumulated a $3.4 billion
debt with Western creditors and was forced to reschedule after 1982
(Acciaris, 1984). Vietnam is in debt to the tune of $3.2 billion to
Comecon and $1.7 billion in hard currencies (in 1984). Since 1983 it
has been compelled to negotiate rescheduling with Japan, Algeria
and Libya. On the advice of the International Monetary Fund, the
dong has had to be devalued several times since 1985.

(e) Private-sector and foreign investment implementation of the model

Paradoxically, in some countries the socialist model is being implemented with the help of a private sector composed of foreign investment and transnational corporations. Zimbabwe and Zambia are the
best cases in point. This is possibly one of the reasons why the Soviet
Union does not include them in the official listing of SODCs. In
Zambia, foreign companies keep a 49 per cent share in the capital of

'Zambianised' enterprises. This share is low enough to keep the country's controlling interest and high enough to ensure access to modern technology and new capital. In Zimbabwe, political leaders have married socialist rhetoric with a strong economic pragmatism. Key sectors of the economy are in the hands of transnational corporations, such as Turner & Newall, Union Carbide, Lonrho, Anglo-American and Heinz. The Zimbabwean plan (1982–5) was welcomed by businessmen in the private sector (Bobo, 1983).

There is evidence also of foreign interest to some extent diluting the model in the more orthodox SODCs. Vietnam passed a law welcoming direct foreign investment as early as 1977. It was a flop. A new law passed in 1987 is among the most liberal in the world. Burma published in 1973 the first list of sectors open to private investment, and in 1974 the state rehabilitated sixty-eight former owners in their property rights over enterprises. The Tanzanian National Agricultural Policy now provides incentives for creating private plantations with foreign shares. Benin welcomes direct foreign investment. In Cabinda, oil is still extracted by Gulf Oil, but the Angolan State has also attracted Texaco, Total, Elf, Petrobras, Nafta, Agip and Mobil.

All in all, more than half of the twenty-one SODCs have based the model of planned industrialisation development on extraneous factors. A prime example of this strategy is South Yemen, combining Comecon aid (Al Khadat, 1985) with repatriated incomes of Yemeni migrant workers (Cigar, 1985). One-third of the Yemeni labour force works abroad, bringing home incomes in hard currencies which cover 50 to 75 per cent of the foreign trade deficit.

(f) The odd case of North Korea

Compared with the other SODCs, North Korea performs well. The planned industrialisation model has been implemented in an orthodox manner, strongly resembling Eastern European experiences of the late 1940s and the 1950s. In 1945, North Korea inherited an industrial base set up largely by the Japanese. Still, the share of industry in the national material product grew from 28 per cent in 1946 to 74 per cent in 1969 (Brillouet, 1975). The country is well endowed with raw materials and energy, but its exports of these products are limited. Self-reliant for 92 per cent of its energy consumption (Sokoloff, 1984) and for its food, the country had developed the production of electricity, steel, cement, fertilisers, and textiles (Breidenstein, 1975) fairly successfully. On the other hand, compared with South Korea, North Korea has, since the end of the 1960s, increasingly been lagging behind, especially in the production of consumer durables and electronics.

Despite occasional Soviet or Chinese aid, North Korea is probably one of the least dependent among the SODCs. Its foreign trade in 1979 was distributed between socialist countries (51 per cent), developed market economies (24 per cent), and developing countries account for the remaining 25 per cent (Brillouet, 1983). However, the North Korean dollar debt reached $2.4 billion in 1984, which is a large amount for a country with fairly small dollar exports. Since 1977 North Korea has been obliged to negotiate a rescheduling of its debt, beginning with Japan. In addition to debt, the North Korean economy is plagued with the usual problems of a centrally planned system: bottlenecks, overconsumption of energy and materials, poor quality, lack of hard currencies. This has hindered the successful fulfilment of the 1978–84 plan. According to the CIA, the GNP growth rate was 0 per cent in both 1982 and 1983.

4   ENVIRONMENTAL FACTORS AND THE PLANNED INDUSTRIALISATION MODEL

One of the Soviet model's claims to fame was its supposed effectiveness in protecting socialist countries from crises generated in the capitalist world economy or of their own making. But the developed Comecon countries have experienced a slowdown in their economic growth since the late 1970s. The slump was tremendous in 1981 and 1982 in Eastern Europe (Andreff, 1985). Moreover, all Comecon countries have also developed considerable foreign debts (Andreff and Lavigne, 1987). It has become clear to most observers that centralised planning and heavy industry do not provide an insurance against domestic economic crisis and external influences. This important fact has contributed a great deal to the disillusionment about the socialist-orientated model of development in the Third World.

Economic adjustment policies and institutional economic reforms in Comecon countries have also adversely affected the standing of the model. In a nutshell, these policies included brakes on imports, incentives to export and an austerity policy for consumers and enterprises. The austerity policy was accompanied by industrial modernisation through a change in priorities among sectors. The development of skill-intensive products (computers, robots, biotechnologies, and so on) has displaced the traditional heavy industries in the ranking of priorities. These adjustment policies are not what many SODCs themselves are ready to accept. Nevertheless, the spirit of new economic reforms emphasises a cold sense of economic efficiency and seems to be chasing voluntarism and 'revolutionary' enthusiasm out of the planned system.

The consequence of the above 'environmental' changes is that the euphoria about Comecon–SODC economic relations is coming to an end. In coping with the external constraint, Comecon countries are now obliged to rationalise their economic relations with Third World countries (Lavigne, 1986b). Even Soviet economists now recognise that something has changed in East–South relations. At least one thing is sure: no country in the Third World, even an SODC, can now expect to receive Soviet hard goods and credit without delivering commodities of interest to the Soviet Union and without insistence on reimbursing existing debt. This is even more the case with other East European partners.

Although it would be risking their economic independence, some SODC leaders may have dreamt of benefiting from the same aid as Cuba, Vietnam and Mongolia. It is now demonstrated that this can only be wishful thinking. SODC leaders will now find a single word written on Comecon's door: closed. By rejecting the applications of Mozambique and Laos to join Comecon, the Soviet Union has helped to stabilise the borders of the sphere of influence of its industrialisation model.

5   TOWARDS ADJUSTMENT POLICIES AND REFORMS IN THE 'SOCIALIST THIRD WORLD'

Among the twenty-one SODCs we have studied, eleven rely on exogenous factors for implementing the planned industrialisation model, and a further eight are practically unable to implement it. Economic performance, which periodically inspired hope in the 1970s, has deteriorated in the 1980s. As a result, in all twenty-one SODCs the trend in the late 1980s is to implement adjustment programmes, austerity policies and economic reforms. Four countries – Benin, Congo, Tanzania and Madagascar – are regulated by the IMF. Five countries implement austerity policies of their own: Iraq since 1983, Ethiopia since 1985, Syria since 1986 and to a lesser extent, Algeria and Cuba. In nine SODCs an economic reform is

under way. This is often not actually admitted for ideological
.reasons. Such is the situation in Algeria, with its export incentives and
a private sector. A deeper reform is not inconceivable in the near
future. Burmese economic reform has been under way since 1977,
restoring the private sector, rehabilitating the market economy,
reinforcing exports and, since 1985, promoting joint ventures with
foreign companies. North Korea has adopted a policy promoting
exports since 1979, and passed a law welcoming foreign investment in
1984. The Guinean economy has been radically reformed since the
political changes of 1984. Private trading of agricultural products has
been re-established in Laos. In Madagascar, the privatisation process
is in place and foreign capital has been welcome since 1986. The
Mozambican reform started in 1980 with what was called a 'mini-
NEP', and has gone as far as joining the IMF. Since 1984 Tanzania
has been denationalising the so-called *parastatales* – that is to say,
state enterprises – and providing incentives to private investment. In
Vietnam the reform was launched in August 1979, resulting since in
widening the free market and private ownership, freeing prices,
restoring profit criteria and bonuses for management, issuing state
bonds, encouraging exports, welcoming foreign investment, and even
making some workers redundant. Although they have escaped both
austerity and reform, countries such as Angola, Kampuchea and
Nicaragua may be described without doubt as 'economies in crisis'.
The civil war adds to the disorganisation of the Afghan economy. In
South Yemen the regime has been destabilised by a restructuring
within the party in power. Only Mongolia has overcome the obstacles
and seems to be doing well in this generally difficult period. But
clearly it would not be easy to convince many in the Third World that
the planned industrialisation model is still beneficial on the strength
of this Mongolian experience alone.

6 CONCLUSION

The problems which the SODCs have experienced since 1973 have
put to the test the model of planned industrialisation development
which appears to have failed, at least in its unadjusted and unreformed version. Several developing countries contest the model as
well as Soviet aid and the role of East–South foreign trade. The new
attitudes were well expressed by the late Mozambican leader, Sa-
mora Machel: 'Africans must use Marxism, but Marxism ought not to

use Africans.' It has now been realised that the Soviet-type model is not a magic formula able to transform poverty and underdevelopment into a developed socialist economy.

Notes

1. With military expenditure financed by foreign borrowing, it is estimated that the Iraqi debt was $50 billion in 1985, not $12 billion as Table 12.2 reports.
2. It should be noted that in the SODCs the so-called reliance on transnational corporations was clearly substituted by reliance on foreign borrowing from public agencies, Comecon countries, and sometimes private banks.
3. At least this was so until 1985. In the years since 1985 Soviet oil has been no cheaper than Western oil.

References

Acciaris, R. (1984) 'La dette cubaine envers l'Ouest', *Le Courrier des Pays de l'Est*, no. 284, May.

Al Khadat, D. (1985) 'The Role of Foreign Financial Aid in the Financing of Capital Investments in People's Republic of Yemen', *Soviet and Eastern European Foreign Trade*, vol. XXI, no. 1–2–3, Spring–Summer–Autumn.

Andreff, W. (1985) 'The External Constraint in the Economic Crisis of East European Countries', in *Research in Political Economy*, eds. Paul Zarembka and Thomas Ferguson (Greenwich, CT: Jai Press).

Andreff, W. (1987) 'Le modèle d'industrialisation soviétique: quelles leçons pour le Tiers-Monde?', *Revue Tiers-Monde*, vol. XXVIII, no. 110, April–June.

Andreff, W. and G. Graziani (1985) 'Contrainte extérieure et politiques d'aptation', in *La réalité socialiste*, eds. Marie Lavigne and Wladimir Andreff (Paris: Editions Economica).

Andreff, W. and A. Hayab (1978) 'Les priorités industrielles de la planification algérienne sont-elles vraiment industrialisantes?', *Revue Tiers-Monde*, vol. XIX, no. 76 October–December.

Andreff, W. and M. Lavigne (1987) 'A Way out of the Crisis for the CMEA Economies?', *Soviet and Eastern European Foreign Trade*, vol. XXIII, no. 3, Autumn.

Bobo, N. (1983) 'The Zimbabwe Lesson', *Monthly Review*, vol. 35, September.

Breidenstein, G. (1975) 'Economic Comparison of North and South Korea', *Internationales Asienforum*, April.

Brezinski, H. (1986) 'Economic Relations between European and Less-developed CMEA Countries', in *East European Economies: Slow Growth* in the 1980s, ed. Joint Economic Committee, US Congress, vol. 2, 28 March.

Brillouet, A. (1975) 'Economie de la République populaire démocratique de Corée', *Revue d'Etudes comparatives Est-Ouest*, vol. 6, no. 4.

Brillouet, A. (1983) 'Le commerce extérieur comme illustration de l'insertion de la République populaire démocratique de Corée dans le concert mondial', *Revue d'Etudes comparatives Est-Ouest*, vol. 14, no. 2.

Chung, S. (1977) 'Le bilan corée: idéologie, politique, économie et développement, réunification et relations extérieures', *Revue d'Etudes comparatives Est-Ouest*, vol. 8, no. 4.

Cigar, N. (1985) 'State and Society in South Yemen', *Problems of Communism*, vol. XXXIV, no. 3, May–June.

Fenichel, A. and Azfar Khan (1981) 'The Burmese Way to Socialism', *World Development*, vol. 9, no. 9–10.

Gottheil, F. (1981) 'Iraqi and Syrian Socialism: an Economic Appraisal', *World Development*, vol. 9 no. 9–10.

Graziani, G. (1985) 'The Non-European members of Comecon: a Model for Developing Countries', III World Congress for Soviet and East European Studies, Washington, November, unpublished paper.

Hirschbein, S. (1981) 'Tanzania: the Non-Marxist Path to Socialism?', *Monthly Review*, vol. 32, January.

Kahn, M. (1984) 'La situation économique de la Mongolie' *Le Courrier des Pays de l'Est*, no. 286, July–August.

Kofi, T. A. (1981) 'Prospects and Problems of the Transition from Agrarianism to Socialism: the Case of Angola, Guinea-Bissau and Mozambique', *World Development*, vol. 9, no. 9–10.

Kornai, J. and X. Richet (1986) *La voie hongoise* (Paris: Editions Calmann-Lévy).

Kuuya, P. M. (1983) 'Transfer of Technology: an Overview of the Tanzanian Case', in *Technologie et Industrialisation en Afrique*, ed. Fayçal Yachir (Algeria: OPU).

Laidi, Z. (1984) *L'URSS vue du Tiers-Monde* (Paris: Editions Karthala).

Lavigne, M. (1986a) 'Eastern Europe – LDC Economic Relations in the Eighties', in *East European Economies: Slow Growth in the 1980s*, ed. Joint Economic Committee, US Congress, vol. 2, 28 March.

Lavigne, M. (1986b) *Les relations Est–Sud dans l'economie mondiale* (Paris: Editions Economica).

Mathonnat, J. (1985) 'Financement extérieur, planification de la production et des échanges: le cas de l'Afghanistan', *Mondes en Développement*, no. 50–1.

Saul, J. (1979) *The State and Revolution in Eastern Africa* (New York: Monthly Review Press).

Sokoloff, G. (1984) 'L'autre Corée', *Economie Prospective Internationale*, no. 19.

Theriot, L. H. and J. N. Matheson (1979) 'Soviet Economic Relations with the non-European CMEA: Cuba, Vietnam, Mongolia', in *Soviet Economy in a Time of Change*, ed. Joint Economic Committee, US Congress, vol. 2, 10 October.

Tiberghien, R. (1983) 'Le développement industriel de la République Unie de Tanzanie', *Cahiers IREP-Développement* (Grenoble), no. 6.

Tiraspolsky, A. (1983) 'Le CAEM et ses partenaires privilégiés du Tiers-Monde', *Le Courrier des Pays de l'Est*, no. 274, June.

Weaver, J. H. and A. Kronemer (1981) 'Tanzanian and African Socialism', *World Development*, vol. 9, no. 9–10.

Wiles, P. (ed.) (1982) *The New Communist Third World* (London: Croom Helm).

Zamostny, T. J. (1984) 'Moscow and the Third World: Recent Trends in Soviet Thinking', *Soviet Studies*, vol. XXXVI, no. 2, April.

13 Industrial Management and Reforms in North Korea

Myung-Kyu Kang

1 PREFACE

At the second session of the 8th Supreme National People's Congress (21 April 1987), the North Korean Prime Minister, Lee Keun-Mo, submitted a report entitled 'The Third 7-Year Plan (1987–93) for the Development of the People's Economy'.[1] According to this report, there are plans to increase the national income of North Korea at an annual rate of 8 per cent and industrial production at a rate of 10 per cent. The 10 per cent target is, however, relatively modest given that the goal set for the annual growth rate of industrial production during the Second 7-Year Plan (1978–84) was 12.1 per cent. It is therefore not surprising that the Prime Minister, in another report entitled 'For the Successful Completion of the Third 7-Year Plan', called for an improvement in the management of the economy and for higher productivity growth. This call reflects the renewed recognition by North Korean authorities of the seriousness of their economic problems, the official claims of high growth rates notwithstanding. Specifically, the report argues for rationalisation of economic management, including an 'independent accounting system', efficient use of resources, significant cost reductions, and improved product quality and labour productivity. Moreover, at the meeting, the communist leader Kim Il-Sung himself emphasised that the accomplishment of the great goals stated in the New Perspective Plan would not be possible without decisive innovations in the methods of guiding the economy and the management of enterprises.[2]

What, then, is the specific position of North Korea with respect to reforming its economy? Can we notice any sign of significant changes there which resemble economic reforms in other socialist economies? If such changes do occur, when did they start, what do they consist of and what are their prospects for success? This chapter is intended to answer these questions.

2 CHANGED SETTING IN THE NORTH KOREAN ECONOMY

There is no clear evidence yet of the presence of a North Korean equivalent of the Chinese determination to reform, of the kind demonstrated at the Third Session of the IV National People's Congress (1978) or in a document entitled 'The Decision on Reform of the Economic Structure' (1984). Nevertheless, North Korea seems to have been making desperate efforts to adapt its economy to changing internal and external conditions, which also include a revision of its traditional Soviet-type system.

The beginning of the new policy may be traced to Kim Il-Sung's repeated calls for improvements in his New Year messages of 1984 and 1985. In the 1984 message he noted that 'this year we need to improve decisively management and guidance of the people's economy. . . . By correct use of the independent accounting system we have to run our economy more scientifically and rationally.' A year later he stressed that there is an urgent need to improve methods of guiding the economy and to manage enterprises 'by effective use of economic measures'.[3]

Secondly, North Korean authorities declared their support for a much-increased opening of their economy to the outside world. According to the 'Decision to strengthen the South–South [North Korea and developing countries] co-operation and external economic relations [with all other countries] to further develop trade', they plan to increase foreign-exchange earnings by multiplying trade with socialist countries by more than ten times over the years 1985 to 1990 and by strengthening economic relations with capitalist countries, even those with which North Korea has no diplomatic relations.[4] In September 1984 the 'Joint Venture Law' was passed, aimed at attracting foreign capital.[5] This latter measure reflects interest in enlarging the inflow of foreign technology, mainly through exchanges and contacts with capitalist countries.

Thirdly, the authorities reorganised government offices in charge of economic affairs and initiated a large-scale reshuffle of the personnel in these offices. The number of divisions in the central government was reduced from thirty-four to twenty-four in November 1985 and the power of local governments was extended by reorganising the 'Committee for Guidance of the Provincial Economy' into a new 'Committee for Guidance of the Local Government and Economy'. The authorities also took some measures to spread the adoption of 'the Associated Enterprise System', which has been experimented with since 1975.[6] It should also be noted that after the appointment of Kang Sung-San as Prime Minister in January 1984, fourteen ministerial positions were filled with practical-minded technocrats. The power of technocrats was strengthened further under Prime Minister Lee Keun-Mo, with the appointment of technocrats also to key party positions.[7]

Fourthly, since 1984, overseas visits by North Korean leaders have become more frequent, especially to the Soviet Union, China, and East European countries. Kim Il-Sung himself visited the Soviet Union and seven East European countries in May 1984, for the first time in twenty-three years. Fifty North Korean delegates visited the special economic zones in Shanghai and Shenzhen in July 1984. In August 1984, Prime Minister Kang Sung-San and his economic officials met the Chinese Party Chairman Hu Yaobang. In 1985, 500 North Korean delegates, including young workers, soldiers, and peasants, visited Beijing, Shanghai, Nanjing, and Shenzhen. More importantly, Kim Il-Sung and Jong-Il went to China to witness China's open-door and decentralisation policies at first hand and, being impressed by the success of these policies, made a statement in their support. The North Korean leaders were thus giving the impression that they were eager to consider changes in their own economic policy along Chinese lines.[8]

Finally, the North Korean authorities have recently been promoting with renewed emphasis both the 'light industry revolution' and the 'service industry revolution', in order to improve the living conditions of the people. This policy change was supported by the slogan that the ultimate objective of socialism is to stabilise people's material and cultural lives, and that this is where the superiority of socialism lies.[9] In economic terms, the new policy can be seen as an attempt to correct the distortion in resource allocation resulting from the long-standing emphasis on heavy industry at the expense of the consumer goods industry. The North Korean authorities have also shown serious determination to foster technological innovation. Kim Il-Sung devoted a substantial part of his 1986 New Year message to this theme, saying that one of the most important projects facing

North Korea is the 'technology revolution'. The Third 7-Year Plan assigns 3–4 per cent of the North Korean national income to research and development.[10]

All this confirms that it was in the first half of the 1980s that North Korean leaders became reform-minded. By 1984 North Korea sought a revitalisation of its economy by 'reform-like' measures, a policy change influenced in part by reforms in China and some European countries.[11] I shall argue that these measures will not produce any satisfactory results unless enterprises are substantially transformed. For the real 'technological revolution' to take place, innovations should be eagerly sought and adopted by direct producers. Co-operation with foreign capital through joint ventures and trade will be fruitless unless enterprises respond actively to new opportunities. Institutional changes at government level need to be radical enough and appropriate to produce such enterprise-level activities. In other words, the key issue in the reform of the North Korean economy, it seems, lies not in the change of political institutions or guidance at government level, but in allowing for an autonomous decision-making power at enterprise level. The North Korean policy-makers have started to recognise that 'relative autonomy' of enterprises is needed, but so far they still continue to put enterprises under the tight control of central government and party leadership.

In December 1984, the 10th session of the Sixth Central Committee of the North Korean Workers' Party discussed, and passed, the 'Provisions on the Independent Accounting System in the State Enterprises'.[12] In the next section I shall investigate the nature of the North Korean economic management system, focusing on these 'provisions'.

3   THE ENTERPRISE WORK SYSTEM AND THE INDEPENDENT ACCOUNTING SYSTEM

It is difficult as yet to identify any radical economic reform measures in North Korea comparable to those adopted by China in 1978 and 1984, or Hungary in 1968 and 1982, or even by the Soviets in 1965 or by Bulgaria in 1987.[13] However, among several measures taken by the North Korean authorities, the renewed emphasis on the independent accounting system (IAS) in 1984 can be considered one of the most important. Although the IAS was first adopted in 1955 for the purpose of increasing fiscal revenues, it was in 1984 that the system became the focus of attention as a possible solution to the desperate endeavour to renovate the economy. What economic effects did the North Korean authorities intend to achieve by the 1984 reform of the IAS? Are the new operating mechanisms of the IAS adequate for the desired goals?

Let us first look at the organisational structure of the industrial enterprise in North Korea. North Korean industrial enterprises are run not by individual managers but by the Factory Party Committees, which have apparently been set up in the spirit of the so-called 'Dae-an Work System (DWS)'. This system has been in operation since 1961 and is the basic model of organisation of North Korean factory management. The system seems to be regarded as very important, because even the Constitution, in Article 30, states that North Korea guides its economy according to that system, calling it an advanced socialist model of the management of the economy. The DWS was named after the Dae-an Electrical Machine Factory, where Kim Il-Sung offered some on-the-spot guidance in December 1961. The idea was to apply the *Chungsan-ri* agricultural management system to industrial enterprises. This original system was so named when Kim Il-Sung provided on-the-spot guidance at Chungsan-ri in February 1960. According to the so-called *Chungsan-ri* spirit, higher officials are supposed not just to issue commands but to go and stimulate enthusiasm and initiative as well.[14]

Accordingly, DWS implies that industrial management is to be based on collective leadership and the 'line of the masses'. It replaces the one-man responsibility system (which showed such shortcomings as individualism, red tape, and formalism) with collective manage- ment by the Factory Party Committee (FPC). It also aims to intensify the political and ideological mobilisation of people, the 'subjects' (not 'objects') under the system of socialist ownership.

The highest decision-making power lies in the Factory Party Com- mittee. In the Dae-an Electrical Machine Factory, with 5000 workers (in 1976), the FPC consists of thirty-five members elected by party members.[15] An FPC usually has between twenty-five and thirty-five members, of whom six to nine constitute the Executive Board. Managers, engineering staff, and workers are equally represented, and meet once a month. The Executive Board is in charge of day-to-day operations, and its core consists of the party secretary and managers.[16]

Shifting to collective management has brought large and increasing interference with managerial decision-making from party functionaries, chief engineers, and workers. Moreover, the party-centred environment enforces the priority of the party secretary's opinion, especially in cases of disagreements among FPC members. The chief engineer devises enterprise plans to achieve centrally assigned goals, and is responsible for the technological aspect of the desired goal of 'Scientific Management'. The manager is in charge of overall administration, except for the technological aspect, and is helped in this work by four deputy managers, assigned to supervise material supply, personnel management, workers' welfare and financial accounting. With the introduction of the DWS, the North Korean material supply system became highly centralised.

Another feature of the DWS is that especially assigned deputy managers, in co-operation with the workers' district administrative committee, are responsible for such tasks as taking care of workers' welfare and securing adequate supplies of consumer goods and services. An important merit of this so-called 'backward supply system' is its ability to satisfy workers' basic needs. Nevertheless, the problems of low quality and limited choice still remain.[17]

Workers' representation in FPC may not be effective in any case due to their limited knowledge of relevant information. The so-called 'masses line' seems to be simply a device for political and ideological indoctrination, and it would appear that workers are mobilised 'passively'. Moreover, since bonus payments are based on team rather than individual performance, they are not particularly effective in stimulating hard work. The authorities have felt obliged to supplement this incentive system by using mass-mobilisation campaigns such as the 'Three Revolutionary Members' (February 1973), the 'Seven-day Speeding Battle' (1974), the '200-day Speeding Battle' (1977–8), the 'Technology Brigade' (1979), the 'Dae-an Speed' (1980), and the '1980s Speed'. In 1979 Kim Il-Sung himself admitted that these speeding battles generated sectoral disequilibria and excessive use of labour, material, and equipment. The operation of the new centralised material supply system also met with some difficulties: the form of commodity exchange through contracts raised the question of the correct price for each commodity in transactions. In this regard, the problems at issue were 'realistic accounting, 'prompt account settling', and violations of payment agreements. Administrative prices, by not taking into account the relation of demand and supply, were thought to be encouraging violations of contracts. There have also been many cases of flagrant inefficiency: excessive use of energy and other materials, especially in chemical and metallurgical industries, unused or underused facilities, errors in accounting, and so forth.[18]

To revitalise their enterprise management, the North Korean authorities combined the DWS with a modified IAS in late 1984. The basic idea of these modifications was to give more autonomy to enterprises. However, this 'autonomy' is still regarded as a 'necessary evil' required by the transitional nature of socialist society. It is in any case doubtful how much autonomy can actually be attained when politics is given priority over economic management, itself remaining highly centralised.

The modifications concern three basic principles to be observed in enterprise management:

(1) Economic categories, such as prices and profit, must be used and be based on the law of value and commodity–money relations; material incentives are allowed and are to be used more extensively.
(2) Each enterprise has to meet its expenses with its own revenues, after making a proper contribution to the state budget.
(3) The evaluation of enterprise performance is to be based solely on the execution of centrally assigned goals.[19]

In evaluating enterprise performance, the IAS uses several performance indicators for each work team or workshop in the enterprise. These are physical production quantities, value indicators of profits, exports and costs, and input productivities. Among these, physical quantities have the highest rank, to be followed by exports. Only those products which pass quality examinations are supposed to count. Provisions on fixed investment and material management require that each firm pays depreciation allowances and a rent for using fixed capital to the state.

Under the Provisions, compensation for labour consists of basic wage, bonus, and prices. The basic wage rate is affected not only by a government estimate of basic living expenses but also, within the limits set by the wage fund, by the fulfilment of plan targets. Each work team in an enterprise is awarded a different rate, according to performance. The wage rates also take into account careers, types of skills, and qualities of labour.[20] Bonuses are paid for over fulfilment of all the centrally assigned goals. Prizes (usually in the form of money) are awarded to honourable individuals or work teams. The actual amounts of prizes are proportional to basic wages. The authorities also award honorary citations for workers or managers with special accomplishments. The source fund for prizes is the 'enterprise fund', which comes from profits and is the money which can be retained only when physical goals are met.[21]

The new IAS aims at achieving *'won's* control' over the management. The idea seems to be that financial control is more effective than physical control. Each enterprise is required to give workers access to financial summary statements for each day, every ten days, monthly, and quarterly.

I have described the new IAS, which was adopted with the intention of revitalising North Korean industrial management. Can this new system be successful? My answer will be negative. As Professor Gert Leptin observed, the system might be regarded as a 'renewed attempt to solve old problems by old methods'.[22] In the next section I analyse the problems with the new IAS, both institutional and theoretical. The main issues are economic efficiency, compatibility of enterprise autonomy with the central plan, and the consistency between plans in financial and physical terms.

4   LIMITATIONS TO THE NORTH KOREAN INDUSTRIAL REFORMS

To begin with, we may consider the perception by the North Korean authorities of their industrial management as reflected in the IAS provisions. Some old concepts and slogans are certainly being less emphasised. These include centralised planning, mass participation, moral incentives, physical planning, and confiscation of most of the enterprise profits. The newly popular concepts are material incentives, enterprise autonomy, scientific and rational management, *won's* control, cost reduction, productivity, and financial control. Their somewhat uncomfortable coexistence with the old concepts is a 'new' phenomenon. The change betrays the authorities' loss of faith in *'Homo Sovieticus'* as an ideal human being under socialism who works efficiently with revolutionary passion for moral or other social reasons. It also reflects the authorities' reluctant acceptance that the people living in contemporary socialist countries, including North Korea, continue to be *'Homo economicus'* and therefore respond primarily to material incentives.[23]

I can detect several potential problems that the North Korean authorities might encounter in implementing their new industrial management system. The first source of problems is the collective leadership in the form of the FPC. Although collective leadership and mass participation are good for initial mass mobilisation and motivation, the system has important inherent limitations. First, there is a problem of clear division of roles inside the Factory Party Committee between political and purely managerial members. Although officially 'there is no party project independent from economic projects',[24] the present system may cause confusion and inefficiencies. The collective leadership may also interfere with the requirement that decision-makers should have executive responsibility. Otherwise situations can arise in which the collective avoids taking responsibilities for the results of its projects on account of the manager being the final executor.

Since the Factory Party Committee consists of professional managers as well as people who are ignorant of management, such as workers and party officials, there is also little room for the use of outstanding entrepreneurial talent in enterprise management.

The next source of problems is the weak North Korean enterprise autonomy. There are still too many strong obstacles in the way of full autonomy. First of all, the 'unitarisation and particularisation'[25] of the state economic plan involve many detailed performance indicators, centralised material allocation, and confiscation of enterprise profits. In the absence of market competition as a disciplinary mechanism, administrative control of the enterprise by central and local governments and party officials is necessary, but this leaves almost no room for enterprise initiatives. The decentralisation so far has mainly involved a delegation of some decision-making power from the centre to local governments. There has been no real enterprise-level decentralisation.

Lastly, I would like to point out that the 'masses line' envisaged by the DWS might not be so effective as expected in stimulating workers' creativity. Since most workers do manual labour, group discussion as one of the main forms of mass participation adopted in the DWS is unlikely to lead to technological or managerial innovations of practical importance, although it might help to maintain workers' political morale. It is rather the case that workers' participation in management prevents managers from fully exercising their professional managerial skills and innovative abilities, although under the present system of central control these skills and abilities cannot be fully used anyway. Furthermore, collective labour compensation and low profit retention do little to motivate workers and managers.

5 CONCLUSION

The North Korean economy can be regarded as a typical centrally planned economy (CPE), one which A. Brown and E. Neuberger defined with the following six characteristics: socialist ownership, command economy, pressure economy, priority economy, extensive growth, and closed economy.[26] Its foundation lies in multilevel controls by physical economic targets within an environment of 'taut planning'. Although the North Korean CPE had performed relatively well until the late 1960s,[27] it has started to show some undesirable symptoms since the mid-1970s,[28] giving rise to the view that positive potentials of the CPE have been exhausted. However, the North Korean experiments with a new IAS cannot be considered a direct attack on the core of the CPE, but a search within the old system for a cure of the system-inherent diseases.[29]

Although one of the main purposes of the new IAS is to improve the performance of enterprises with the use of material incentives and economic measures, not administrative commands, the highest priority in enterprises' goals still goes to physical products, not to profits, a practice which implicitly places a low premium on cost reductions. The result is a state of confusion rather than improvement. The confusion is well reflected by the recent remarks of Kim Il-Sung:

> Nowadays enterprise workers pay less attention to physical planning since evaluation of the plan has been increasingly based on value indicators. It *might be better if* we reformulate the main criteria of enterprise evaluation from value indicators to physical ones.[30]

It is useful to ponder about the objective function of North Korean enterprise managers. It may be assumed that they are motivated by private benefits, such as money and status. Since these two benefits go hand in hand, the managers must be bonus-maximisers.[31]

The source for bonus funds is retained extra profits, and managers can retain part (50 per cent) of profits only after they first fulfil physical production targets. However, the usual socialist practice of 'taut planning' makes satisfaction of this condition difficult. Besides, even if managers were able to succeed in surpassing this year's targets, the practice of 'ratchet principle' could see to it that next year's targets are set high, thus discouraging hard work this year.

North Korea is very proud of its planning scheme whereby workers determine their own 'preliminary production figures' and send them up to central planners before the centre assigns 'control figures' to enterprises. These voluntary, preliminary targets are to 'solve the problem of utilising the production capacity to the limit'.[32] However, given our discussion above it is highly doubtful that North Korean managers and workers report their true capacity to the centre.

In conclusion, it seems to me that the new North Korean IAS is an unpromising endeavour to open the long-closed door of the North Korean economy with the weak hands of managers who, under DWS, continue to be highly controversial bureaucrats rather than powerful innovative entrepreneurs.

Notes

1. *Roding Sinmun*, Pyongyang, 22 April 1987.
2. *Roding Sinmun*, Pyongyang, 24 April 1987.
3. Kim Il-Sung, New Year Message, 1 January 1984, *The Monthly Korean Affairs* (Japanese), February 1984, pp. 12–17; Kim Il-Sung, New Year Message, 1 January 1985, *The Monthly Korean Affairs* (*MKA*), February 1985, pp. 2–7.
4. North Korean Central Yearbook (in Korean), Pyongyang, 1985, p. 124.
5. The Joint Venture Law of DPRK, *The Monthly Korean Affairs*, November 1984, pp. 18–20.
6. *South and North Korean General Survey* (Japanese), 1987, pp. 330–34.
7. Kim Soon Bae, 'Key Personnel Changes and Policy Orientations in North Korea', *Material for Unification Education in Korean*, no. 29, Seoul, April 1987, pp. 15–22.
8. Kim Ki-Dae, 'New Tasks of Economic Policy in DPRK', *MKA*, June 1986, pp. 28–31; *Economist* (Japanese), 22 October 1985, p. 60.
9. Kim Jong-Il, 'Let Us Raise the Living Standard of the People Higher', *Social Sciences* (Korean), no. 4, 1984.
10. Kim Il-Sung, New Year Message, *The Report of the Bureau of Secretary*, Committee of National Peace and Unification, Pyongyang, January 1986, pp. 5–6.
11. It is known that Chinese persuasion was most influential. See John J. Metzler, 'The China Connection and North Korea's Emergence from Isolation', *American Asia Review*, Winter 1985, p. 122.
12. For the revised Provisions, see *Democratic Korea* (in Korean), Pyongyang, 13 February; 1, 7 and 20 March; 4, 24 April; 1 May 1985. Also see the Literature Collection on New Economic Trends in DPRK (Japanese), by Asian Economic Institute (Tokyo), March 1986, pp. 7–32.
13. Peter Humphey, 'Bulgarian Leader Stuns Nation With Reform Package', *The Korea Herald*, 8 August 1987.
14. E. Brun and J. Wersh, *Socialist Korea*, 1976, pp. 334–60; *The Economic Dictionary* (Korean), Pyongyang, 1985, vol. i, pp. 460–1.

15. E. Brun and J. Wersh, *Socialist Korea*, p. 353.
16. M. Bunge, *North Korea, A Country Study*, 1981, p. 130.
17. *Economic Dictionary*, p. 461.
18. M. Bunge, *North Korea*, pp. 134–5.
19. Chapter I, Article 2 of the Provisions, in Literature Collection, pp. 8–9.
20. Chapter V of the Provisions, ibid., pp. 18–24; *Economic Dictionary*, pp. 189–90.
21. *Economic Dictionary*, vol. ii, pp. 31–2.
22. Gert Leptin, 'The German Democratic Republic', in Hohmann *et al.* (eds), *The New Economic Systems of Eastern Europe*, 1975, p. 72.
23. Joseph Berliner, *The Innovation Decision in Soviet Industry*, 1978, pp. 401–2.
24. *Killoja* (Korean), Pyongyang, 1986, no. 6, p. 47.
25. *Economic Dictionary*, pp. 34–6.
26. A. Brown and E. Neuberger, 'Basic Features of a Centrally Planned Economy', in M. Bornstein (ed.), *Comparative Economic Systems*, fifth edn, 1985, p. 179.
27. J. Robinson, 'Korea, 1964: Economic Miracle', in *Collected Economic Papers*, vol. 3, 1965, pp. 207–15.
28. While the 5-Year Plan (1957–61) achieved the targets one year before the end of the plan period, the first 7-Year (61–67) Plan took ten years, and the next 6-Year Plan (71–76) and the second 7-Year Plan (78–84) needed two or three years of adjustment periods.
29. Of course, there are IAS successes. In Pyong-Chŏn gu, a housing construction and clothing factory reduced costs by 3.5 per cent in 1985 and increased profitability by 120 per cent. However, their discontinuous incentive system tend to produce more 'failure cases'. See *Kulloja*, 1986, no. 1, p. 64.
30. Kim Il-Sung, *Collected Works*, Pyongyang, no. 28. pp. 126–7.
31. Chang Young Kim, 'Profit Levers and Its Reasonable Use in the IAS Enterprises', *Social Sciences*, Pyongyang, 1985, no. 1 (from Literature Collection, pp. 50–6).
32. *Economic Dictionary*, p. 328.

Part V
General Aspects

14 Socialist Incentive Schemes and the Price-Setting Problem

Jean Benard

Socialist central economic planning, as it has been practised and theorised in the Soviet Union and most Eastern European countries, has long neglected the issues of decentralisation and pricing. Although this has been less the case since the reforms of the late 1960s, the emphasis of those reforms too has been on organisational and management rules rather than prices.

The basic question is this: can a decentralised system of incentives be consistent with centralised optimal prices, or does it require decentralised market-determined prices? We shall try to answer this question by considering in turn the role of prices and the various methods of price-setting in the two types of national economic organisation: closed hierarchy and open hierarchy. In an introductory section we define these two organisational structures and their pricing problem.

The first section examines the decision-making process within a closed economic hierarchy, typified by an asymmetrical distribution of information among its agents, especially between the Central Planner and firms. Even when firms operate under a socialist system, their management and workers' collectives are assumed to enjoy a private asset: information of which the Centre is ignorant. The incentive schemes, through the use of bonuses, aim at making managers use their private information and total capacities to maximise the social welfare as defined by the Central Planner.

If prices are exogenous to the socialist firm, the problem of knowing how they have been centrally determined remains. And if the very functioning of incentive schemes has some feedback upon prices, the problem is even more intricate. From a partial equilibrium analysis, we come then to a general equilibrium one. This extension of analysis is complicated further if this endogenisation of prices encompasses, as it ought to do, consumers' behaviour and its links with the activities of the Central Planner.

The second section summarises the recent theoretical studies of the socialist managers' decision and reward mechanisms which aim at making the mechanisms 'incentive compatible'. As we are interested in price-setting, we shall distinguish between non-price and price-incentive mechanisms.

The third section will remind us how dynamic procedures of decentralised planning, proposed by Lange, Malinvaud, Heal and others, determine simultaneously an optimal allocation of resources and an optimal price structure through an iterative dialogue between the Centre and the firms. We then inquire into their respective costs, their strategic manipulability and examine the incentive mechanisms which they may incorporate in order to become 'manipulation-proof' (or 'strategy-proof', defined by Green and Laffont [1979, p. 293] as 'strongly individually incentive compatible'). Apart from the theories which allow non-convexities (externalities and increasing returns) and non-lump-sum redistribution, all these planning procedures, in the end, amount to simulating market mechanisms. If so, we ask why not benefit from this efficient 'old lady', called 'invisible hand', directly, assisted when necessary by a well-devised socialist 'radar'? This combination would constitute what is called an open hierarchy.

The fourth and last section tries to draw some tentative conclusions. These stress the necessity of reintroducing market mechanisms inside the socialist production sector, but give more weight to forecast and control in the short term and to long-term explorations.

I   THE HIERARCHICAL ECONOMIC ORGANISATION: ITS PRICE-SETTING AND INCENTIVE PROBLEMS

An economic organisation is a group of individuals seeking through a common effort to achieve an efficient production of goods. To do so the group has to maximise a common objective, even if each member's own objective does not coincide with that of the organisation.[1]

1.1   Hierarchy

A hierarchy is an organisation whose members are ranked along a pyramidal scheme with horizontal tiers and vertical sectors. The members belonging to the same tier and the same sector are subordinate to a head belonging to the tier immediately above. Heads of neighbouring sectors belonging to the same tier are led by a head located at the second higher level and so on, until the whole network, so designed, is towered over by a supreme head.

Within such an organisation, information circulates only vertically. From one sector to the next, information always has to pass through the higher level which links the related sectors.

A *centralised hierarchy* is one where all decisions are taken at the overall summit for all the members. A *decentralised hierarchy* delegates decision-making power for some purposes to various intermediate levels.

As decisions imply information, centralisation is committed to information circulation. We say that a centralised hierarchy is *closed* because every member communicates with all other members only through the summit. A decentralised hierarchy is *open* because, while the summit communicates only with the general environment, the intermediate levels communicate with their respective local environments.[2] But if the summit has the power to define what are 'general' and 'local' environments, it can reduce decentralisation and opening to very little indeed.

Soviet economic planning since 1929 may be represented as a closed centralised hierarchy, a 'command economy' in the parlance of Western economists. From 1965 onwards it has repeatedly been the subject of decentralisation reforms, aimed at accommodating hierarchy with autonomy. Until now these reforms have not been very successful. One of the reasons for this failure has been that, if the price-making authority was left with the centre of the Soviet economic hierarchy, the methodology of setting prices consistent with the physical decentralised planning has never been clearly defined. Even the very existence of this problem has never been acknowledged by Soviet planners.

1.2 The price-setting problem

As Arrow (1970) underlines, any organisation aiming at producing outputs from given resources efficiently has to maximise an objective function subject to its resource constraints. If the organisation's controlling Centre were omniscient, it could solve the problem through the well-known Lagrangian-type methods. Its solution would give both optimal quantities and optimal (shadow) prices. By transmitting these shadow prices to all levels in charge of output, the Centre would offer them the opportunity to determine optimal outputs which would also correspond to the overall optimum.

1.3 The incentive issue

Thus the Centre which has perfect information and ability can sort out all the details of the optimal physical output of the whole organisation. But how can shadow prices be calculated if the Centre does not have this knowledge and ability?

In recent years, socialist countries and Western economists have concentrated their analysis upon internal organisation problems, emphasising the role of economic incentives. They are perfectly right, but this is not the end of the story. For, assuming that there is a procedure to compute shadow prices, the question is how to make sure that, given incentives, this procedure is consistent with the output-decision-making procedure? This is the question we shall be addressing in the following sections.

II INCENTIVE-COMPATIBLE MECHANISMS INSIDE A HIERARCHICAL ORGANISATION

The incentive problem arises within an organisation as soon as information is asymmetrically distributed among its constituent members. Moreover, as transmitting information is costly, some information becomes a private good that no member gives up without receiving compensation. In the absence of such compensation he may gain by 'cheating'. Even if incentives are devised to meet this problem, uncertainty and unobservability of the inferior members' effort by higher hierarchical levels produces situations in which 'adverse selection' and 'moral hazard' problems arise, reinforcing the motives for cheating and providing opportunities for strategic manipulation.

The academic literature on incentive schemes within planning systems has concentrated upon the problem of avoiding strategic manipulability, somehow neglecting the pricing problem. From this rich literature we shall select only two examples: one with prices assumed as given, the other with prices endogenously determined.

2.1 Non-price-incentive schemes

A scheme of the first category was developed by Holmstrom (1982). It models the functioning of a planning organisation as a non-co-operative game. It may be recalled that the traditional Soviet bonus formula was:

$$S_o(x) = \bar{B} + (\beta - \alpha)(x - \bar{t}), \text{ when } x \geq \bar{t} \tag{1}$$
$$= \bar{B} + (\gamma - \alpha)(x - \bar{t}), \text{ when } x < \bar{t}$$

where $\bar{B}$ is the fixed remuneration of the firm's manager, $0 < \alpha < \beta < \gamma$, $\bar{t}$ is the output target and $x \leq \bar{x}$, $\bar{x}$ being the maximum output possible.

The new bonus formula, introduced in a 1972 Soviet proposal, is:

$$S_1(x) = \bar{B} + \beta(x - \bar{t}) - \alpha(x - t), \text{ when } x \geq t \tag{2}$$
$$= \bar{B} + \beta(x - \bar{t}) - \gamma(x - t), \text{ when } x < t$$

Members have the right to substitute output targets of their own for those proposed by the Centre. Their rewards are a function of the gaps between achieved output x and the centrally proposed target $\bar{t}$ as well as their own target t.

It is easy to show, as Weitzman (1976) does, that (2) dominates (1) in the sense that it induces the management to propose and meet maximum possible targets, that is, $t = \bar{x} = x$. The new bonus formula seems therefore more advantageous for both firms and society.[3]

Holmstrom demonstrates that, in addition to the superiority above, 'a linear revision scheme in which the targets only may increase, can be dominated by a delegation scheme with this same restriction.'

A delegation scheme is one in which the Centre refrains from setting targets and leaves the firm to do it, but builds a reward mechanism whose parameters are set in such a way that the firm itself selects what the Centre would like it to select. Prices enter into such mechanisms as soon as there are many outputs or many inputs.

Another group of studies of non-price-incentive mechanisms goes further by considering situations where private information leads to 'adverse selection' and (or) 'moral hazard' problems.

Loeb and Magat (1978) starting from Weitzman's (1976) formulation of the Soviet bonus systems, showed that if the Central Planner keeps the right to allocate to firms physical resources, such as basic equipment or key raw materials, and bases this allocation upon firms' proposals, then even the 'new' bonus formula, such as Holmstrom's, granting firms the opportunity to substitute their own targets for those of the Central Planner, would not be immune to manipulation (strategy-proof).

The only way to avoid this risk of strategic manipulation is to introduce into the bonus formula a 'pivotal mechanism' of the Clarke-Groves family.

For instance, if the output of every firm i is linked to some capital input K_i which is centrally allocated to it, and to a locally controlled resource Z_i known only by the firm, the bonus formula (2) must now be written:

$$S_i(x_i,\bar{E}_i) = x_i(K_i,Z_i) + \sum_{j \neq i} \bar{E}_j(K_j,Z_j) - A_i(\bar{E}_{-i}) \qquad (3)$$

where $-i$ denotes all enterprises except the ith.

In equation (3) the success or pivotal bonus indicator for the firm i has three components:

- the achievements of the firm (output or profit), given the allocation of central resource K_i and the use of its own resource Z_i, $x_i = x_i(K_i, Z_i)$;
- the output proposals of all the other firms, $\sum_{j \neq i} \bar{E}_j(K_j,Z_j)$;
- an amount which depends on the proposals of all the other enterprises.

The 'pivotal bonus' is defined to measure the loss which the whole economy would incur if enterprise i could not work because no central resource would have been allocated to it ($K_i = 0$). It is the social opportunity cost for firm i.

It has been demonstrated (Loeb and Magat, 1978; Conn, 1979) that such a pivotal bonus mechanism is manipulation-proof, since it gives any firm a lower reward if it cheats than if it tells the truth.[4]

More recently, Conn (1982) has gone still deeper into the complex issue of principal–agent relations inside the hierarchical planning system. As has been frequently observed, the firm's achievements are a function not only of allocated resources and technology, but also of hidden variables such as managers' effort. In that case, even the

Groves pivotal incentive mechanism, as devised by Leob and Magat, is no longer immune to manipulation. Conn proposes to deal with this problem in the following way. Suppose that each manager i maximises a separable and additive utility function:

$$U_i = S_i - V_i(e_i) \tag{4}$$

where S_i is his bonus and $V_i(e_i)$ his disutility of effort. The Centre allocates scarce resource K among firms by solving the following problem:

$$\text{Max } [\sum_i x_i(K_i, e_i) - \sum_i V_i(e_i)]$$
$$\text{subject to } \sum_i K_i \leq \bar{K} \tag{5}$$

Conn shows that the corresponding pivotal bonus formula must then be of the form:

$$S_i(x_i, y_o) = x_i(K_i(y_o); e_i) + \sum_{j \neq i} E_j(K_j(y_o); e_j(y_o))$$
$$- \sum_{j \neq i} m_j(e_j(y_o)) - \bar{\bar{A}}(t_{-i}) \tag{6}$$

where $y_o = [\bar{E}_1 \ldots \bar{E}_n; m_1 \ldots m_n]$ is the vector of both targets ($\bar{E}_j$) and effort disutilities (m_j), as communicated by the firms to the Centre. With these declared values the Centre will solve (5) finding the optimal allocation of the resource K among the firms. This allocation, together with the effort disutilities, and the term A_i (which must be independent of $\bar{E}_i$ and m_i, but may depend on $\bar{E}_j$ and m_j for $j \neq i$), does appear in the bonus formula.

Formula (6) is a clever extension of formula (3), taking account of the manager's disutility of effort. It also represents a Clarke-Groves pivotal mechanism and, as such, is both 'strongly, individually, incentive-compatible' and 'satisfying' – that is, both strategy-proof and Pareto-optimal.

Again, as with Weitzman and Holmstrom, so also Loeb–Magat and Conn implicitly assume that the price system is determined elsewhere in a consistent manner, through a free or regulated market or by the Central Planner.[5] They do not say anything about it. They thus work in a partial-equilibrium setting.

2.2 Price-incentive mechanisms

At the other extreme of the organisational spectrum, the centrally set targets disappear and firm managers are allowed not only to choose freely their outputs and inputs but also to set prices. They are supposed to do this through maximising their rewards. The Centre now has just to design a rewards scheme so as to induce price-setting managers to produce at the socially optimal output level.

Mo Yin Tam (1981) proposes a 'negative price incentive structure' (NPIS) which may be written in the following way:

$$S(p) = \bar{B} + \alpha\pi(p) - \text{ß}p = \bar{B} + \alpha[\ pq(p) - C(q(p))\ ] - \text{ß}p \qquad (7)$$

where S is the bonus, π the profit of the firm; q the output and p the price.

The manager is given a reward directly proportional to the firm's profit and inversely proportional to the price he will set. Maximising this reward with respect to p gives

$$q + (p - C')q' = \frac{\text{ß}}{\alpha} \qquad (8)$$

with $C' = \frac{dc}{dq}$, marginal cost, and $q' = \frac{dq}{dp}$. Aiming at social welfare optimum, the planner wants $p = C'$, which requires that

$$q^* = \frac{\text{ß}^*}{\alpha^*} \qquad (9)$$

Unfortunately the planner does not know the cost function of the firm, $C(q)$, so that he cannot know what q^* is. He therefore engages in an iterative process, modifying α and β from step t to t+1, by applying the rule:

$$\frac{\text{ß}_{t+1}}{\alpha_{t+1}} = q_t \qquad (10)$$

from an initial step $t = 0$, where he observes the quantity fixed by the manager, to a terminal step T where $q_T = q^*$. Tam demonstrates that such a dynamic process monotonically converges towards the optimum q^* at which the condition $p = C'$ is satisfied.

As it is easy to check, NPIS happens to be equal to the producer marginal surplus less its total cost in the previous period

$$S_t(p) = \Delta PS_{t-1} - C_{t-1} \tag{11}$$

where ΔPS_{t-1} is the variation of producer surplus in response to a price variation $p_t - p_{t-1}$.

In a subsequent discussion (*QJE*, February 1985), Finsinger and Vogelsang, as well as Gravelle, showed that such a mechanism was efficient only for myopic behaviour on the part of the manager. If the latter maximises the discounted flow of his future rewards, the mechanism must be modified to take account of the *variations* of profit and prices. The bonus formula proposed by Finsinger and Vogelsang is that, for every future period t,

$$I_t = B + (\pi_t - \pi_{t-1}) + q_{t-1}(p_{t-1} - p_t), \text{ or} \tag{12}$$

$$I_t = S_t + C(q_{t-1}) \tag{13}$$

which in view of (11) gives:

$$I_t = \Delta PS_{t-1} \tag{14}$$

This bonus is just equal to the procedure surplus variation.

The non-myopic manager will maximise

$$\underset{p}{\text{Max }} I = \sum_{t=0}^{\infty} (1+i)^{-t} I_t(p_t, p_{t-1}) \tag{15}$$

Neglecting the income effects upon consumer demand and surplus, the authors demonstrate that such a formula leads the manager to revise the price p_t from period to period until it equals marginal cost. They also show that this process is monotonously increasing in terms of surplus. Moreover, it cannot be strategically manipulated as the NPIS can, for it is never more advantageous for the manager to set prices in another way.

Both the Tam and the Finsinger–Vogelsang bonus formulae are

very attractive, since they do include explicit reference to prices and are informationally quite simple. Moreover, the Finsinger–Vogelsang formula is not strategically manipulable. The Central Planner does not need to know the firm cost or production function; he only has to monitor its production level q from period to period and adjust appropriately the parameters ratio: β_{t+1}/α_{t+1}.

Unfortunately for the Central Planner, this is not sufficient. Let us note first that while the Weitzman–Holmstrom formulae were static game rules allowing the solution to be reached in one step, here we face a *dynamic iterative procedure* that may last a long while. Fortunately, as it is monotonic, it may be interrupted, if necessary, before getting the optimal solution (it is 'well defined' in the Malinvaud sense). But, contrary to classical decentralised planning procedures such as those by Lange, Arrow or Malinvaud, the procedures above are not '*tâtonnement*' processes – that is, they do not have the property that no production, exchange and effective pricing are made before the terminal equilibrium, or the optimum, has been reached. They are *ex post* dynamic procedures, since, before modifying the bonus parameters α and β, the Central Planner must have observed the quantity produced, q_{t-1}. It is a '*non-tâtonnement*' process akin to the Marshallian dynamic adjustment of price and quantity through the well-known Cobweb diagram. So it generates a sequence of unstable successive situations, converging towards a stable one, which is the only Pareto-efficient equilibrium.

A second remark is that the firm considered by Tam and Finsinger–Vogelsang is either a monopoly or at least a monopolistic competitor. The bonus formula is designed to prevent its manager behaving like a monopolist by reducing the output and charging a high price, thereby inducing him instead to price at marginal cost. But with a natural monopoly this policy would presume the knowledge of optimal deficits and lump-sum transfers, which is not practically feasible. At the same time, the formula is prone to strategic manipulations.

This latter defect may be suppressed by imposing on the natural monopoly firm a budgetary constraint which appears in the bonus formula, through a high penalty for losses. Then the mechanisms will converge towards a second-best optimum and prices will be of the Ramsey–Boiteux type.

But, once more, as Finsinger and Vogelsang underlined in their 1981 article, 'all [these] incentive mechanisms are discussed in a *partial equilibrium framework*' (p. 390).[6]

III JOINT DETERMINATION OF OPTIMAL QUANTITIES AND PRICES THROUGH THEORETICAL DECENTRALISED PROCEDURES

3.1 The decentralised dynamic procedures

Apart from shadow prices associated with an optimising megamodel for the whole economy, if one existed, we are left with the so-called dynamic decentralised planning procedures.[7] Most of these are of the *gradient type*, where the planner has only, at each successive step, to adjust either prices to the gap between aggregate supplies and demands proposed by the firms, or quantities to the gap between firms' own MTRs which they send to the Centre and the corresponding average MTR centrally computed. The first type are 'price procedures' and were initially devised by Lange, Taylor, Lerner, refined later by Arrow and Hurwicz, and are now known as LAH procedures. The second type are 'quantity procedures' such as Heal (1973) and Malinvaud (1970–71), Dreze–De La Vallee Poussin (1971), and are known as MDP procedures.

Decomposition programming procedures give the Central Planner a more important role by letting him approximate the firms' production sets in the neighbourhood of their optimal programme, from their successive proposals. Again we meet 'price procedures' (Malinvaud, 1967) and 'quantity procedures' (Kornai-Liptak, 1965; Weitzman 1970).

As is well known, all these procedures determine iteratively both an optimal allocation of physical goods – that is, an optimal production programme – for each firm, and an optimal price vector. There is no ranking or split between these two operations; they are intimately connected through the various iterative steps. Only the task of adjusting either prices or quantities is given to the Central Planner, while the making of related proposals, for either quantities or prices, is left to the firms. And, as it is a '*tâtonnement*' procedure, nothing is implemented before the whole chain of calculations has been worked out. Optimal quantities and prices are mutual dual variables. Consequently the Centre cannot limit itself to price calculations by ignoring the quantity proposals issued by the firms, nor can these limit themselves to quantity programming, ignoring price adjustments resulting from the central balancing of their proposals.

3.2 Their drawbacks

Although theoretically satisfying, because they lead to general equilibrium and a Pareto optimum, the decentralised planning procedures have several drawbacks which prevent their practical use.[8]

First, no existing theoretical procedure is universal in the sense that it deals with informational exchanges either between the Central Planner and firms (all of them except MDP) or between the Central Planner and households (MDP). Their inner logic should make them encompass both exchanges. And, as only Heal and MDP can successfully deal with increasing returns, they would be the best candidates. But this extension of the iterative procedure to households would be cumbersome and costly and might be feasible only in the age of generalised home computerisation.

The second drawback of decentralised planning procedures, even limited to the firms, is their heavy information and calculation cost. One way of reducing these costs is to shorten the procedures once the progression towards the social optimum is considered satisfactory enough. In doing so, however, the planner must be sure that, in Malinvaud's words, the procedure is 'well defined' – feasible at every step and increasing in social utility from each step to the next. As we know, this is warranted only for 'gradient quantity type procedures' (Heal and MDP) and for 'decomposition price procedures' (Malinvaud).

The third defect is their strategic manipulability as soon as we assume that firm managers do not behave 'competitively' or – in a socialist planning framework – 'faithfully'. Here we again meet the incentive problem.

Recently, many studies (mainly by French economists)[9] have been devoted to the strategic properties of two gradient procedures: the MDP and the LAH. If we limit to three the possible strategies (in terms of the theory of games) – dominant strategies, Cournot-Nash strategies and maxi-min strategies – played by the firms, we can summarise the results obtained by J. J. Laffont (1985) in the following manner:

(i) With maxi-min strategies, the MDP procedure is immune to manipulation, globally as well as locally.
(ii) With Cournot-Nash myopic strategies, MDP may be manipulated but the manipulation effect will be limited. It will affect

more the planner's distributive objectives than the Pareto efficiency of the plan. If Cournot-Nash strategies are global (that is, extend to the whole iterative sequence), the terminal equilibrium will be competitive and therefore Pareto-optimal, but without any planned redistribution. The planner's distributive role is then entirely swept away.

(iii) With dominant myopic strategies, in the MDP procedure manipulation possibilities appear as soon as there are more than two firms and in any case of global dominant strategies.

(iv) As for the LAH procedure, Laffont (1985) has shown for a two-goods economy that it could be made locally incentive-compatible within dominant strategies, if the Centre sends to the firms 'non-linear prices' instead of mere provisional prices, all along the iterative process.

So in both respects, information and calculation cost and susceptibility to manipulation, the decentralised planning procedures are more attractive from a theoretical viewpoint than from a practical one.

3.3   Pivotal incentive mechanisms and general equilibrium

Can the incentive mechanisms which we have discussed above lead to general equilibrium (and Pareto-optimal) prices?

If the prices which they use (implicitly, as in Holmstrom, Loeb–Magat and Conn or explicitly as in Tam, Finsinger–Vogelsang and Kotulan) are given exogenously, they are arbitrarily determined and so there is no hope. But if firms do negotiate among themselves through a generalised market system, prices would become equilibrium prices.

This is clear in the case of the Tam, and Finsinger–Vogelsang mechanisms, as firms' marginal costs do converge towards their respective prices. This may be obtained through the market, if oligopolistic coalitions are excluded and the incentive bonus rule is enforced. The only difficulty is that the economy will confront temporary disequilibria on the way to equilibrium.

As for the Groves pivotal mechanisms advocated by Loeb–Magat and Conn, we have to distinguish between their Pareto-optimal result and their general market equilibrium achievement. The first quality is always achieved; a Clarke-Groves pivotal mechanism always leads to a Pareto optimum and it does so through only one exchange of messages between the Centre and the agents (in this sense it is a static procedure and is cheaper than a dynamic one). As for its possible decentralisation through a general equilibrium system, there is a difficulty since it generates a global non-zero surplus which cannot be redistributed without inducing agents to anticipate and so to manipulate it. This global surplus can be considered as the social opportunity cost of the manipulation-proof mechanism. So the whole economic system is not equilibrated, since the Central Planner (or the government's budget), which receives the pivotal tax, has an excess surplus. Meanwhile Green and Laffont (1979) consider that this difficulty can be overcome in two ways.

The first shows that in economies with a large number of agents, the pivotal mechanism incurs a relatively small aggregate surplus so that, once redistributed to the agents, it will be neglected by them when devising their optimal answer to the Centre. So a general approximate equilibrium will be reached.

Furthermore, the authors demonstrate that even if the agents take into account the redistribution of the aggregate pivotal surplus, 'their optimal strategies will be approximately truthful in large economies and that the decision taken as a result almost always coincides with the true optimal decision' (Green and Laffont, 1979, ch. 9).[10]

So we may conclude that if it were practically possible to use Groves pivotal mechanism every time adverse selection and moral hazard occur from hidden information or action, this strategy-proof and Pareto-optimal mechanism should be used, and that its use would not seriously disturb the general equilibrium.

3.4 Pricing under increasing returns

Before we leave the price-planning procedure, we must consider the theoretical and practically important point of *increasing returns and natural monopoly*. Socialist planning cannot let socialist firms behave as capitalist monopolies, but since a first-best policy with pricing at marginal cost would entail losses for natural monopoly firms and would stimulate strategic behaviour, a Ramsey-Boiteux (RB) price rule, with budgetary constraint, seems to fit better, though it would lead to second-best optimum. The pricing formulae are more or less complicated depending on whether the firm environment in question is competitive or monopolistic. The reason is that as the priced goods are independent or have substitutes or complementary goods, and so on,[11] the RB pricing formulae have to be combined with incentive mechanisms, for instance of the Finsinger–Vogelsang type, in order to ease their implementation by making them strategy-proof.

It should be noted that if socialism precludes private ownership of productive capital assets, it cannot then utilise competitive entry into markets to regulate them. So the case of Baumol's 'contestable competition',[12] which could, theoretically, dispense with regulating natural monopolies, cannot be considered here. For the same reason, if socialist firms are not allowed to hire the best managers and if badly managed firms are not allowed to go under, there can be no operational device to select efficient and devoted managers.

IV FOR A CO-OPERATION BETWEEN COMPETITIVE MARKETS AND CENTRAL PLANNING

4.1 Why simulate and not practise competitive market pricing?

As we near the end of this overview of the planned-price issue, we cannot forget that all the decentralised gradient planning procedures in the final analysis amount to simulating perfect market functioning. On the other hand, incentive-compatible mechanisms aim at eliminating strategic behaviour which precludes markets moving either to first-best Pareto optimum or, when natural monopoly situations or other non-convexities cannot be dealt with by first-best pricing rules, to a second-best optimum.

So everything pushes competitive general equilibrium into the foreground. It would therefore be inappropriate to postulate that market mechanisms must necessarily be excluded from the inner planning organisation – that is, from the economic interrelations among socialist firms.

A more logical and economically more efficient way of dealing with the organisation issue would possibly be to set it in terms of benefit-cost analysis. We do not intend to do this here, but wish only to register some tentative proposals arising from our survey.

4.2 Some tentative proposals

(i) Incentive-compatible mechanisms are necessary in order to stimulate socialist firms managers to be efficient. The best mechanisms are those which 'delegate' to the managers the task of determining the firm's production programme and reward them with bonus formulae fitted to this delegation process.

(ii) Every time the firm behaves strategically, the incentive system must include a pivotal mechanism.

(iii) Every time a natural monopoly situation occurs, second-best pricing rules with incentive-compatible reward systems are to be devised for the related firms.

(iv) Consumption goods prices and labour wages should clear their respective markets and enter into the production prices computation.

(v) The use of fixed equipment and land must be compensated through rental payments, and financial loans through interest payments. As the socialist state is considered the owner of production means, it must receive these rental and interest payments.

(vi) All production prices should be computed through first- (or eventually second-) best optimising devices, whether centralised or decentralised. As centralised optimal pricing devices cannot be run independently of iterations dealing with both quantities and prices, since this would be costly and prone to strategic behaviours, it seems better to use such methods only for key products such as energy, transportation, credit and foreign exchange and for some 'merit goods'. All other current products would be priced by the firm themselves, with trading on actual socialist markets.

(vii) When competition between socialist firms begins to appear too weak, splitting enterprises into smaller units would become necessary every time increasing returns to scale are not present. Another incentive for more competition lies in widening foreign trade, as the European Common Market and South Korea experiences have proved.

(viii) A corollary of this reform would be the discontinuation of administrative material allocating and rationing institutions such as *Gossnab* in the Soviet Union.

(ix) As soon as physical and central price plannings leave the stage, the taxation problem comes in. The government budget will continue to be supplied by direct levies upon firms' planned profits and by indirect buffer taxes between production and consumption prices. But in a would-be optimal planning system, the tax rates can no longer be arbitrary. In order to achieve economic efficiency, and leaving aside the distributive problem,[13] the rates should be structure-price neutral. To this end, a uniform value added tax (VAT) would seem to be the best practical instrument, while excise taxes and subsidies should be limited to a minimum.

(x) In fact the historical experience of planning decentralisation in socialist countries, such as those attempted in Yugoslavia, and more recently in Hungary and possibly in China, have more or less followed this scheme. No theoretical decentralised procedure has been applied; instead various kinds of actual market have been allowed to develop.

4.3   The remaining role of Central Planning

Such a reform would be a 'revolution' to some and a 'restoration' to others. If it were actually implemented, what would be left of Central Planning?

In our own view, rather little in the field of current (short-term) *ex ante* detailed planning and still less in terms of current implementation or bureaucratic control tasks. On the other hand, a wide range of economic analysis, observation and computation would be opened up, relative to short-term macroeconomic control and to medium- and long-term planning. The mathematical tools of economic modelling, both for multi-level programming and for applied general equilibrium models, would be very useful, as has already been experienced both in Eastern and Western governmental or academic economic research institutes.

As a corollary of such a reform of the planning system, the present socialist economies would no longer be pure 'hierarchical organisations' in their current functioning. Not only would their opening have been increased, but also an element of 'polyarchy' would have entered them since socialist firms would be directly transacting with each other, albeit under some central control.

But as long as the collective ownership of production means and enterprises continues, with its corollaries for creation, mergers, splitting and disappearance of firms, the hierarchical organisation will remain but be transferred to the long-term domain.

Will this transfer prove viable? This is an open question.

4.4   Necessary behavioural changes

Another question, closer at hand, relates to the necessary transformation of agents' economic behaviour. Will it prove easy for socialist firm managers to take risks and financial responsibilities, to negotiate contracts, to be attentive to demand and supply fluctuations, even to price fluctuations, and so on. Until now, most of them have instead been used to filling out administrative files, memorandas and reports, finding out the best channels for pushing their projects along the bureaucratic labyrinth or finding the raw materials or equipment they need in order to implement the planned targets before the end of the year. Still more challenging would be the attempt to transform bureaucrats into efficient managers. These problems are more sociological than strictly economic and that is why we feel we are not qualified to deal with them. In any case, we sincerely wish that solutions can be found.

Acknowledgements

I am grateful to Michel Mougeot for enhancing my information and to Pierre Picard for helpful comments. All errors and deficiencies remain mine.

Notes

1. This definition follows K. J. Arrow (1970).
2. Organisations, hierarchies and centralisation have been recently defined more formally by Th. Marschak (1986). We think that our more descriptive definitions do not contradict his own.
3. Discussions of these formulae may be found in Weitzman (1976), Loeb and Magat (1978), Holmstrom (1982) and Kotulan (1985).
4. More precisely, the mechanism is 'strongly individually incentive-compatible'.
5. In a recent survey of planning theory, R. G. Heal notices that Loeb–Magat must assume monoproduction and one input only in order to avoid the aggregation problem without market prices (Heal, 1986, p. 1505).
6. An article on the same topic was recently published by Cox and Isaac (1987). But again the problem of determining prices in a general equilibrium setting is left aside.
7. For an accurate presentation and analysis, see Heal (1973) and Picard (1979).
8. These drawbacks do not seem to have played a major role in the Soviet planners' refusal to try them. Ideological reasons (Marxian as against marginalist theory of value), political and sociological factors (weight of party and state bureaucracy) may have been more powerful causes.
9. For example, the works of Champsaur, Laroque, Laffont, Rochet.
10. Note that if the implementation problem had been set in terms of 'Bayesian strategies' (where the agents have subjective probabilities

about their partners' strategies) instead of 'dominant strategies', the negative surplus generated by the pivotal mechanism might have disappeared (cf. d'Aspremont and Gerard-Varet, 1979).
11. On this topic see R. Guesnerie (1980), D. Bos (1986).
12. Baumol (1982).
13. As already mentioned, we are not disregarding the importance of distributional problems for socialist economies, nor the considerable theoretical (and applied) literature on the subject. We have simply chosen to limit this chapter to efficiency issues.

References

Arrow, K. J. (1970) 'Control in large organizations', pp. 223–38 in *Essays in the Theory of Risk Bearing* (Amsterdam: North Holland).
Baumol, W. (1982) 'Contestable markets: an uprising in the theory of industry structure', *American Economic Review*, vol. 72, no. 1, March.
Benard, J. (1986) 'Economie Publique' (Economica).
Bos, D. (1986) 'Public Enterprise Economics' (Amsterdam: North Holland).
Conn, D. (1979) 'A comparison of alternative incentive structures for centrally planned economic systems', *Journal of Comparative Economics*, vol. 3 no. 3.
Conn, D. (1982) 'Effort, Efficiency and Incentive in Economic Organizations', *Journal of Comparative Economics*, vol. 6, no. 3, September, pp. 223–34.
Cox, J. C. and Isaac, R. M. (1987) 'Mechanisms for Incentive Regulation: Theory and Experiment', *Rand Journal of Economics*, vol. 18, no. 3, Autumn.
D' Aspremont, C. and L. A. Gerard-Varet (1979) 'Incentives and Incomplete Information', *Journal of Public Economics*, vol. 11, pp. 25–45.
Dreze, J. and De La Vallee Poussin (1971) 'A tatonnement process for public goods', *Review of Economic Studies*, vol. 38, April.
Finsinger, J. and I. Vogelsang (1981) 'Alternative Institutional Framework for Price Incentive Mechanisms', *Kyklos*, vol. 34, fasc. 3, pp. 388–404.
Finsinger, J. and I. Vogelsang (1985) 'Strategic Management Behavior under Reward Structures in a Planned Economy', *Quarterly Journal of Economics*, February, pp. 263–9.
Green, J. and J. J. Laffont (1979) *Incentives in Public Decision Making* (Amsterdam: North Holland).
Guesnerie, R. (1980) *Modèles de l'économie publique*, (CNRS).
Heal, R. G. (1973) *The theory of economic planning* (Amsterdam: North Holland).
Heal, R. G. (1986) 'Planning', in Arrow– Intrilligator, *Handbook of Mathematical Economics* (Amsterdam: North Holland) vol. III, ch. 29.
Holmstrom, B. (1982) 'Design of Incentive Schemes and the new Soviet Incentive Model', *European Economic Review*, vol. 17, pp. 127–48.
Kornai, J. (1984) *Socialisme et économie de la pénurie*, (Economica).

Kotulan, A. (1985) 'Theoretical Aspects of Incentive System', *Czechoslovak Economic Papers*, no. 23, pp. 55–74.

Laffont, J. J. (1985) 'Incitations dans les procédures de planification', *Annales de l'INSEE*, no. 58, April–June.

Loeb, M. and Magat, W. (1978) 'Success Indicators in the Soviet Union: the Problem of Incentives and Efficient Allocations', *American Economic Review*, March, pp. 173–81.

Malinvaud, E. (1970–71) 'Procédures pour la détermination d'un programme de consommation colective', *European Economic Review*, Winter.

Marschak, Th. (1986) 'Organization Design', (in Arrow –Intrilligator, *Handbook of Mathematical Economics*, vol. III, ch. 27, pp. 1359, 1440).

Mougeot, M. (1987) Les mécanismes incitatifs dans une économie centralement planifiée', *Journées de l'AFSE-Toulouse*, May, mimeo, 34 pp.

Picard, P. (1979) *Procédures et modèles de planification décentralisée* (Economica).

Stalin, J. (1952), *Les problèmes économiques du socialisme en URSS* (Paris: Editions Sociales).

Tam, M. Y. (1981), 'Reward Structures in a Planned Economy: the Problem of Incentives and Efficient Allocation of Resources', *Quarterly Journal of Economics*, vol. XCVI no. 1, pp. 111–28). *Discussion* of TAM's paper by Finsinger and Vogelsang and by Gravelle, and Tam's reply (*QJE*, vol. C, no. 1, 1985, pp. 263–89).

Weitzman, M. (1970) 'Iterative multi-level planning with production targets', *Econometrica*, vol. 38, no. 1.

Weitzman, M. (1976) 'The New Soviet Incentive Model', *Bell Journal of Economics*, vol. 7, Spring, pp. 251–7.

15 Contemporary Socialist Systems and the Trends in Systemic Reforms Worldwide

Branko Horvat

Historical developments call for an analysis and an extrapolation. I developed what I regard as a complete theory of socialism elsewhere (Horvat, 1982). In this chapter I should like to draw attention to only a couple of its central arguments and propositions.

All socialist revolutions were fought under the banner of justice. An analysis shows that the constituent elements of justice are the three ideals of pre-socialist revolutions: liberty, equality and fraternity. Moreover, each of these ideals, to be really meaningful, requires the other two. Traditionally, socialists build on equality. Contrary to conventional wisdom, equality is an operational concept; it can be defined very precisely. We are surely equal if we are equal in performing all our basic social roles. There are only three such basic roles: as producers, consumers and citizens. They are basic in the sense that we cannot live in a society without performing them, and only them. Equality of producers implies equal access to social capital. In other words, it implies social property and self-management. A basic precondition for genuine self-management is a free market (full market autonomy of producers). Equality of consumers implies a distribution of income according to work. The basic precondition for that is planning which must ensure equal starting positions for all producers (perfect competition, in the terminology of classical economists). As is well known, actual markets under capitalism function poorly. Planning is or would be used to eliminate market imperfections. Finally, equality of citizens implies self-government and political liberties. That, in turn, requires decentralisation and deconcentration of political power.

Again, if we are to provide the shortest possible definition of the socialist system, we might say: socialism is about political and social

234

democracy. For that it needs social property, market and planning. Unlike private property, social property is compatible with economic democracy. Individual initiative, the greatest developmental achievement of capitalism, belongs to social property as well, but changes its nature. Private property generates an exclusive and antagonistic individual initiative, while social property generates a co-operative one. Planning and market are no longer in opposition to each other: planning makes market work well; market is by far the most efficient instrument of planning. The way that socialism tries to solve contemporary social problems is by deconcentrating power, economic as well as political.

1 ETATISM

In the preceding section I described the basic socialist creed and suggested its consequences, but socialist movements and thinking also follow two sidelines. One is anarchism.

Anarchists believe that human beings are by nature good and sociable and only the state and the concentration of power makes them wicked. Consequently, social evils will be eliminated if compulsory organisations are replaced by spontaneous associations. Anarchist movements occasionally came to be quite important, as for instance in Ukraine at the time of the Russian Revolution and in Spain at the time of the Spanish Civil War. But their power never lasted long.

Diametrically opposed are the ideas of state socialists as exemplified by the Second International and, in particular, by the Third International. They shunned any spontaneity and insisted on strong organisation and the role of the state. The socialists of Marx's and Engels's generation believed in the withering away of the state. This idea was somewhat nebulous at the time it was formulated, but it may be made quite precise if it is realised that the modern state performs two very different functions: it is a repressive organisation backed by force and it is also an organisation providing social services. The oppressive function of the state should wither away; the service function should be maximally expanded.

Socialists of the two later Internationals did not care much about such subtleties. They were mesmerised by the organisational potentials of the state. Stalin openly proclaimed that Engels was ignorant and wrong: state power must increase, not wither away. Even the relatively mild social-democrats and labourites believed that genuine socialist reforms require a widening of state control and a nationalisation of industries. After the Second World War, left-orientated governments in various countries carried out extensive nationalisations. The proportion of nationalised industries came to be considered as an index of socialist achievements. Very soon both governments and workers were disappointed: governments because efficiency did not improve, workers because this socialism was not much different from the previous capitalism.

Class oppression and social differences were particularly great in the countries lagging behind in development. For this reason such countries were foremost candidates for social revolutions. But lagging in development meant illiteracy and absence of political democracy. With these two ingredients, revolutions were not likely to be socialist. Rather early – in 1902 – Lenin expressed his profound doubts in the ability of the working class – not to mention the peasants – to carry out a socialist revolution. He insisted that, instead, an organisation of professional revolutionaries, a party acting as a social *avant-garde*, should accomplish the task. Clearly, there can be only one *avant-garde*.

When socialist revolutions actually broke out – with the exception of the pioneering Paris Commune – a quite plausible theory of post-revolutionary order already existed. A vanguard party should seize power and use the state to mobilise the uneducated population in order to build socialism in the interest of all. Revolutions themselves generated everywhere attempts at spontaneous self-management and self-government. But the party was soon able to use its political monopoly to establish an all-embracing state control. *Socialist* revolutions ended up generating *etatist* systems. This historical joke is still a source of great confusion.

Socialism is about self-determination, individual freedom, political and economic democracy, elimination of social hierarchy, deconcentration of political and economic power. Etatism, on the other hand, established the political monopoly of one party, introduced a rigid political and, consequently, social hierarchy, eliminated political pluralism, replaced markets by bureaucratic controls, replaced private property by state and not social property. Consequently, it blocked individual initiative and established an extreme concentration of political and economic power. Socialist producers are self-managers; socialist citizens are free and equal individuals. Etatist producers are wage labourers hired by the state; etatist citizens are obedient servants of the state, subject to the comprehensive controls of a monolithic, hierarchically structured political bureaucratic apparatus. Etatism is clearly antiethical to socialism. To confuse the two is more than a small error in comparative systems analysis. The strengths and the weakness of etatism lie in the characteristics of the system just enumerated. Let me first deal with the strengths.

A country substantially lagging behind in development has a poor, uneducated community with enormous social and economic differences generating class polarisation. Under such circumstances fast growth is unlikely and backwardness tends to be perpetuated. If in such a country capitalism is replaced by etatism – which, however, is not the only possible alternative – growth possibilities are greatly enhanced. The state is converted into a collective entrepreneur, the nation is mobilised to carry out development plans, wasteful social and political conflicts are replaced by organised action and single-mindedness of purpose. All that becomes possible if the population can be made to believe that the change is worthwhile. This is where socialist ideology (not socialist theory!) enters the picture. Etatism is a bureaucratic collectivist system with socialist ideology.

As long as the ideological grip is operative, the system works. Etatist countries achieve high rates of growth.

Not only is the rate of growth high, the gains from growth are, generally, more equally shared. Basic welfare may be defined in terms of three social indicators: life expectancy at birth, education (measured as the number of university students relative to the population) and health (measured in terms of medical services – that is, the relative number of physicians and hospital beds). In order to eliminate differences in economic development, the sixty most highly developed countries are ranked according to gross national product per inhabitant and these rankings are compared with the rankings of social indicators. If the resulting difference is positive, the society in question provides its common members with more basic goods than other societies. A comparison of the rankings shows that in etatist societies the broad mass of the population lives longer, receives more education and enjoys much better medical care than would usually occur under alternative social arrangements at the same level of economic development.

The achievements of the etatist countries have been quite impressive. Their failures are also substantial. As the economy develops and becomes more complex, administrative planning becomes less and less efficient. Data indicate that for GDP *per capita* above $1000 (in

1968 prices) etatist growth rates fall steeply, some to sink below capitalist growth rates. Technological progress, as conventionally measured, also falls below the rates common for capitalist countries. Centrally Planned (or Managed) economies begin to lag behind the general world development. In the words of Enrico Berlinguer: the developmental potential appears exhausted.

Nor is that all. The gap between socialist ideology and etatist practice is widening and the population cannot fail but become intensely aware of that. The resulting credibility gap substantially reduces the state's mobilisation capability. Increasing corruption and cynicism characterise attitudes. Radical reforms have become overdue. This is essentially the current state of affairs.

Reforms are necessary, but it is not easy to carry them out. Powerful interests collude to prevent change. Any radical change means expropriation of the political power of the ruling bureaucracy – which has in the meantime constituted itself as a ruling class – and it is not willing to be dispossessed of power and privileges. On the other hand, egalitarian ideology degenerated into what Jozo Županov (1979) described as an 'egalitarian syndrome': whatever the results or the lack of results of our work, we are all equal and entitled to equal earnings. Radical change introduces uncertainties, requires productive differentiation, and that is not attractive for the large segments of the population accustomed to security of employment, poor work and no responsibility. Thus many workers, as well as the ruling bureaucracy, support the *status quo*. It is extremely difficult to fight such a powerful conservative alliance.

Like capitalism, etatism has its own contradictions. The main contradiction appears to be between socialist ideology and etatist practice. The liberation of man is made impossible by an authoritarian state control. A classless egalitarian society is replaced by a rigid hierarchy of status privileges. The main legitimation of the system – the high rate of growth – is no longer possible.

Again, a short definition of the system might read: etatism is based on political and economic control by the state. For that reason I followed Sveta Stojanović in adopting the term etatism as the most adequate term to describe the social systems of the USSR, China and Eastern Europe (Stojanović, 1973). Political control implies the monopoly of one party. Economic control implies state ownership of the means of production – state economic monopoly. As a consequence market is undesirable and planning is strictly administrative. The main historical role of etatism seems to be to speed up economic growth in order to catch up with the more advanced countries. Once this task is more or less achieved, etatist institutions become dysfunctional.

2 REFORMS

Reforms are not a specific feature of the current world scene. Every new crisis generates new reforms and there is a continual occurrence of reforms, both in the West and in the East. Not all reforms are of equal importance, but all seem to be pointing in the same direction.

Predatory capitalism, with a ruthless class war, is (at least within national boundaries) behind us by now. Crucial reforms were inaugurated as an outcome of the world economic crisis of the 1930s. At that time the planned economy of the Soviet Union did not experience the unemployment and stagnation which plagued the capitalist West. Something had to be done, and so the welfare state and government stabilisation policy were invented. Welfare state improved the lot of the poor and underprivileged. When it was inaugurated, the welfare state represented a remarkable change in social consciousness – it charged the state with social responsibility. But today that begins to look like a bureaucratic paternalism. The current generations ask for more than mere survival.

Taylorism, which treated workers like oxen, and authoritarian 'management prerogatives' which were ideologically justified by property rights, are also behind us. The two landmarks were the two world wars. At about the time of the First World War, the autocratic organisation of a typical capitalist firm began to encounter strong resistance. The need to expand war production and avoid strikes induced governments and employers of the belligerent countries to experiment with some mild forms of workers' participation. Although similar attempts had already been made, particularly in Germany, British joint consultation, as exemplified in the Whitley Councils of 1917, may be taken as a landmark. Joint consultation means that the employer is obliged to consult his employees before making decisions that affect their work and income in some important way. However, the final decision is his.

The next step towards democratisation of management was made in Germany after the Second World War when codetermination was introduced. Under the pressure of the 1918 Revolution, when German workers demanded the socialisation of the economy, the Weimar Constitution envisaged codetermination. But this constitutional provision was never enacted. After the last war a series of laws was passed providing for workers' participation in the boards of directors – in some industries on the parity basis – and also reserving the post of the personnel director for the trade-union representative. Today all West European countries, and many others, have some form of codetermination. The merits of joint consultation and codetermination are now being rediscovered in the etatist countries as well.

Further development led towards full-fledged workers' management. This was both revolutionary and reformist. As a result of a social revolution, workers' management was established in Yugoslavia on a national basis in 1950. The reformist way was also pioneered by Peru in the 1970s under President Velasco Elvarado (it was called *democracia social de participation plena*), but the development was mostly reversed after his death. The same idea was taken over, and more successfully implemented, by the Swedes in the 1980s. Genuine democratisation of management requires also a change in property relations; workers must have control over invested capital, at least in part. Swedish Wage Earners' Funds are financed by a certain percentage of annual gross profits and a payroll tax. The funds buy shares in the companies and are controlled by the unions. That, of course, is not full workers' management – the economy is still privately owned and unions are centralised organisations. But the Swedish reform marks a successful beginning of a reformist transition period.

Capitalism began with the establishment of political freedoms and seems to be ending by introducing economic freedoms. That is how the conflict of the two incompatible organisational principles – political democracy and economic autocracy – is approaching its resolution. In this respect the activities of the United Nations are quite illustrative. In 1948, the UN passed the Universal Declaration of Human Rights which confirmed the classical principles of political democracy already proclaimed in the American Declaration of Independence (1776) and in the French Declaration of the Rights of Man (1789). Only a few years later another document was passed, complementing political rights with social and economic rights. The modern list of human rights is quite inclusive, but still not completely so. Characteristically, self-management does not appear on the list. The reason is obvious: it is incompatible with both private and state ownership.

It is clear that the etatist reforms will proceed in the opposite direction: from economic security to political liberties. The first wave of liberalisation occurred after Stalin's death thirty years ago (and with some delay in China after Mao's death). The second wave has just been inaugurated with the Soviet *perestroika*. Complex and rapidly changing modern economies cannot function without competition of ideas and individual initiatives, and neither is possible without political reforms. Thus, political liberalisation is an existential precondition for development. In the economic sphere it will lead to an expansion of the market and increased independence of firms. But radical political liberalisation is unlikely to occur soon, because that would change the nature of the system. The ruling class will try to preserve its political monopoly as long as it possibly can. Therefore etatist countries are most likely to begin to experiment more seriously with economic rather than political democracy. Joint consultation and various kinds of codetermination – inappropriately called workers' management – are being tried out and are likely to be extended in the near future. In this way the need for a radical social-political reform might be postponed for another generation.

In both West and East, reforms are encountering the resistance of powerful vested interests. In the West it is private ownership which prevents efficient social planning and workers' management. In the East it is the political monopoly of the ruling bureaucracy which prevents independent initiative and social innovation. As a consequence, capitalism develops through a series of economic crises, etatism through a series of political crises.

Almost forty years ago (1949), in his address to the American Economic Association entitled 'The March into Socialism', Joseph Schumpeter predicted an etatisation of the economy with the bureaucracy replacing entrepreneurs and called that socialism (Schumpeter, 1950). This prediction was doubly wrong. First, etatism is nearly as different from socialism as is capitalism. Second, etatism is now in deep crisis and is clearly not the ultimate social system towards which the world is moving.

Yet some trends are discernible. Capitalism is not converging to etatism, as Schumpeter thought in 1949. Neither are the two systems converging to each other, as Jan Tinbergen asserted two decades later. Both systems are converging, but to something different. This different system will be, in my view, what in this chapter I describe as socialism.

References

Horvat, B. (1974a) 'The Relation between Rate of Growth and Level of Development', *Journal of Development Studies*, pp. 382–94.
Horvat, B. (1974b) 'Welfare of the Common Man in Various Countries', *World Development*, pp. 29–40.
Horvat, B. (1982) *The Political Economy of Socialism*, M. Sharpe, (New York: Armonk).
Schumpeter, J. A. (1950) *Capitalism, Socialism and Democracy* (New York: Harper).
Stojanović, S. (1973) *Between Ideals and Reality* (New York: Oxford University Press).
Županov, J. (1979) *Sociologija i samoupravljanje* (Zagreb: Školska knjiga).

Index

For Product Safety Concerns and Information please contact our EU
representative GPSR@taylorandfrancis.com
Taylor & Francis Verlag GmbH, Kaufingerstraße 24, 80331 München, Germany